CAMTASIA STUDIO®
AND BEYOND

CAMTASIA STUDIO®
AND BEYOND

By
Stephanie Torta
Stacey Dunbar

MERCURY LEARNING AND INFORMATION
Dulles, Virginia
Boston, Massachusetts
New Delhi

Publisher: David Pallai
MERCURY LEARNING AND INFORMATION
22841 Quicksilver Drive
Dulles, VA 20166
info@merclearning.com
www.merclearning.com
1-800-758-3756

This book is printed on acid-free paper.

Stephanie Torta and Stacey Dunbar. *Camtasia Studio® and Beyond.*
ISBN: 978-1-936420-33-9

The publisher recognizes and respects all marks used by companies, manufacturers, and developers as a means to distinguish their products. All brand names and product names mentioned in this book are trademarks or service marks of their respective companies. Any omission or misuse (of any kind) of service marks or trademarks, etc. is not an attempt to infringe on the property of others.

Library of Congress Control Number: 2013944476
131415321

Our titles are available for adoption, license, or bulk purchase by institutions, corporations, etc. For additional information, please contact the Customer Service Dept. at 1-800-758-3756 (toll free).

The sole obligation of MERCURY LEARNING AND INFORMATION to the purchaser is to replace the disc, based on defective materials or faulty workmanship, but not based on the operation or functionality of the product.

ACKNOWLEDGMENTS

Many people helped with the making of *Camtasia Studio and Beyond*. Although there are too many to name, I would like to mention a few whose support went above and beyond. First, "Thank you," to Allison DiRienzo, Antonio Lopez, and Cara Torta and Jonathan Torta for all of their help in creating the sample projects used in this book. To Vlad, Eric, Emily, David, Don, Paul, and Kristen and all my friends who gave us their support. Thanks, also, to my brother, Jon, for taking the time to help however he could, and to the rest of my family. Most of all, I would like to give thanks to my mother; without her support this book would not have been possible. Thank you.

S. Torta
Boston, MA

CONTENTS

*P*REPARATION

CHAPTER 1

OVERVIEW

IN THIS CHAPTER

In this chapter, we take an overall look at powerful screen capturing, recording, and editing tools by TechSmith. Camtasia Studio provides an innovative multimedia recording and editing program. Snagit works more as a screen capturing and image editing program. Jing deals with quickly sharing your captures, both screen and short video, online. All of these programs are part of the company TechSmith and can work separately or seamlessly together.

Once you've completed this chapter, you will be able to:

- Recognize TechSmith tools such as Camtasia Studio, Snagit, Jing, and Screencast.com
- Know some of the features and capabilities that are available
- Understand the technical writing style that will be used in later chapters
- Learn ways to share your projects for others to see

Files: All figures in this chapter are in color located in the chapter folder on the DVD.

1.1 - Programs of TechSmith

TechSmith is a leading provider of screen capture and recording software for individual and professional use. Some of this software includes Camtasia Studio, Snagit, Jing, and the Screencast.com hosting site. With powerful capabilities and an easy user interface, these programs are used by both professionals and amateurs alike. Visit the TechSmith Website for the latest information on products and technical support.

1.1a – Camtasia Studio

Camtasia Studio is a leading professional-level application for recording, editing, and producing your screen casts, PowerPoint presentations, or additional video, audio, or image projects. With the mix of a user-friendly interface with industry leading capabilities, Camtasia Studio is perfect for both professionals and beginners to create professional looking projects with ease.

Project: Watch the sample projects representing a few different types of projects created using Camtasia Studio.

- **Torchwork** – a sample of a story or blog report

- **Presentation Tips video** – sample of a work or school teaching tool

- **Presentation Tips presentation** – a sample of a PowerPoint presentation recording

- **InDesign Tutorial** – a sample of a screen capture tutorial

- **Overtime** – a sample of an animated storyboard

- **Cat's Inner Thoughts** – a sample of a home movie

This very powerful group of programs has three main phases: recording, editing, and producing. Most of the work will be done with the Camtasia Recorder and Editor (See Figure 1.1). The recorder and editing phases can work independently from each other. For example, there might be times you want to edit photos together with a music track and use just the editing and producing phases.

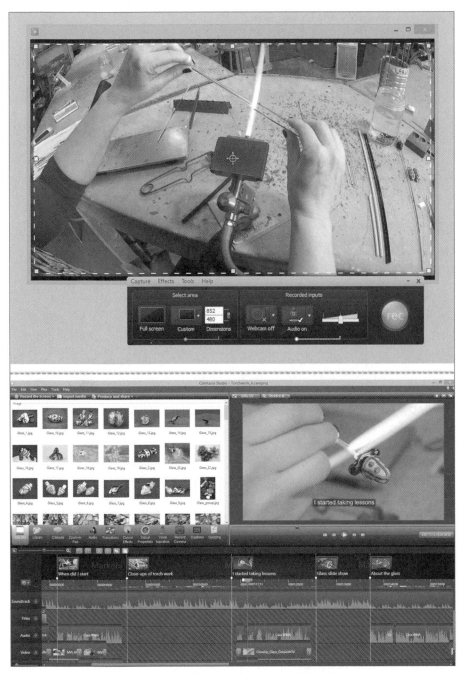

FIGURE 1.1 — Screenshots of Camtasia Studio, Recorder (top), and Editor (bottom).

Camtasia Studio's Main Sections

The Recorder – The Camtasia Studio Recorder is used to record your computer screen. An external video camera can be used and recorded during the screencast recording. System sounds and external audio can be recorded and split onto a separate track in the timeline.

The PowerPoint Add-in – Camtasia Studio installs an Add-in to the **Microsoft PowerPoint** program. This added feature will record your presentations as they are or with added voice narration and additional camera picture-in-picture capture. Notes within PowerPoint can be added as a caption track within Camtasia editor.

(Key Term) **Microsoft PowerPoint** – Microsoft Office's slide and multimedia presentation program.

The Editor – The editor includes tools such as the clip bin and library, task tab, preview window, and timeline. Using these tools, you can add video and audio clips and special effects, arrange your clips, and preview media within your project.

The Production Wizard – Once you are done editing your project, it is time to use the Production Wizard for a step-by-step walkthrough to render your project into a playable or sharable video or audio file. Once rendered, these files can be transferred to a device, burned to a CD/DVD, saved to your computer, or uploaded onto a Website.

System Requirements

Camtasia Studio will be able to run on most computers but it does take some computing power. The more powerful your computer, the faster rendering, the higher quality, and the more complex projects you can create. For the most up-to-date minimum system requirements and instillation directions, check the TechSmith Website.

(Net Search) **Camtasia Studio Minimum System Requirements** – Go to www.techsmith.com for the latest up-to-date minimum system requirements and instillation tech support.

Camtasia Studio for Mac

Camtasia Studio also has a version that runs on the Mac operating system. The basic idea and features are mostly the same as the version for the Windows operating system although the location of the menu items and key commands might be different. This book uses the Windows version of Camtasia, however, if you are using the Mac version you will be able to follow along with only slight modifications.

NOTE *All of the recording and editing projects on the book DVD were created using Camtasia Studio and Snagit.*

1.1b – Snagit

Snagit is a program by TechSmith that captures all or part of your screen plus audio output. These captures can be still shots or short videos. Snagit enables you to add more visual impact to your project and PowerPoint presentations by easily adding pictures, logos, special effects, or short video clips. The flexibility of Snagit lets you be creative and work easily on both your desktop and online.

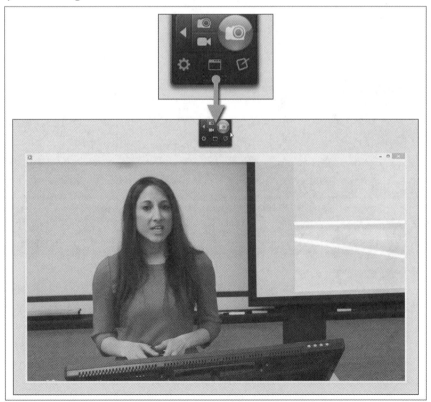

FIGURE 1.2 — Screenshot of Snagit capturing interface and its default placement on the computer screen.

Snagit's Main Sections

Capturing – With just one click, you can capture everything on your screen or a select portion of your screen. Snagit can also capture short videos and increase the scale of your screenshots. The Snagit interface is located in a movable pop-open menu (See Figure 1.2). This menu has selection, video, image, hotkey, and setting controls.

Editing – Snagit also includes editing features that allow you to enhance and manipulate your captures. Some of the features include creating custom graphics and adding special effects such as spotlighting, text, and arrows (See Figure 1.3).

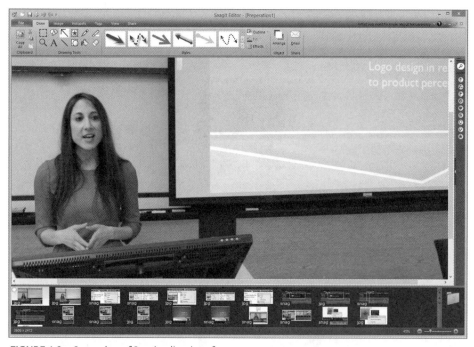

FIGURE 1.3 — Screenshot of Snagit editor interface.

Sharing – Save your captures in a variety of different file formats on your computer or open them within the Snagit editor for enhancement. You can also share your videos with a number of social sites including YouTube, Twitter, or Facebook.

> **NOTE** *All of the screenshots in this book were taken and enhanced using Snagit.*

1.1c – Jing

Jing by TechSmith is a free screen capturing program that takes a picture or short video (up to five minutes) of your screen and uploads it to the clipboard, an FTP site, Websites, or your computer. It has a simple one-click format and can quickly be uploaded, saved for reference in libraries, or shared with your friends. Jing captures can be easily shared on sites including Screencast.com, Flickr, Twitter, and Facebook. Jing can help improve your online conversations by creating images and short videos while sharing them instantly. Like Snagit, Jing has a one click pop-up menu for selection (See Figure 1.4). After the selection, a preview window will open where you can make adjustments before saving or sharing your file.

FIGURE 1.4 — Screenshot of Jing capturing interface and its default placement on the computer screen.

1.2 – Creating and Sharing

There are many reasons to use Camtasia Studio, Snagit, or Jing in both your professional occupation and personal use. You can create everything from complex to simple projects by arranging video, audio, and images on a timeline. With so many options to record, edit, and produce your project, you can always find new ways to be creative. Here are some highlighted features and tools.

1.2a – Equipment

A minimum amount of equipment is required to capture or record your screen. Although some computers or laptops have an internal camera, microphone, or mouse, it is recommended to use external devices for better quality. Technology is always changing, so you should research for the best equipment your budget will allow. Once you have your equipment, always perform performance and quality tests before recording. Do these tests every time you record because recording conditions might change.

Some of the equipment you may need includes:

- A mouse
- A camera
- A microphone
- A tripod
- Extra batteries or power cords

1.2b – Screen Capturing and Recording: Selected Features

With Camtasia Studio, Snagit, and Jing, we have a multitude of recording options and features. Captures can record all or only a select area of your screen. Here are a few highlights of the types of recording features that will be covered in-depth in later chapters.

Picture-in-Picture – Camtasia Recorder and PowerPoint Add-in include a picture-in-picture feature where you can show PowerPoint or desktop screen actions with a video of yourself or lecturer speaking from a different place (See Figure 1.5).

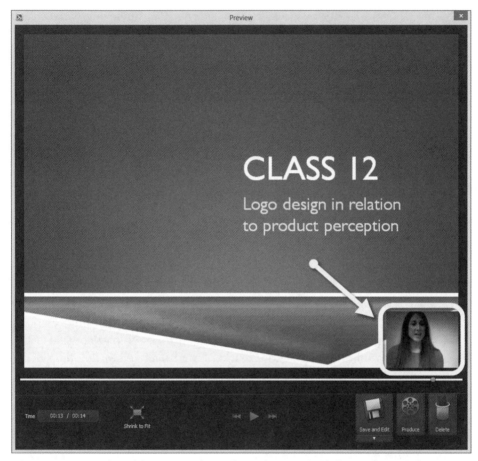

FIGURE 1.5 — Screenshot of the picture-in-picture feature being used with the Camtasia recorder.

 Picture-in-picture (PIP) – One picture is shown on a full-size screen and one or more pictures are shown as an insert window.

ScreenDraw – During the recording phase, you are able to draw lines, arrows, boxes, and free flowing pen lines on your screen. The color, shape, and width of these marks and objects can be adjusted. Draw marks can also be added during a paused state of the recording (See Figure 1.6).

Drawings and objects added during the recording phase cannot be edited; they are burned onto the recording clip. So, this function is mostly used for recordings that will not be edited or will not need to be posted before they are edited. For example, a sports coach reviewing video plays can draw and highlight the clips during a presentation or send a recording to players and coaches showing the highlighted area of the video.

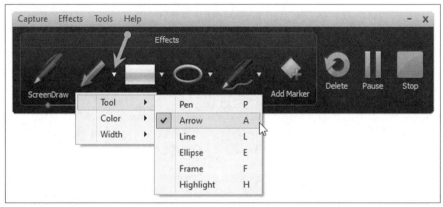

FIGURE 1.6 – Recorder shows the drop down of the tool tab and then the arrow tab.

Adding Markers – Markers are like a sticky note you can add at selected points during the recording or editing phase. During recording, you can mark a mistake that needs to be edited, a spot for a table of contents title, or an area to split the clip. These markers can be moved or deleted during the editing phase making them a perfect streamlining workflow tool.

PowerPoint Add-in – Included with Camtasia Studio is a PowerPoint Add-in for recording presentations that can be shared to sites or saved to be edited using Camtasia Editor. The Add-in records the slide presentation along with any audio and video played during the recording. An additional camera can be used to capture a speaker or other subject during the recording in a picture-in-picture overlay. This extra footage can be moved and edited on a separate timeline track.

 Markers – Creating recording notes, setting points to split long videos into multiple videos, and making navigation points.

1.2c – Powerful Editing Tools: Selected Tools

Both Camtasia Studio and Snagit come with editing tools. These editors can add special effects, text, and other enhancements to add to your projects. Here are a few highlights that will be detailed fully in later chapters.

Timeline — Timeline is a section of the Camtasia Editor used to combine and manipulate video, audio, images, and special effects together. The timeline has multiple video and audio tracks that you can add, delete, group, move, and lock (See Figure 1.7).

FIGURE 1.7 — Screenshot of the timeline showing video and audio tracks along with special effects.

Task Tabs – The Task Tabs menu bar holds many of the special effects that can be added to your projects. Some of these effects include callouts, transitions, captions, zoom-n-pans, quizzes, and mouse effects (See Figure 1.8).

FIGURE 1.8 — Screenshot of the Task Tab menu bar.

Most of the tab tools function with just a click or a click-and-drag maneuver. They will add these professional looking features to your timeline and project. For example, to add a **callout**, simply click the **Add callout** button to add a new callout onto your timeline. In later chapters, we will show a step-by-step on the finer details, such as placing, moving, and adjusting the callouts.

Callout – Graphics overlaid on the video or image to show an important process or object.

Library — You can import a variety of media and add video, audio clips, and images and edit them into your project. The library comes packed with a variety of images you can use or you can store your own media for use across projects (See Figure 1.9).

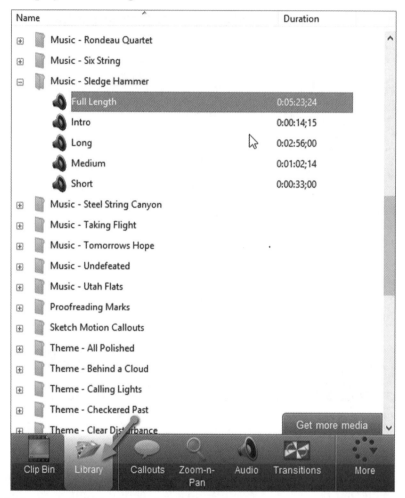

FIGURE 1.9 — Screenshot of the Library tab with file selections.

TechSmith adds additional downloadable content for your library on their Website. These include music tracks, callout themes, and images.

 Library – Holds timeline sequences, audio, images, and video clips to use in your project.

Captions — Camtasia Studio supports enhanced captioning. This feature lets you use **ADA (The Americans with Disabilities Act)** or **Section 508** compliant closed and open captions. Captions can be imported, typed, or translated using the voice recognition feature by using the Camtasia Editor. Captions also can be added by importing your notes from a PowerPoint presentation.

Key Term   **ADA** — The Americans with Disabilities Act - federal anti-discrimination act to make sure qualified people with disabilities have the same opportunities people without disabilities have.

Key Term   **Section 508** — An amendment to the Rehabilitation Act of 1973 where as people with disabilities have access to technology.

The captions are placed on a separate timeline track for easy editing and can be moved and rewritten if your project changes. The style, color, and position can all be modified to fix your needs (See Figure 1.10).

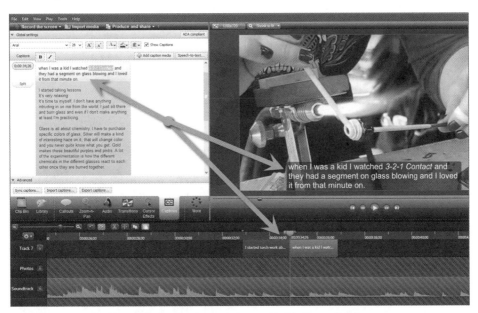

FIGURE 1.10 — Screenshot of the caption feature being used inside Camtasia Editor.

Captions can be used as a search tool for your video project and can be open or closed during the start of the video.

1.2d – Share Your Projects: Selected Formats

After your video is recorded and edited, you can post your project directly to social media sites, or produce them in a number of different file formats. Camtasia Studio has the ability to develop a table of contents, quizzes, and searchable videos by posting to Screencast.com or using Flash.

You will be able to produce a number of videos in a variety of formats:

■ **MP4 – Flash/HTML5 Player** – .mp4 – Motion Picture expert group 4

■ **WMV – Windows Media Video** – .wmv – Window Media Video

■ **MOV – QuickTime movie** – .mov – Quick Time Movie

■ **AVI – Audio Video Interleave video file** – .avi – audio video interleave video file

■ **M4V – iPod, iPhone, iTunes compatible video** – .m4v – MPEG-4 Video file from iTunes

■ **MP3 – audio only** – .mp3 – MPEG 1 or MPEG 2 audio Layer 3

■ **GIF – animation file** – .gif – Graphics Interchange Format

Share your videos quickly and directly to sites like:

■ **Screencast.com** – TechSmith sharing site

■ **YouTube** – Video sharing site

■ **SCORM** – Compliant Learning Management System (LMS)

A production wizard will walk you through all the available options for rendering your project (See Figure 1.11). Depending on the file format, you will have the option to add watermarks, a built-in player, metadata, and a table of contents.

1.3 — About the Book

This book splits the preparation work and description of the interface and fractures apart from the step-by-step procedure lists located in the later chapters. This was done to streamline the step-by-step portion as much as possible. To further keep the steps as clear as can be, each section starts off with a quick overview and a step list before an in-depth detail explanation.

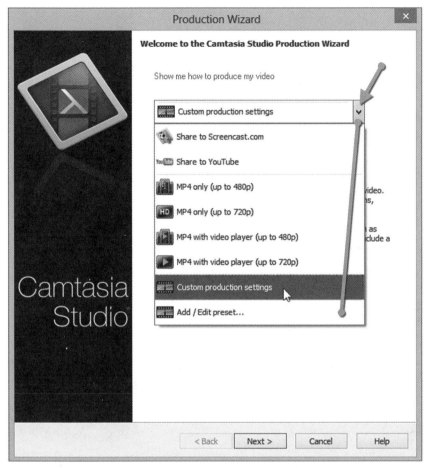

FIGURE 1.11 — Screenshot of Production Wizard.

This book also includes a number of additional materials that are included on a DVD. Callout signs will indicate when a file or video is located on the DVD for review.

1.3a – Chapter Layout

The chapters in this book are split and divided to maximize learning and ease in finding the features or menus you are searching for. Chapter 2 holds information for preparing your project including writing a script, equipment needed, and tips for a clean recording. Chapter 3 will serve as the blueprint for the Camtasia Studio interface. All of the menus are documented with their functions described. Chapters 4-9 are step-by-step lists on how to perform tasks and add features such as recording your screen, adding callouts, and sharing your video. The first part of each of these chapters will have a list for quick reference followed by an in-depth look at the process.

A breakdown of the chapters:

- **Chapter 2** – Preparation set-up work for your project for the best possible recording or editing

- **Chapter 3** – Overview of Camtasia Studio menus and interfaces

- **Chapters 4–9** – Provide step-by-step instructions on how to perform tasks or add features

- **Chapters 10–11** – Learning Snagit and Snagit Editor

- **Chapter 12** – Learning Jing

1.3b — Terminology

During Chapters 4–9, we will be discussing in detail step-by-step instructions on how to record, edit, and produce your project. These chapters are heavy in computer, project, and program terminology. Many of these actions and locations have the same name. I will be using a common and user-friendly technical writing system of using a bold face font to describe menu item names, buttons, file formats, programs, interface parts, and keyboard keys. This style is used to differentiate between a work action and programs, formats, or terms.

In addition, file formats will be written using their actual file extension for clarity. This is how they are viewed on your computer screen and you will be able to quickly identify them.

For example, the action step-by-step list to record:

1. Open **Camtasia Studio Recorder**.

2. Select the area of the screen to capture (Full or Custom).

3. *Optional:* Click the **Custom** button. Enter or select size once custom options is expanded.

4. *Optional:* Click the **Webcam** button to activate camera recording.

5. *Optional:* Click the **Audio** button to activate audio recording.

6. Hit the **F9** (default) hotkey or the **Record** button to start recording.

7. Watch the 3-2-1 countdown and get ready for the recording to start.

8. Record your screen project.

9. *Optional:* Add effects to the recording.

10. Hit **F10** (default) hotkey or the **Stop** button to end recording.

11. Preview the recording in the **Recorder Preview Window**.

12. Click the **Save and edit** button to save the file as a **.camrec** file and open the recording within the **Editor** for editing.

13. Click the **Produce** button to open the **Production Wizard** to create the video without editing.

And the paragraph:

> When you are ready to record, open the **Recorder** through the **Menu Options** and press the **Rec** button. Once you are finish with the screen capture, click the Stop button. The default setting is to save the capture as a **.camrec** file that can be edited within the **Editor**.

Both examples show how similar the terminology and action names are. Without differentiating them, what you need to do could get lost in where it is located. With the bold lettering highlighting the menus, interface areas, file formats, and programs from the explanation of the work action, the action becomes clear.

1.3c – On the DVD

Included in this book is a companion DVD. This DVD holds a variety of important information that collaborates with the book.

Some of these features include:

- **Mini tutorial videos** — showing the actions talked about in the book

- **All images in color** — to see more detail color coding used by the programs

- **Project files** — create your own projects using supplied sample files

- **Sample projects** — completed project created by the programs

1.3d – Book Callouts

There are also a number of different callouts for further information including additional files on the DVD and research ideas for the Internet. With changes in technology, you will want to research the latest information for your project. The callout Net Research will indicate an ideal topic for a further information search.

- **Net Research** — Changing or using dependent information that should be research for the latest updates

- **On the DVD** — Extra files on the DVD

- **Quick Clip** — Quick tutorial videos on the DVD

- **Tip/Note** — Useful information and tips for a project

- **Key Term** — The meaning of an important word or phrase

CHAPTER SUMMARY

This chapter provided an introduction to Camtasia Studio. We quickly gave you an introduction to TechSmith's other programs, Snagit and Jing, which will be covered in more detail in later chapters. This book will help you understand each of the applications. In the next chapter, you will develop a competence in all basic tasks to successfully prepare, record, and share your first presentation.

CHAPTER PROJECTS

1. Write in a journal the most important information and thoughts you have after reading each chapter in this book. Brainstorm how you might use this information.

2. Write your own definition of Camtasia Studio and include all of its features.

3. Define a Timeline and how you would use it.

4. List five features you are interested in using and why you might use them.

5. What is ADA and Section 508 and why are they important?

6. List the difference between Jing and Snagit and explain which you would use and when.

7. Describe an idea you have and what features you would like to use that are in Camtasia Studio.

8. Make an exact list of all of your equipment (mouse, cameras, microphones, tripod, extra batteries or power cords) and perform a performance and quality test. Do you need any additional equipment? If you do, research the possibilities.

9. Explore the library and describe five clips you might like to use.

10. List ten key terms or words from Chapter 1 or the glossary you did not know before reading this book and write the definitions in your own words.

11. Search on the Internet the minimum system requirements of Camtasia Studio (www.techsmith.com).

Bibliography

U.S. Environmental Protection Agency. *Section 508: Accessibility* (n.d.). Retrieved April 26, 2012 from http://www.epa.gov/inter508/faqs/index.htm#1

CHAPTER 2

PLANNING AND PREPARATION

IN THIS CHAPTER

Camtasia Studio makes it easy to record your computer screen to create and share your Microsoft PowerPoint presentations, screencast tutorials, personal movies, or voice narrations. Many of us are excited about our projects and want to start recording them right away. However, before you begin to record your screen there are important steps to take to make those recordings professional and polished. In this chapter, we will focus on the importance of prepping your files, recording space, and equipment before recording your project.

Once you've completed this chapter, you will be able to:

- Learn the advantages of a streamlined script or outline
- Understand storyboarding
- Define your goals for your audience
- Choose a good recording location
- Take prerecording steps for a smoother recording
- Prepare your equipment and settings
- Perform a project run-through
- Record your presentation with editing in mind

 Files: All figures in this chapter are in color located in the chapter folder on the DVD.

2.1 — Starting Your Project

Camtasia Studio can be used for both professional and personal projects. Videos, screencasts, and presentations can range from family scrapbooks to interactive classroom quizzes. Video projects can be simple and quick or complex with advance features. This wide range of end use makes Camtasia Studio very versatile.

Some project examples are:

- Work presentations
- Personal trip or event videos
- Tutorial training
- Marketing materials
- Family movies
- Classroom support
- Distance learning
- Classroom lessons or quizzes
- Family scrapbooks

Once you have outlined the overall objective and have an idea of who is going to see the project, it is time to start building your project. It is important not to rush into the recording phase. The more you flush out your project in the preparation phase, the smoother the recording and editing phases will be.

2.1a — Write a Script

A common mistake in creating a video project is to focus only on the visuals. The visual part of the project is what people will see, therefore, much of the time in preparing centers around this aspect of the presentation. However, having a clear narrative to tell the story or message you are trying to convey to your audience is just as important. It does not matter how pretty your presentation looks if your audience loses attention or misses the point you are trying to convey. Your project will not be as effective as it could have been.

Define the Goals of the Presentation

It is easy to stray off topic when narrating or constructing a project. Defining the goal of the overall project can keep you focused on the relevant and important content rather than extra miscellaneous information.

Ask yourself this question:

Is this something the viewer really needs to know?

If the information is not essential, then cut it out of the project. If you still want to add the information, try using supplements. For example, I have two case studies I want to share, but only one that is directly related to my video. I can add the additional information in a separate document such as a .pdf or a smaller video for further review. This keeps my main video project streamlined while still presenting all the information I wanted to share.

 .pdf — Portable Document File — Multi-platform format by Adobe Systems.

Use a concise headline structure for a clear hierarchy of important topics. Having a lot of talking points can get confusing for a viewer especially if it is detailed information. Grouping the information in smaller bites using a hierarchy can keep both you and the audience on track.

Know Your Audience

If you are going to share the project with a larger audience or if you are trying to convey a specific message, you should ask yourself the following questions:

- Who is your audience?
- Who is likely to see the project?
- When and where are viewers going to see it?
- What message do you want the viewers to see when watching the video?
- Is there information you want gathered from this project?

Answering these questions will narrow who your target audience is and the ways to reach them. No video or script will appeal to everyone you are trying to reach. Having an in-depth idea of who your target audience is the higher chance you have of your message reaching them. The appropriate length for videos for your audience can help your presentation. You can lose the attention of your viewers if you do not have your audience in mind.

A Strong Script

With a strong and concise narrative, you will be able to articulate complex messages clearly and confidently to others. A script does not have to be detailed to be effective. Even a loose outline will keep a clear focus and your project streamlined.

A list of points to write an effective script:

- Content should be short and to the point

- Try and stay on topic and focused on the content

- Think about holding the audiences' attention from beginning to end

- Know your topic and do research for the most updated information

- Break complex techniques or concepts down to multiple segments, around 3–4 steps each

- When possible, demonstrate, summarize, or show examples

- Reference real-life situations and use analogies your audience can relate to

- Understand the difference between having fun and being funny, and remember that funny is hard to accomplish in a group setting

- Keep visual assets and availability in mind when writing

During the recording stage, a script or outline will help reduce mistakes and a bad voice recording by keeping you focused on your content. Mistakes will happen during a recording, but a clear script or outline will quickly get you back on track.

Often transition sounds like "um" and "like" and "you know" are spoken and will need to be removed during the editing phase. Many times we say these words without knowing we are even saying them. An outline or script will help limit them by having a map of what we are going to say during the recording.

Closed Captions and Table of Contents

An added benefit of writing an outline or script is that it can be easily converted into captions and a table of contents for your videos. It is always a good idea to add captions when possible. Captions can be closed on playback or burned into the video. Your viewers might have hearing impairments or be in a location there they cannot play the audio. Having captions will help with both situations.

2.1b — Storyboarding

The narrative is not only the spoken word, it is also your video and images. When you are creating a video project, think about how the images work in conjunction with your script. One of the first steps to turning the outline or script from the written word to a visual project is a storyboard.

A storyboard starts to integrate the visual materials with your script. Storyboards are a series of drawings, slides, or photographs that visually conveys your story. Adding your outline, script, or dialogue to the storyboards will give a closer look to what your final project might look like.

A lot of time can be wasted during the recording stage if you do not have a clear idea of what you need to record. Storyboards can find any potential problems that might occur during the recording stage. They serve as a tool with the goal of streamlining production details. Where and when you use the visuals can be mapped out before you start recording, allowing you time to fix any issues, both technical and with the flow of the narrative.

Use your script or outline as a guide for your storyboard (See Figure 2.1). Then, add any still images of your visuals at important steps or draw a quick sketch if you do not have an image. A rudimentary sketch is fine; the goal is to represent a recorded visual, therefore detailed art is not required. Stick figures are perfectly fine for representation.

Although you might be only using a script storyboard, there are a number of different types of boards to show the representation of a script or idea into a visual form.

When narrating a screencast or giving a lecture your voice will greatly affect the audience in positive or negative ways

Watch these two videos and think about how the difference in voice affects the outcome of the speech.

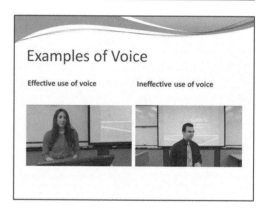

FIGURE 2.1 — Sample of a storyboard with an accompanying script.

A few types of storyboards

- **Outline or table of contents** — uses outline material with image highlights

- **Full action script** — script and images with camera movement notes

- **Concept boards** — detailed illustrations focusing on a location, background scenery, or event

- **Editorial or production boards** — reflect the story and the camera shots in detail

- **Commercial boards** — normally in color on large sheets of paper and are very detailed

- **Graphic novel or comic-book boards** — very detailed boards that tell a story without camera action notes

 Project: Fill in blank script and storyboard frames.

2.1c — The End Use of Your Project

Before you start recording your project, you should think about how your project will be used after you complete it. With the new technology and viewing patterns, there are more ways for your audience to view your project.

How your audiences will view the video will affect the file size, file format, aspect ratio, and destination. Some are hard to change after the recording stage and might need to be redone. It is best to think of how the video will be used before recording so you set your project files up correctly during the recording stage.

How to determine end use

- How will you record your project?

- How will this project be shared?

- Where will the video be watched?

- If the project will be shared over the Internet, are there bandwidth or accessibility issues?

- What will be the video aspect ratio?

- How long is the project?

A Mobile Audience

There are a number of advantages for creating and sharing videos and tutorials. Once the videos are created, students, friends, or coworkers will be able to view the videos anywhere or anytime on different devices.

Preparing Project Files

If you know the video end use, you can optimize your files to fit the playback location or device. For example, if you know the video will be playing back at a widescreen ratio, you can create any background images to that size to use during the recording or editing phases.

Interactive Projects

With advances in technology, the ability to create distance learning and training tutorial videos has become easier. This includes adding interactive features such as quizzes into the video project. You can take advantage of interactive features to reach and test your audience.

Distance learning

Students do not have to be in the classroom to view updated videos. By sharing projects to Web servers, students can watch the videos at any location on multiple devices and basically bring the classroom around with them.

Quizzes

Video projects can be helpful for students or coworkers to review project notes by adding a quiz to the video to test what they just watched. After they see the results, they can review the video again, if needed. You are able to gather the results of the quizzes through e-mail or online services.

2.2 — Preparing the Recording Area

Preparing an area for recording can solve a number of possible issues relatively easy. The area includes your computer screen and the location you will be working. The work you do preparing and selecting a calm location, decreasing background sounds, and cleaning your desktop will increase the quality of your recording.

2.2a — Choosing a Recording Location

Choosing a recording location will depend on what type of project you will be recording. Many of the location factors have to do with the recording phase. If you are just working with Camtasia Studio Editor, like creating a family album, then the location may not be as important. In choosing a recording location, think about what distractions are in that location. Everyplace will have problems that will hinder your recording, the goal is to select a place with less and fix any distractions you can.

When recording from a desktop, try and soundproof the area as much as possible. Turn off any electronics that you will not be using. Many devices will have sounds like motor hums and alarms. The goal is a silent area for a clear audio recording. Natural sounds, like traffic or birds, could also affect the recording.

When working outside, wind will be a big factor. Even a small breeze can be picked up with your recording device. Try and minimize wind sound by recording around or in shelter. There are microphone wind covers the will help defuse the wind sound. A quick audio test recording will check if the wind sound is being picked up.

When recording a lecture in a large room, placement of the camera and microphone will be important. Web cameras have a limited recording distance and perspective. Additional audio devices might be needed to capture the speaker and not the rest of the room. Marks on the floor might be needed to show where the camera recording area ends.

Create a Designated Recording Space

If you are going to be creating a number of recordings, it is recommended that you customize a designated recording space. This will save you setup time and keep the quality of your recordings consistent. Configuring a designated recording account on your computer will also streamline the setup process.

To help with keeping a consistent recording space, you can create a designated user account on the computer you are using. Keep this account only for your recordings and keep the desktop and taskbar clear of extra information or icons.

Consistency for a Cohesive Recording

Once you prepare a spot, try and use it for any recordings while using the same equipment. This will keep a cohesive look between clips especially if you are making the recordings in segments or on different days.

2.2b — Background Noises and Acoustics

Your recording area greatly affects the quality of any audio that you are recording. A bad audio recording location can ruin an otherwise good recording. Time will be wasted if you are forced to rerecord a full new recording or audio.

Examples of Background Sounds

The recording location can be affected by room size and shape. Each room has different acoustics and could affect the overall sound. Background location sound such as trains, a dog barking, or air conditioners, could be caught in your audio and ruin the recording. Perform an audio test at the desired volume level and check the background sounds.

Some background examples are:

- Construction and traffic noise
- Dog barking
- School buses
- Trains

Additional computer sounds:

- Computer fan or hum
- Headphone and microphone cords clicks
- Keyboard and mouse sounds
- Operating system or program alerts

Additional domestic sounds

- Air conditioners
- Size of room and room acoustics
- Squeaky floors or furniture

Additional office sounds

- Office workers talking
- People passing by the recording area
- Phones

Without talking, perform an audio test recording. Capture all the background sounds you might miss while concentrating on your project then playback the recording with a headset on and listen to the sounds. There are a lot more background sounds that you might realize.

Keeping a consistent recording area will help with audio continuity. A change of recording location or equipment can change the quality or sound of the audio. Some adjustments can be made in the editing phase or with software to try and level out the audio tracks, but it is more efficient and professional to check your audio during your initial recording.

2.2c — Preparing Your Computer and Screen for Recording

Once you are all set with your dialog and gathering your files, there are still a few more steps to take before recording to assure a clean and professional looking project. Distractions in your recording can draw the attention of your viewer away from your video.

Desktop Background and Computer Operating System

A simple and clear desktop and recording area is needed. A solid color background is preferable. It is less distracting to the viewer. Messy or complex backgrounds should be avoided (See Figure 2.2).

Some steps for keeping a clean recording screen are:

- Clear extra **icons** on the desktop

- Empty recycle bin

- Hide or auto-hide the **taskbar**

- Hide or delete personal files or folders

- Use a simple arrow for the mouse pointer

- Make the desktop background a solid color

- Turn off any theme system sounds that you do not want recorded

Icon — An image object displayed on the computer screen to navigate to a file on the computer or device.

Taskbar — A bar that contains tabs or icons that can be used to change from one task to another.

FIGURE 2.2 — Example of a messy and distracting desktop.

QUICK
CLIP

Messy verses a clean recording background — A quick clip comparing a complex recording area verses a simplistic one.

With a simple and clear desktop, the focus of the audience will remain on what you are presenting. Screen objects and mouse movements are easily distinguished and followed (See Figure 2.3).

The taskbar and other operating system features can also interfere with your project. For example, if you have a clock in your taskbar and pause your recording the time will appear to skip. It might be small but it is noticeable to your viewer. The same skip can appear if you cut or slice your recording clip during editing.

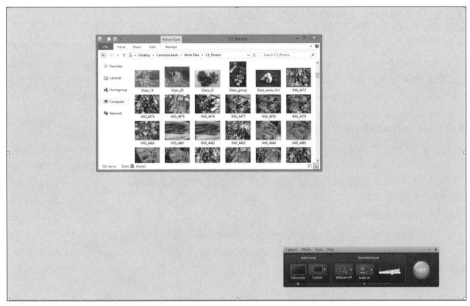

FIGURE 2.3 — Sample of a clean background and screen recording area that is not distracting.

Open Files and Programs used in Your Recording

Before you start, have all the files you will be using ready and accessible for use.

- Outline, script, or storyboard
- Files you are going to open or show should be easy accessible folders
- Open programs that you will be using and close the ones you are not using

2.3 — Equipment

This book will assume that you have already installed all relevant software including Camtasia Studio. If you have any issues with the instillation, it is best to go to the TechSmith Website for more up-to-date program information, software instillation, and technical support.

 TechSmith — A software company that publishes leading screen recording programs such as Camtasia Studio, Snagit, and Jing.

2.3a — Software Install and Compatibility

There are times where you might have to use equipment or a computer that you are not familiar with. New equipment or updates might be needed for compatibility. Leave time before your presentation to install or update any software required for a smooth running of your presentation.

Software Install and Updates

Before you start recording, it is good practice to check your equipment and update all your software that you will be using. Sometimes software will have automatic notification that might activate during your recording.

Equipment Compatibility

Determine all technical specifications and compatibility of the external equipment and your computer you will be making the recording on before you start.

Use External Devices

External devices generally are better quality than any built-in features because they are designed for that function. For example, if you are on a laptop, use an external mouse with a smooth mouse pad over the touchpad. The external mouse will have smoother and crisper movements. When recording any audio, use an external microphone over the one built in to the laptop.

Samples of external devices.

- External microphone
- Web camera
- External mouse
- Internet access

Depending on the computer you are using, an external connection to the Internet might be needed if you are sharing the project online.

2.3b — Using a Camera

Choosing a camera to fit your needs can be wide-ranging. As with other types of technology, new models and processes are developed every year.

The camera type will also be dependent on how you will use the camera during your project.

Camera Types and Reviews — Perform a camera device search including types of cameras including video and Web cameras. Compare the type of recording, budget, and end product of your project to select the best recording device.

Before selecting a camera, research the device types and how the camera is going to be used in your projects. How the camera is going to be used will affect the type of camera that would work best.

Choosing a Camera

Selecting a camera type depends on how you are going to use the video and what you are going to capture with the camera. For use during the recording phase, a Web camera is ideal (See Figure 2.4). For video work being edited within the timeline depends on the quality, size, and budget of your project. Multiple cameras can be used at the same time for different purposes. For example, during a lecture a Web camera might be used to capture the speaker during the presentation while a separate video camera might be used to capture the room, props, or other views to be edited into the project.

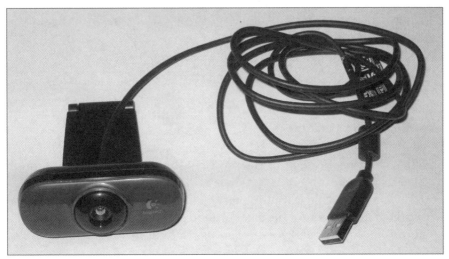

FIGURE 2.4 — An example of a USB Web camera.

Connecting and Calibrating the Camera

You want to make sure that your camera is working and is receiving video. Be sure to perform any pre-recording test to check and make sure your camera is installed or setup properly. Use both the video Preview Window and a short recording to be sure. If the camera is not showing video, you might need to check both the camera settings and the Recorder settings.

Web Camera

Use a Web camera for any picture-in-picture recording using the Recorder, Editor, or PowerPoint Add-in. When installed properly, the video preview window will show the live streaming camera input.

Key Term   **Add-in** — An enhancement to a base program.

Video Camera

While not available to be used for picture-in-picture recording through Camtasia, other types of video cameras can be used to record for use within the Editor.

Positioning the Camera

With both the **Camtasia Recorder** and **PowerPoint Add-in**, there are camera preview windows that show the live stream camera input. Use this window to make sure you are capturing what you want in your video (See Figure 2.5).

An otherwise good recording can be ruined if the camera placement is wrong. Marks on the floor can provide a speaker a marker as to where the camera view ends.

Recording with the Camera

When working with one stationary camera, the placement of the subject within the camera point-of-view will be a little easier than with multiple cameras or a moving subject. When working with more than one camera, plan your camera angles and shots for each camera. With a moving subject, test the point-of-view of the camera and mark the area for reference. If you are unable to add markers, try and use natural markers like trees, desks, or signs.

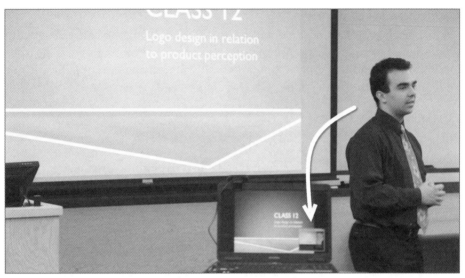

FIGURE 2.5 — An example of bad blocking as the subject is stepping outside of the camera recording area.

Set or check Web camera and deployment — Once you have the video camera working, you need to make sure that the speaker or the subject of your recording stays within the recording zone.

2.3c — Audio Setting and Microphone Use

Good audio is essential to a professional-level recording. Bad audio or miscellaneous background noises could easily ruin your recording. People tend to skip videos with bad audio. Because of this, good audio capturing during the recording phase is very important. There are some modifications that can be done to edit and enhance audio tracks, but those techniques take time and might not always work.

Net Search **Microphones types and reviews** — Perform an audio device search including types of microphones. Compare the type of recording, budget, and end product of your project to select the best recording device.

Choosing a Microphone

Each microphone type will have different strengths and vary greatly depending on how you are going to use them. For example, a headset microphone (See Figure 2.6) works well while sitting at a desk, but is not good for a classroom setting.

Types of microphones

- **Headset** — worn on the head keeping your hands free

- **Lapel, or attachable** — can be attached to clothing or objects

- **Desktop** — sits on the desktop or flat surface

- **Hand-held** — a directional microphone to be pointed at the subject to be recorded

- **Shotgun** — very narrow recording area that can be mounted or hand-held

FIGURE 2.6 — An example of a headset microphone.

Key Term **Shotgun Microphone** — A very narrow recording area that captures sound in an outward cone in front of the device.

Try and use an external microphone because generally they offer better sound quality. Internal microphones are not the best quality and also might catch keyboard-clicking sounds. Use an external **USB** plug-in microphone if you are recording from a laptop. It is good to carry a microphone in your computer bag.

Key Term **USB port** — Universal Serial Bus (computer port).

Do not use internal microphone unless that is your only option because the sound quality will not be as good and might record keyboard-clicking sounds.

Attachable microphones, such as a lapel microphone, work best for hands free and are not intrusive during the recording. Knowing how you will be using your microphone during your project will help you pick the type of microphone that will best fit the needs of the recording.

Additionally, you can use a separate hand-held external audio recording device for separate audio track and a backup.

Connecting and Calibrating the Microphone

When you first start learning about using audio and creating recordings, it is advisable to use the **default** audio settings. The default setting works well for most recording projects and will record system sounds to a separate track within the **Timeline**.

Key Term **Default** — A value that is preset when user does not set values.

Positioning the Microphone

The type of recording you will be doing will determine how you position the microphone. For example, narration recording where you will be sitting at a desk will work best with a headset microphone or a desktop microphone that is away from the keyboard. The microphone can pick up keyboard strokes and other computer noises.

Types of placement and locations:

- Desktop recording

- Classroom recording

- On a set location

- An outside location

Each location will have a different set of possible issues to overcome. For example, outside locations might have wind noises that the audio recordings will pick up.

Keep the microphone a constant distance from your mouth and try and keep this distance consistent every time you use it. If you start to see the audio levels changing drastically, it could be your microphone moving out of position. Six inches generally is a good distance for a desktop microphone, while a headset microphone will be positioned a few inches from the corner of your mouth. It should not be directly in front of your mouth.

Do some practicing with your microphone and settings. Every microphone is slightly different. Record some test audio using the microphone for the best placement and volume settings. The goal is to capture a clear mid-level audio track without extra noises such as breathing or clicking sounds.

Recording with the Microphone

The recording programs in Camtasia Studio, Snagit, and the PowerPoint Add-in all have live audio volume levels indicator that can be checked before you start your recording (See Figure 2.7).

FIGURE 2.7 — Screenshot of audio volume levels inside Camtasia Recorder.

The **Automatic gain** on the microphone could accidently pick up additional background noises. Turn the device input gain off or on low.

Automatic gain — An adaptive system inside your audio recording device that reduces the volume if the sound is strong and raises the volume when it is weak.

To be confident on your audio settings, perform a quick recording and open the clip in Camtasia Editor. The audio clip will show in the timeline in a **waveform**. This wave should be in the middle portion of the clip. Too high or too low indicates potential problems with the audio quality (See Figure 2.8).

FIGURE 2.8 — Screenshot of an audio wave clip inside Camtasia Editor.

Adjust the audio volume levels on the recorder, or device, and check the placement of the audio device. Then preform another check to see if the wave is now in an acceptable zone.

Waveform —The shape of a signal in the shape of a wave.

Portable Audio Recording Device

It is very handy to have a portable audio recording device with you during any on-location casting. Built-in microphones, within a Web camera for example, might not capture clear audio and have a lack of mobility. Good quality backup or separate audio tracks will allow more flexibility during the editing process. Portable audio recording devices are made to capture sounds and generally have a better quality audio recording (See Figure 2.9).

Natural Sound

Having a separate audio recorder will allow you to capture natural sound around your recording area. These sounds can be added into your video during the editing phase to enhance your project.

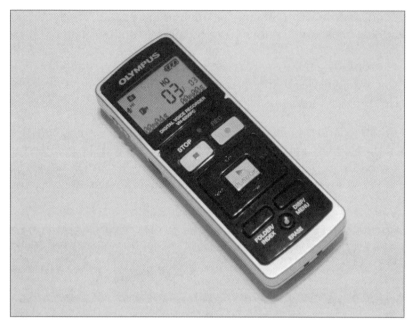

FIGURE 2.9 — An example of a hand-held audio recorder.

Key Term **Natural Sound or Wild Sound** — Sound recorded in the environment of the recording area that might not be picked up in the initial recording or additional sounds for enhancement.

Examples of natural sound:

- Phone ringing
- Dog barking
- Paper rattling
- Door closing
- Cars or trains
- Office, crowd, or nature sounds

Interviews or other types of voice recordings are another useful feature for using a portable audio recorder. The camera microphone might not record the best voice track, using a second device will serve as primary or back-up audio clips.

2.3d — Internet Connection

If you are broadcasting or recording over the Internet, you will want to check your bandwidth and connection to the Internet. It is recommended to perform a full run-through of your project to test the Internet and equipment settings. Additional access logins might be required.

2.4 — Effective Recording Techniques

There are a few simple techniques that can make your project have a professional look. These techniques can also make your editing easier and more efficient. Take your time with the recording stage. You need a good recording; it is the heart of the project.

2.4a — Perform a Full Run-Through

Gather all your materials and open all of the programs you will be using. Like sports, practice will make your performance better and save time in the recording phase.

Computer checklist:

- Clear the last window and Internet searches from the search fields

- Delete extra tabs open in an Internet browser

- Open all your windows or programs you will need

- Close all programs that are not needed

Perform a run-through with all mouse movements and practice the steps you will be taking. Look for good places for pauses. This will keep your project clean and free flowing during your recording.

Recording checklist:

- Take your time and do not rush

- Work from an outline or script

- Keep your recordings precise and to the point

- Gather all your materials and have them ready

- Check any audio and video device input settings

- Record in a quiet area

- Record in the same location for consistency

- Perform a quick test recording to check audio levels and camera input

- Record background music separately and add later with the **Camtasia Editor**

 Camtasia Editor — The editing portion of the program Camtasia Studio.

2.4b — Making Mistakes

If you make a mistake, just pause, then keep going where you left off. You not have to do every recording in one take. Mistakes will happen during a recording. To manage and edit these mistakes, use a pause after the mistake before continuing. In the editing process, you will be able to spot these pauses in your timeline and make a clean edit.

Managing and using your mistakes:

- Don't be rattled if you make a mistake

- After a mistake, pause then repeat the dialog line or perform the action again

- Use the pause button within the **Camtasia Recorder** to pause the recording

- Use the paused time to gather your thoughts

- Pauses work as editing queues, signaling where an edit is needed

 Camtasia Recorder — The recording portion of the program Camtasia Studio.

2.4c — Voice Narration and Speech Recording

With posting projects online and distance learning, you might never see users. In recording dialog, it is best to narrate as if you are talking to a real person in the same room.

Delivery is as important as content. How you present the dialog will convey its own message to your audience.

Voice narration and speech recording tips:

- Talk in sound bites and short phrases

- Speak clearly and pronounce each word and each syllable

- Speak conversationally and try to be relaxed

- Do not be timid, be confident in what you are saying

- Speak with a dynamic rhythm by changing the speed, volume, and pitch of your voice

- Change tone of voice and try not to be monotone

- Speed up on unimportant items and slow down at interesting points

- Punctuate your pauses, use the pauses as tools

- Avoid transition sounds, such as "er," "um," and nervous coughs

- Project your voice and speak loud enough for your audience or microphone to clearly hear you

- Control your body language by standing tall, keeping your head held high, and maintaining relaxed movement

- Enjoy what you are doing, it will be reflected in your voice

- Make eye contact by looking around to your audience and focus on one person at a time

Although a number of points in the list might sound like they are only for a group presentation and not a recording at your desk, they will still increase the overall quality. For example, the tip about projecting your voice might not sound useful for recording a narration at a desk while you are alone talking into a computer microphone. However, if you speak as if you are talking to a small audience, the narration recording will sound more natural.

2.4d — Use Pauses

Pauses will be one of the biggest helpful queues when editing. Pauses can also help you gather your thoughts. **F9** (default **hotkey**) starts and pauses the Camtasia Recorder. Use it whenever you have a mistake, long pause, or need to rework your recording area.

Using pauses:

- Voice and mouse pauses

- Pausing for editing queues

- F9 (default hotkey)

Use pauses not only with voice but also with your mouse. Try not to move the mouse when the recorder is in pause, or move it back as close as possible to the original location. Otherwise the mouse will appear as if it is jumping around the screen. In editing, it is better to pause and say a line again with the mouse in the same spot. If it is not and later you edit and cut that part of the video, your mouse will appear to jump locations on the video.

(Key Term) **Hotkey** — Keyboard key stroke commands that act as shortcuts to menu actions.

2.4e — Manage Mouse Movement

Mouse jumps occur after editing video clips or moving the mouse when paused. The mouse appears to jump from one position to another area of the screen. This can be very confusing to the viewer and should be avoided.

There are a number of tricks in the editing process we can use to try and fix jumps but they do not always work. An otherwise perfect recording can be ruined with bad mouse jumps.

Mouse jumps can cause real headaches in editing. It is good practice to try to move the mouse as little as possible. And if you do have to redo a part and are still recording, try and move the mouse as close as possible to the last location before the mistake.

Mouse movement tips:

- Try not to move the mouse and talk at the same time

- Move mouse — pause – talk – pause – move mouse

- Try to show what you are saying and say what movements you are doing on screen

- Do not move the mouse or other screen objects around quickly

- Watch where you place what you move with the mouse

- Avoid the mouse buttons or the scroll wheel unless you tell the viewer, because they cannot see your mouse actions

Try and describe your actions and your mouse movements. Remember your viewer cannot see your keystrokes and it is sometimes difficult to follow quick movements with the mouse. You do not want to lose or confuse them so remember to speak your actions. This includes the scroll buttons. We use these key commands or buttons in regular day use and it is easy to forget during a screen recording that the viewer cannot see or know the actions unless you describe them.

It is hard to follow the mouse when watching a screen video. There are mouse features inside Camtasia to highlight the viewer's being able to follow the mouse; however it is good practice to make minimal mouse movements. This will also aid in the editing process.

Be careful where you leave your mouse when narrating or recording action on your screen. You do not want your mouse to cover up important information, words, or images.

If your recording has multiple windows open, try and keep their movement to a minimal. It is common to keep moving the window around the screen but it is both distracting to the viewer and will make it harder to edit your recording.

2.4f — Screencast Recording

When you are recording your screen, imagine your audience watching over your shoulder as you are talking. Remember they cannot see your keyboard or mouse movements so it is good habit to always try and speak these movements so the viewer can follow along.

Screencast recording tips:

- Invite them to take the same actions on screen.

- Remember, you have no personal feedback during the recording.

- Do not say "just click here" or use a Hotkey Commands without saying the key combination.

- Each step must be showed on screen and spoken. There are special effects that can be used, however, it best to develop the habit of speaking the movements.

- Give directions and user action.

- Content should be short and to the point, stay on topic.

- 3–9 minutes overall with 5–7 minutes being ideal.

2.4g — PowerPoint Slide and Image Design

When building your PowerPoint presentation slides or designing images that you will use during your recording, visibility, and legibility will be important features. These visuals are not helpful if the viewer cannot understand them. There are a few techniques you can incorporate to make them look professional and easy to view.

PowerPoint slide and image design tips:

- Suggested **Font** and size: 32 point Arial (or another simple sans serif font) as it is easier for the viewer to read.

- Use simple and cropped images.

- Use simple and clear animations and backgrounds.

- Spell check any captions or text being used.

- Use contrast to highlight important information.

- In PowerPoint, use the Notes field for reference and to import into the Editor for captions.

- In PowerPoint, the Title is imported as your marker and table of contents, add a placeholder title if you want to create or mark a spot in the recording.

- In PowerPoint, use an animation or slide transitions within your presentation during the recording. You can add them using the Editor, but it is faster and smoother to use what you already setup.

- Try and use the same transitions or animation styles throughout the project for consistency.

(Key Term)   **Font** — Characters of text in a certain style and size.

2.4h — Using Sound

Sound recording is more than the voice or narration audio. Background and natural sound will also be a factor when you are recording. During the editing phase you can add sounds on different tracks in the timeline to enhance your project. If you are recording on a location, listen to your surroundings for any wild or natural sounds you can additionally record. For example, if your project is about a hiking trip that you have still photos for, recording background birds, waterfall, or other sounds can be added to the timeline with the photos to enhance the end video project.

CHAPTER SUMMARY

Creating and sharing projects needs planning and preparation to make the recording professional and polished. Defining your goals and knowing your audience will help you focus your ideas for your script and storyboard. You must also know how you are going to use your project because that will help determine how you record it and what you use to record it. To save time and rerecording, preform checks on the background noise, acoustics, computer operating system, files, software, camera, audio settings, microphones, and Internet connection. Learning effective recording techniques such as learning how to handle mistakes, knowing the tips on voice narration and recording, using pauses and managing mouse movements before you start, will also help you to have a professional look to your project.

CHAPTER PROJECTS

1. Discuss the importance of using an outline or script and the ways to use them.

2. In your own words, write a summary of a section of the chapter you feel is most important to you and why it is important.

3. Identify who is your audience for the presentation and what are your goals?

4. How would you prepare your screen and location for recording?

5. Give three reasons why you would change a script.

6. Watch a commercial and write an outline, goals, and the audience it is targeted for.

7. Write a two-page script and assemble a four-frame storyboard to go with it.

8. Read a short story and write a script or create a storyboard about it.

9. Exchange a short script you have written with a friend, classmate, or coworker and receive constructive feedback.

10. Make a checklist of all the equipment you need for a presentation including cameras, audio devices, Internet connections, and software.

11. Share in a discussion or write about any experience you might have with video projects.

12. Write in a journal the most important information and thoughts you have in this chapter. Brainstorm how you might use this information.

13. Search the Internet about the different types of cameras including video and Web cameras. Compare the type of recording, budget, and end product of your project to select the best recording device. Which would you wish you had and which can you afford on your budget?

CAMTASIA STUDIO

CHAPTER 3

MENUS AND INTERFACES

IN THIS CHAPTER

In this chapter, we will review the interfaces and features of the programs within the Camtasia Studio while the later chapters focus on the individual action tasks and a step-by-step guide. Some of the menus are embedded within each other and can be complex in its structure. To keep this chapter as a quick reference guide as well as an in-depth resource, there will be a short overview list before the explanation for important or common features.

Once you've completed this chapter, you will be able to:

- Navigate the Camtasia Studio interfaces
- Understand the menu system
- Know how the Studio programs integrate with each other
- Explore the PowerPoint Add-in
- Adjust hotkey commands

 Files: All figures in this chapter are in color located in the chapter folder on the DVD.

3.1 — Understanding the Interface Menus and Terminology

Before you begin to record or edit your projects, you should understand the different interfaces included in Camtasia Studio. Knowing the interfaces increases your ability to learn what the programs are capable of, what features are available, and how they work together. In return, you are able to integrate and organize these features into your presentations efficiently.

3.1a — Differentiating Similar Names

Actions and menu items sometimes have the same name. In an effort for clarity, this book uses a technical writing style where the menu item names, buttons, file formats, programs, interface parts, and keys will be in bold lettering to differentiate from an action or explanations. For example, the paragraph:

> The default setting is to save the capture as a **.camrec** file that can be edited in with the Editor. When the **Save and Edit** icon button is clicked, the **Editor** will launch with the recording placed in the **Timeline** and **Clip Bin**. This action will also close the **Recorder Preview** window while the **Recorder** will remain open.

The bold lettering in this paragraph highlights the actions for the menu, interface areas, file format, and programs from the explanation of the feature.

3.1b — Menu Terminology

There are a lot of different terminologies for user interfaces. Some can get confusing because they are similar to each other and others have multiple names. For example, a dropdown menu in media source could be called a fly-out or pull-down in another. In this book, common names were selected for the parts of the user interface.

- **Dialog box** —interface window that opens for user interaction
- **Dropdown menu** — a button when clicked opens a list of options that are selectable

- **Icon button** — an image graphic that also acts as a function button
- **Menu Options bar** — a bar commonly located on the top of the interface that has selectable dropdown options and generally controls the overall program
- **Right-click menu** — a menu that will open when the right mouse button is clicked
- **Window** — an area holding a program, dialog box, or user interface and can pop up and overlay over each other
- **Wizard** — a dialog box that will walk the user through a set series of steps

Context Menus

Context menus change to match the tool, location, or task you are working with. For example, when using the Editor, if you right-click on a track in the timeline, a menu for track-oriented tasks will appear. If you select a clip, and then right-click, clip-oriented tasks will appear (See Figure 3.1).

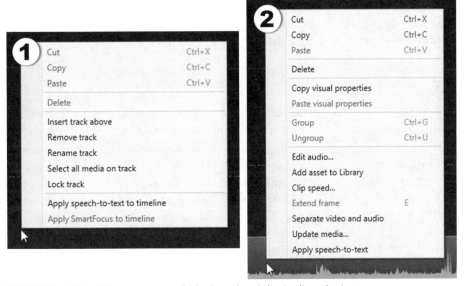

FIGURE 3.1 — Right-click context menus for both track and clip timeline selections.

1. Right-click context menu for a track selection within the timeline
2. Right-click context menu for a clip selection within the timeline

It increases the workflow speed rate to always right-click on an area of the interface, selections, or tool you are working with to see if the action you wish to preform is in the context menu.

Task dependent Menus

Task dependent menus are menu or options only active during certain actions. When not activated, these menus will be grayed or disappear altogether. If you see a menu that is grayed out, the prerequisite task has not been activated. For example, in the Recorder Toolbar, if the camera option is turned off, then the selection to activate the camera toolbar will be grayed out. Once the camera is activated, the selection for the camera toolbar is accessible.

3.1c — Hotkey Commands

Hotkeys are keyboard shortcuts that use keystrokes to activate menu or task actions. For example, within the **Recorder**, the **F9** key will start the recording and **F10** will stop the recording. These actions can be selected through the menus but knowing the key commands will streamline your workflow. Although some of the hotkey commands are customizable, the noted hotkeys in this book are the default commands.

3.1d — Overlapping of Task Commands

The overlapping of task commands and locations can be seen throughout the programs. For example, in the **Camtasia Recorder Menu Options** bar, there is a selection under the **Tools** tab for **Options**. This opens the **Tool Option** task window. The same window dialog box can be opened through both the **Webcam** and **Audio** options dropdown menu in the **Recorded inputs** section. It is the same tool task window dialog box, just located in different interface locations for your convenience (See Figure 3. 2).

1. **Menu Options dropdown** — Menu Options > Tools > Options

2. **Recorder Webcam dropdown** — Webcam dropdown > Tools > Options

3. **Recorder Audio dropdown** — Audio > Tools > Options

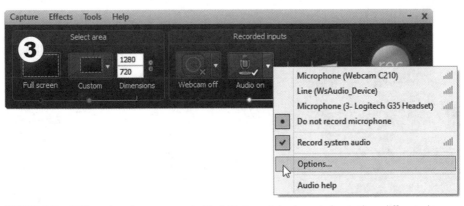

FIGURE 3.2 — Different locations to open the Tool Options dialog box window in three different places.

This redundancy happens in all of the Camtasia Studio interfaces. The overlap is built-in for the user to be able to customize their workflow for increased efficiently. For example, some people like using hotkeys where other people might use the dropdown menus.

3.2 — Launching Camtasia Studio and the Welcome Window

After installing Camtasia Studio, you are ready to launch the program to start creating your screencast or video project.

Net Search — **TechSmith** — **www.techsmith.com** — The site of the company that created Camtasia Studio is packed full of tutorials and help documents along with free downloadable assets to add to your library. The site also holds a community section for tips and creative ideas. It is recommended to have this site bookmarked in your Internet browser for frequent visits.

3.2a — Launching Camtasia Studio

Camtasia Studio is split into two main sections, the Camtasia Recorder and the Camtasia Editor (See Figure 3.3). These sections work as individual programs or seamlessly together to create well-rounded projects. The studio also includes Camtasia MenuMaker, Camtasia Player, and additional features like the PowerPoint Add-in along with other sharing capabilities.

FIGURE 3.3 — Screenshots of the Camtasia Recorder (left) and Camtasia Editor (right).

1. **Camtasia Recorder** — the pre-recording screen capture phase

2. **Camtasia Editor** —the editor with a project opened

Because these programs can be started individually, you can launch them from Menu Options through your operating system or inside each

Camtasia Studio program. For example, you can open the Camtasia Recorder individually through desktop shortcuts or the Start menu. You can additionally open the Camtasia Editor and launch the Camtasia Recorder by clicking the Menu Options, Welcome Window, or Hotkey command (See Figure 3.4).

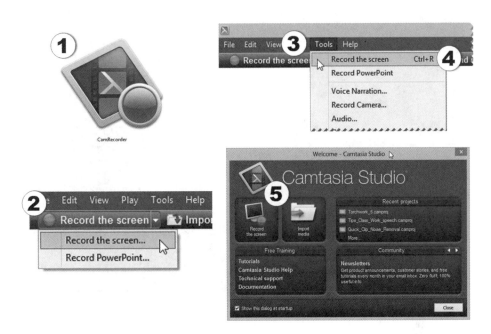

FIGURE 3.4 — A selection of possible ways to launch the Camtasia Recorder.

1. **Shortcut icon** — an icon located on your computer

2. **Record the screen** — a button that opens a dropdown menu within the Editor

3. **Menu Options** — a menu dropdown within the Editor

4. **Hotkey command** — a key stroke within the Editor

5. **Welcome Window** – a dialog box that opens once the Editor is launched

3.2b — The Welcome Window

When you first open **Camtasia Studio**, a **Welcome Window** will pop up with options to record your screen, open a saved file, or help and information navigation (See Figure 3.5).

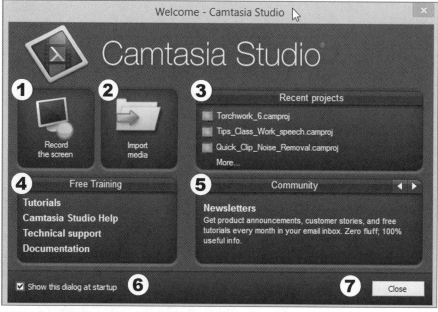

FIGURE 3.5 — This is a screenshot of the Welcome Window that displays options in navigation and help.

1. **Record the Screen** — a one-click option to start the Camtasia Recorder

2. **Import media** — brings up the Import media dialog window

3. **Recent projects** — a history of recent projects that were opened in the Camtasia Editor

4. **Free training** — launches the TechSmith Website with tutorials and downloads

5. **Community** — launches the TechSmith Website to the community section

6. **Show this dialog at startup** — toggles on and off the Welcome Window opening on startup

7. **Close** — closes the Welcome Window

You can disable the automatic startup of the **Welcome Window** at launch of **Camtasia Editor** or keep it active for easy navigation. The **Camtasia Recorder** can be launched individually but will not automatically launch the **Welcome Window**.

NOTE

When you first launch Camtasia Studio, a tutorial video will automatically start playing. This video will only start on first open; however the "getting started project videos" is located in the program folder if you wish to view them again.

3.3 — The Camtasia Recorder Interface

The Camtasia Recorder is used to create screen captures. Once open, the Recorder will overlay the recording area and interface over your desktop. The Camtasia Recorder includes three phases; pre-recording, recording, and post-recording. Each phase has a different interface that includes options and tools needed for that phase of the screen capture (See Figure 3.6).

FIGURE 3.6 — Screenshots of the three recording phases (pre-recording, recording, and post-recording).

1. **Pre-recording phase interface** — tool selection and settings before recording

2. **Recording phase interface** — expanded tools during the recording phase

3. **Post-recording phase interface** — preview of the recording with sharing and saving options

3.3a — Pre-recording Interface

After Camtasia Recorder is launched, the interface will overlay the screen and is ready for recording. The recording area can be adjusted to only capture the selected area of the screen. Input and tool settings can be adjusted before the recording starts.

Two major sections of the pre-recording interface are the Recording Area Selection and the Recording toolbar. The Recording Area Selection shows what portion of the screen will be captured and the Recording toolbar holds the settings for the screencast. The Recording toolbar can be moved independently or connected to the Recording Area Selection box (See Figure 3.7).

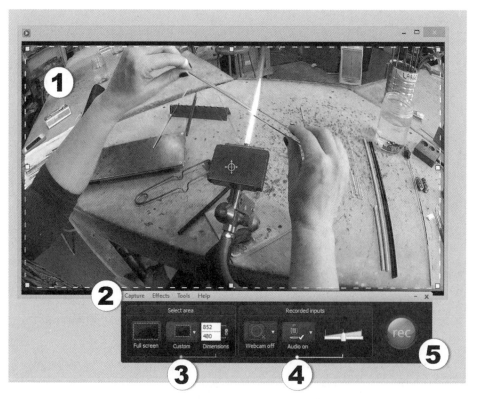

FIGURE 3.7 — Screenshot of the Camtasia Recorder interface overlaid over a video background showing the selection box, menu options, selection area, recorded inputs, and record button.

1. **Recording Area Selection box** — overlay selection of the interface to set and adjust the dimensions of the recording

The Recording Toolbar

2. **Menu Options** — application pull down menu for options features as well as additional tools

3. **Selection Area** — full-screen, preset, and custom recording dimensions linked to the Recording Area Selection box

4. **Recorded Inputs** — controls for input devices such as cameras and microphones

5. **Record Button** — button to start the recordings

Selected Interface Highlights: Pre-recording

Recording Area Selection

The dotted green line shows the boundary of the recording area. Everything inside the dotted box will be recorded while everything outside will not be part of the capture. To move or resize the recording area, click and drag the adjustment handles or the compass (See Figure 3.8).

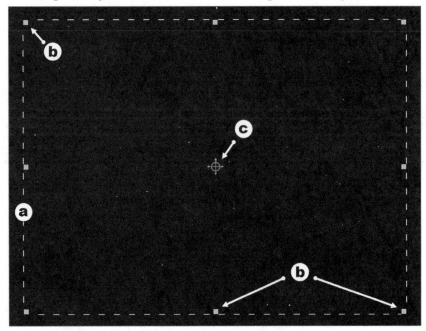

FIGURE 3.8 — Recording Area Selection overlaid over a black background.

A. **Recording Area Selection box** — a dotted green box that outlines the area of the screen to be recorded

B. **Adjustment handles** — little black outlined squares can be clicked on with the mouse and dragged to adjust the Recording Area Selection box to the desired dimension on both the sides and corners of the Selection Area box

C. **Moving compass** — an icon that when clicked allows you to fully move and reposition the selection area while keeping the dimensions

D. **Outside the Capture area** — any portion of the screen outside the dotted box will not be included in the capture

Menu Options

The outline of the **Menu Options** will remain the same in the pre-recording and recording phases with the only changes being particular tools being grayed out and unable to select. The **Menu Options** is located at the top of the **Recording Toolbar** (See Figure 3.9).

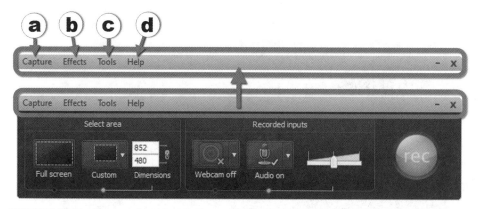

FIGURE 3.9 — The location of the Menu Options within the Recording Toolbar.

A. **Capture** —— selections controlling the recording aspects of the program. These include starting and stopping the recording along with area selection and what input devices will be used.

B. **Effects** —can be included into the screencast during the recording. These include captions, system stamps, and system sounds.

C. **Tools** — launches additional programs included within Camtasia Studio and opens the Tools Options and Recording toolbar dialog boxes.

D. **Help** — additional recourses and help selections.

Effects Options

Within the **Effects** Menu Options is a listing for the **Effects Options** dialog box. This dialog box has **Annotation**, **Sound**, and **Cursor tabs** with task-specific tool options (See Figure 3.10). Click on the tabs at the top of the menu window to select the effect settings. The path to the dialog box is: **Effects > Options**.

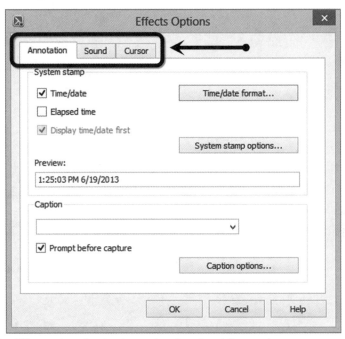

FIGURE 3.10 — Effects options showing Annotation, Sound, and Cursor tabs.

- **Annotation tab** — settings for system stamps and captions including the options to adjust the background, positions, font, color, effects, and style of the stamps and captions

- **Sound tab** — controls the recording sounds or system sounds volume and type of mouse button click sounds

- **Cursor tab** — toggles the activation of the cursor effects being editable in Camtasia Editor or burned into the capture during recording

Within the **Annotation tab** there are a few embedded dialog boxes that hold more in-depth style selections. These include **Time/Date Format**, **System Stamp Options** and **Caption Options**, and font and color selections (See Figure 3.11).

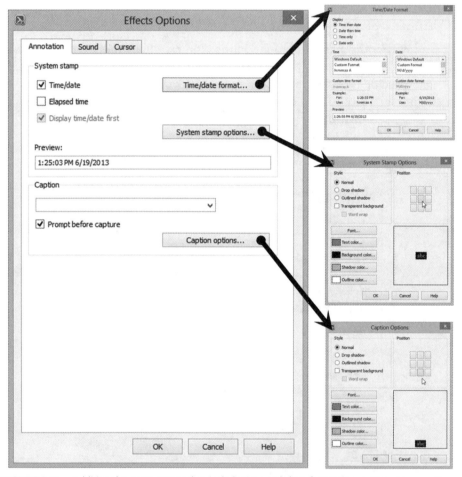

FIGURE 3.11 — Additional pop-up menus that include time and date formatting, system stamp options, and caption options.

The combination of these options allows customizations of the stamps and captions to fit the style and look that best fits the project.

At the top of the **Cursor tab**, there is a checkbox called **Make cursor effects editable in Camtasia Studio** that activates or deactivates the cursor effects during the recording. To activate the mouse effects during the recording, make sure the checkbox is unchecked and the rest of the tab is active for selection (See Figure 3.12).

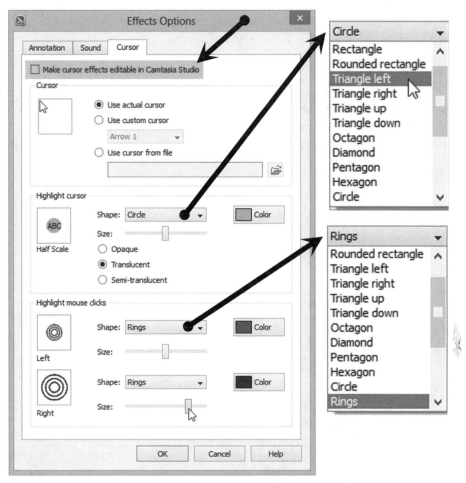

FIGURE 3.12 — Effects Options showing Cursor tab open and "Make cursor effects editable in Camtasia Studio," Circle, and Rings highlighted.

The effects are burned into the capture during the recording stage. These effects will not be able to be edited or removed later. If this box is checked, the rest of the tab will be grayed out and not eligible for selection because all of the effects will be available in the editor and the mouse effects data will be collected, but not burned into the recording.

Tool options

Within the **Tools Menu Options** is a listing for the **Tools Options** dialog box. This dialog box holds **General**, **Inputs**, **Hotkeys**, and **Program tabs** with additional settings for the relative subject. In addition to the Menu Options, both the **Webcam** and **Audio input** dropdown menus have a selection to open the **Tools Option** dialog box to the **Inputs tab** (See Figure 3.13).

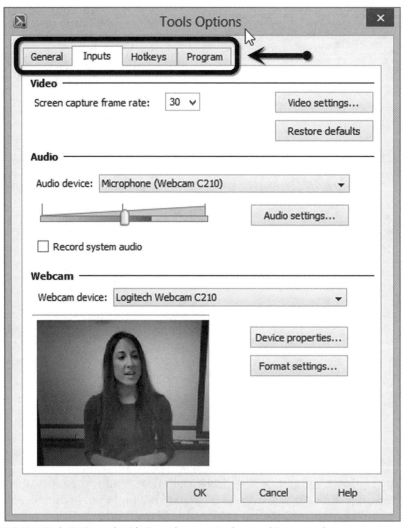

FIGURE 3.13 — Tools Options tab with General, Inputs, Hotkeys, and Program tabs.

- **General tab** — settings for the overall capture and saving location and file options

- **Inputs tab** — preview, selection, and settings for input devices

- **Hotkeys tab** — allows customization of selected hotkeys

- **Program tab** — settings for recording region, workflow, and minimizing the **Recorder**

Click on the tabs at the top of the menu window to select the effect settings. The path to the dialog box is: **Tools > Options**.

Recording toolbars

This dialog box will toggle the activation and display of the tools and statistics during the Recording phase (See Figure 3.14). The path to the dialog box is: **Tools > Recording Toolbars**.

FIGURE 3.14 — Toggles for tool options to appear and use in the Recording phase is on the Recording Toolbars.

Camtasia MenuMaker

Camtasia MenuMaker is a separate program that creates a menu interface to organize and share videos or screencasts for distribution (See Figure 3.15).

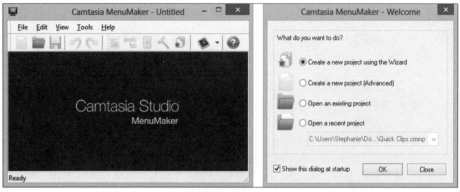

FIGURE 3.15 — Camtasia MenuMaker interface and Welcome menu

A **welcome** dialog box will automatically pop up once **MenuMaker** opens to create a menu interface for video distribution. There are options to use a walkthrough **Wizard** or create a menu without the help of the wizard. Creating a menu for multiple videos is an easy way to organize and display on DVDs, CDs, and drives.

Camtasia Player

This player is very simplistic and plays **.avi** files. It is useful for viewing an **.avi** file saved directly from the Recorder without using the Editor (See Figure 3.16).

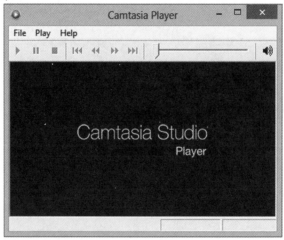

FIGURE 3.16 — Camtasia Studio Player that plays .avi files.

Selection Area

Click the **Custom** button. The custom options expand and enter dimensions into the Width and Height fields. Preset sizes can be selected by clicking the dropdown arrow to select from a list of **Standard** or **Widescreen** dimensions (See Figure 3.17).

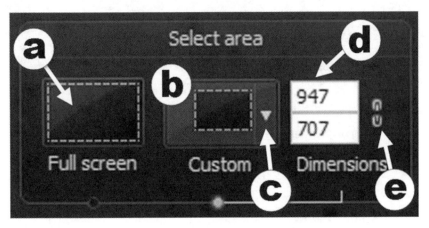

FIGURE 3.17 — Full screen and Custom selections for the Screen Recording Area are shown.

A. **Full screen** — default setting and records all the activity on the entire screen

B. **Custom** — records a selected area on the screen, application, or window

C. **Custom Dropdown menu** — a list of common aspect ratios and recent dimensions

D. **Height and Width (in pixels)** — text fields where the Height and Width of a selection can be entered

E. **Lock/Unlock** — toggle maintaining the aspect ratio with the Width and Height dimensions

Recorded Inputs

This section of the **Recorder Toolbar** controls the activation, settings, and device selections of the **Webcam** and **audio** imputs (See Figure 3.18).

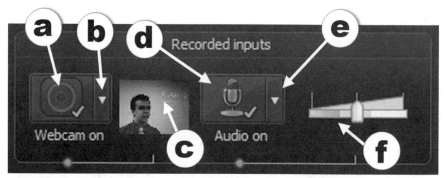

FIGURE 3.18 — Input controls for external and internal devices along with previews.

A. **Webcam on/off** — toggles the activation of the Web camera

B. **Webcam Dropdown menu** — opens Webcam options and device selection

C. **Webcam Input Preview** — previews for both camera input and audio levels

D. **Audio On/Off** — toggles the activation of the audio device

E. **Audio Dropdown menu** — opens audio options and device selection

F. **Audio Input Preview** — live preview of audio levels

A larger live preview image of the Webcam appears when the mouse hovers over the smaller preview image (See Figure 3.19).

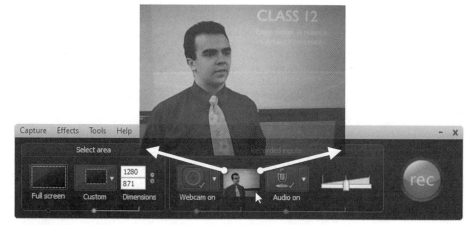

FIGURE 3.19 — A larger image of the Webcam input will appear if the mouse hovers over the input image in the Recorded inputs bar.

The **green checkmark** next to the **Webcam** and **Audio icons** indicates that the input devices are activated and will be recording once the screen capture is started. The **red X** and the closing of the input previews indicate that the input devices are not enabled and will not be recording (See Figure 3.20).

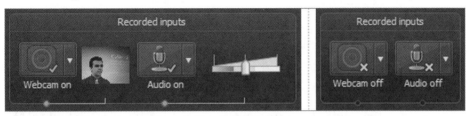

FIGURE 3.20 — Input options turned on (left) and off (right).

Click on the white down arrow to open the dropdown menu with Webcam settings and options.

3.3b — Recording Interface

Once the recording starts, the interface will change to the recording phase. The selection area is represented by blinking corners and the **Recording toolbar** will show the selected tools and settings (See Figure 3.21).

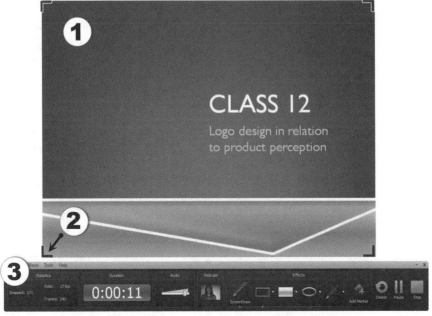

FIGURE 3.21 — Overview of the Recording phase interface shows the recording area, corners, and recording toolbar.

Overview Review — Recording Interface

1. **Recording area** — everything within the area outlined by the corners will be captured in the recording

2. **Corners** — indicate the edge of the recording area and will change color and blink once the recording has started

3. **Recording toolbar** — expanded menu that contain statistics, duration, audio, Webcam preview, drawing effects, markers, delete, pause, play, and stop buttons and information

Selected Interface Highlights: Recording

The **Recording Toolbar** changes depending of what recording tools are activated within the **Recording Toolbars** dialog box (See Figure 3.22).

FIGURE 3.22 – Full expansion of the Recording Toolbar with all tools and information.

The path to open the dialog box to toggle the activation of the tools is **Recorder > Tools > Recording Toolbars**.

The **Effects** section within the **Recording Toolbar** will expand or decrease depending on the effect selected. For example, if **ScreenDraw** is selected, the **Cursor Effects** bar will collapse. If the **Cursor Effect** is selected, the **ScreenDraw** will collapse (See Figure 3.23).

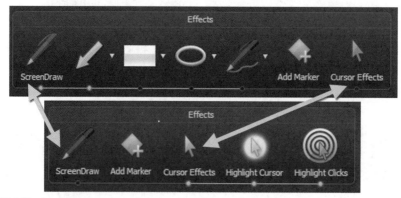

FIGURE 3.23 – The Effects section will change according to what is selected.

3.3c — Post-recording Interface

After the recording ends, the interface will change to the post-recording phase. Use the recording preview windows to review the screen capture and Webcam. If the recording is good, select the save, edit, or produce buttons (See Figure 3.24).

Overview — Post-recording Interface

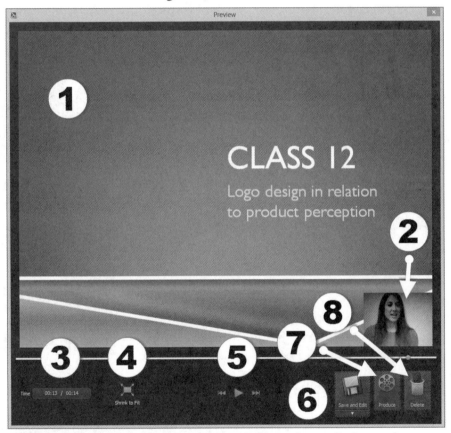

FIGURE 3.24 — Recorder Preview window opens automatically once the recording is stopped.

1. **Video preview** — this area is a preview of the recording

2. **Webcam input preview** — this preview is a live feed of what the camera is capturing

3. **Time** — the location of the playback frame compared to the overall duration of the recording

4. **Shrink to fit/View at 100%** — toggles the video from full size to fitting within the **Video Preview**

5. **Player controls** — buttons for **Restart**, **Jump to End**, and **Start/Pause**

6. **Save and edit** — click the **Save and Edit** icon button to open the recording in the **Editor**

7. **Produce icon button** — opens the **Production Wizard** to create a shareable video

8. **Delete** — deletes the recording without saving

Selected Interface Highlights: Post-Recording

Shrink to fit/View at 100%

The **Shrink to Fit** icon button will shrink the playback video to fit the preview area window. The **View at 100%** icon button will show the playback video at full recording size. If this size is larger than the preview area window, scroll bars will appear along the sides that are longer than the window allows. Only one of these icon buttons will show at a time (See Figure 3.25).

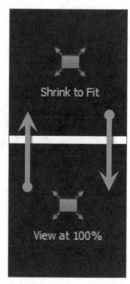

FIGURE 3.25 — Playback video view fitting adjustments.

Save and edit

The default setting is to save the capture as a **.camrec** file that can be edited in the **Editor**. When the **Save and Edit** icon button is pushed, the **Editor** will launch with the recording placed in the **Timeline** and **Clip Bin**. This action will also close the **Recorder Preview** window while the **Recorder** will remain open. By clicking the dropdown menu, a **Save As** selection can change the save location, name, and file format to .avi without opening the **Editor** (See Figure 3.26).

FIGURE 3.26 — Save and Edit selection will Save As....

3.4 — The Camtasia Editor Interface

After you are done recording or gathering media, the Camtasia Editor is used to assemble your project (See Figure 3.27).

Overview — Editor Interface

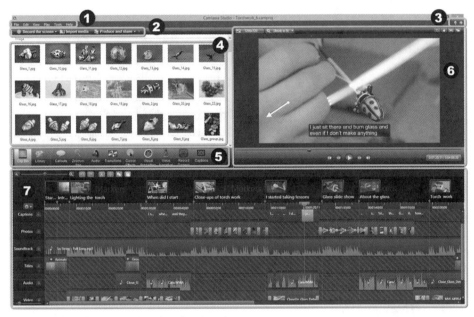

FIGURE 3.27 — The Camtasia Studio Editor interface.

1. **Menu options** — holds navigation, setting, and tasks mostly dealing with the overall program

2. **Application menu** — will launch the Recorder, PowerPoint Add-in, Production Wizard, or import media

3. **Help menu** — launches the help document or online tutorials

4. **Tool and Media preview** — a content area that will change to show the media or tools depending on what media or task tab you are on

5. **Clip Bin and Library tabs** — tabs that store all imported and available media

6. **Task tabs** — tabs that hold tools to create and preform selected features

7. **Preview window** — will show preview for the selected area of the timeline where the playhead is positioned

8. **Timeline** — shows all of the frames, tracks, and features of your project including videos, images, audio, special effects, and other features

Selected Interface Highlights: Editor

3.4a — Application Menu

The Editor Application menu includes icon buttons to launch the Recorder and Production Wizard and imports media (See Figure 3.28).

FIGURE 3.28 — The three icon buttons (Record the screen, Import media, and Produce and share) of the Editor Application menu are shown.

- **Record the screen** — launches the Recorder and minimizes the Editor

- **Import media** — opens a navigation dialog box to select media to import

- **Produce and share** — launches the Production Wizard to render the project

3.4b — Preview Window

The preview window shows the action in the timeline at the point of the playhead along with project playback controls. The media in the timeline can be resized, adjusted, moved, and rotated in the canvas area of the preview window (See Figure 3.29).

1. **Preview Window** — overall area containing the playback controls, canvas, and view options

2. **View Options** — editing dimensions, view options, and video dimensions

3. **Canvas** — video playback with the ability to arrange, rotate, resize, and order the content linked to the timeline

4. **Playback Controls** — controls the video playback with play, pause, fast forward, fast rewind, and shows the time and current frame

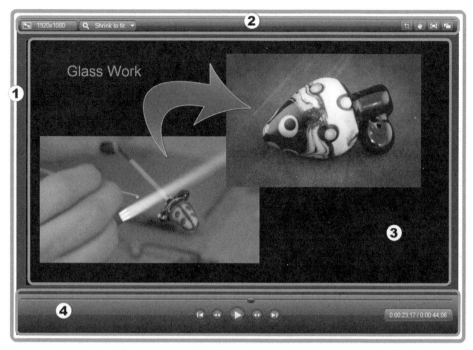

FIGURE 3.29 — This screen shows the preview window, view options, canvas, and playback controls.

3.4c — Task Tabs

Most of the major tasks used when editing your project have their own tab (See Figure 3.30).

FIGURE 3.30 — Task bar with ten task tabs that can be used for your projects.

- **Callouts** — graphics that appear in the video project that highlight important objects or processes

- **Zoom-n-Pan** — gradual change in the focal area will magnify or move the view area

- **Audio** — tools to adjust the audio volume, quality, and background noise

- **Transitions** — a fade or wipe animation combining two clips

- **Cursor Effects** — highlights the cursor and mouse clicks

- **Visual Properties** — enhancements and added effects to media clips
- **Voice Narration** — sound and voice recorder to add as a clip
- **Record Camera** — video and screen recording
- **Captions** — places text or script as a track
- **Quizzing** — interactive questions and answers

Select a tab to display the tools and settings associated with the task.

3.4d — Timeline

All media being used in the project is located within the timeline. The timeline is the main work area of the project with the splitting, cutting, arranging, layering, animating, and adding effects to media tracks (See Figure 3.31).

1. **Timeline Toolbar** — holds the magnifying slider, redo and undo, cut, split, copy, and paste

2. **Tracks** — area lines to add media, animation, and special effects

3. **Add Tracks** — a button to add tracks

4. **Toggle Marker and Quiz Track view** — opens and closes the maker and quiz track

5. **Marker or Quiz Track** — a collapsible track holding the markers and quizzes

6. **Time Duration Tracker** — indicates where in the duration of the timeline the media and playhead are located

7. **Playhead** — a slider that can select and move throughout the duration of the timeline that is linked to the preview area

8. **Markers** — pin points spots within the timeline and production

9. **Clips** — the media pulled or imported from the Recorder, clip bin, and library

10. **Snap guides** — yellow guide lines that pull or snap clips to markers, media, or other clips

11. **Animation indicator** — an icon of a blue arrow that indicates an animation applied to the clip

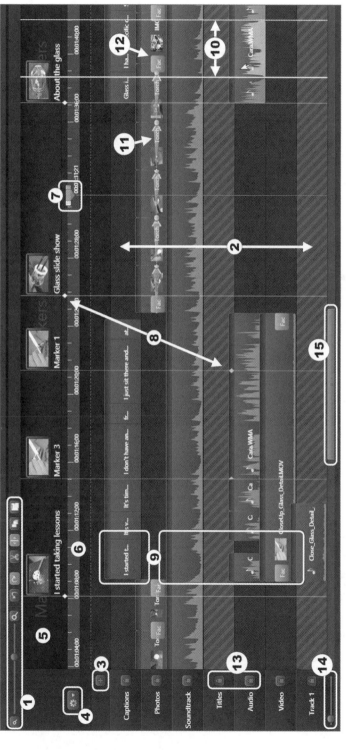

FIGURE 3.31 — The timeline has 15 areas (timeline toolbar, tracks, added tracks, toggle marker and quiz track view, marker or quiz track, time duration tracker, playhead, Markers, clips, snap guides, animation indicator, transition indicator, lock tracks toggle).

12. **Transition indicator** — an icon in-between or at the end of a clip to indicate a transition

13. **Lock Tracks toggle** — locks and unlocks tracks

14. **Track height adjustment** — adjusts the height of the tracks

15. **Navigation slider** — a slider bar that will navigate through the duration of the timeline

Playhead

The playhead consists of three main parts; the **Green in point**, the **Gray middle**, and the **Red end point** (See Figure 3.32).

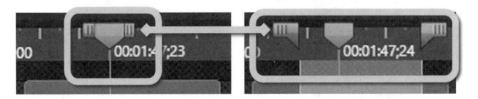

FIGURE 3.32 — The playhead has three main parts (green in point, grey middle, and red end point).

- **Green in point** — an indent movable slider that can mark the start of a selection

- **Grey middle** — the downward point and line represents the current frame and duration location of the playhead and preview window

- **Red end point** — an indent movable slider that can mark the end of a selection

3.5 — PowerPoint Add-in

The **PowerPoint Add-in** enables the presentations to be recorded with audio and video inputs. These recordings are saved in the **.camproj** file format for editing and sharing.

The recording **Add-in** is located in the **Add-in Tab** in the **Menu Option** within **PowerPoint** (See Figure 3.33).

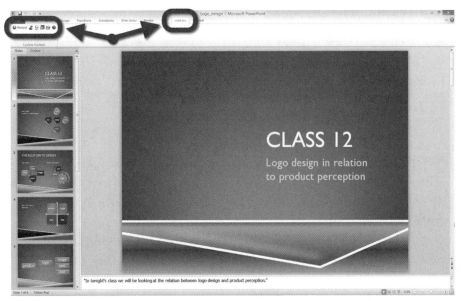

FIGURE 3.33 — Location of the Recording toolbar and Add-in tab.

___

NOTE

___

Depending on the version of PowerPoint installed, the interface might look slightly different. However the Add-in will still be installed.

3.5a — Recording Toolbars

The **Recording Toolbar** holds all the tools and settings for the **Add-in** (See Figure 3.34).

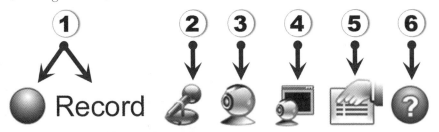

FIGURE 3.34 — Close-up of the Recording Toolbar.

1. **Record icon button** — starts the recording and the **PowerPoint** presentation

2. **Record Audio** — toggles recording the audio input

3. **Record Camera** — toggles recording the camera input

4. **Camera Preview** — launches a window showing what the camera will be recording and what will display during the recording

5. **Recording Options** — launches **Options** dialog box

6. **Help Topic** — launches the **Help Topic** guide

Record Icon Button

The Record icon button will start the presentation in full screen mode. The recorder will start automatically or pause depending on if the **Start the Recording paused** selection is checked in the **Camtasia Studio Add-in Option** dialog box.

The **Record** icon button will change to **Stop Recording** icon button if you are still recording after the end of the presentation (See Figure 3.35).

FIGURE 3.35 — Recording toolbar changed depending on if the recorder is running or stopped.

Camera Preview

If the camera is enabled, the **Camera Preview** button opens a preview window showing the camera input (See Figure 3.36). The preview will also show during the recording phase.

FIGURE 3.36 — Camera preview of what is recorded.

3.5b — Recording Options

Selecting the **Recording Options** button launches the **Camtasia Studio Add-in Options** dialog box (See Figure 3.37). This dialog box has selections for the overall program, video and audio, picture-in-picture, and record hotkeys.

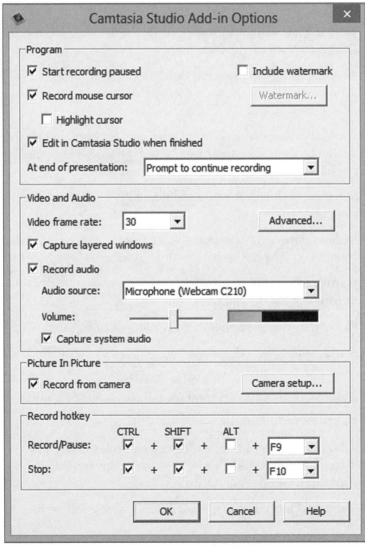

FIGURE 3.37 — The Camtasia Studio Add-in Options menu shows the Program, Video and Audio, Picture-In-Picture, and Record hotkey choices.

- **Program** — options dealing with the program including settings for the mouse cursor, watermark overlay, and recording functions

  - **Start recording paused** — toggles the automatic start of the presentation and recording once the record button is clicked

  - **Record mouse cursor** — toggles if the recording will include the mouse cursor and its movements within the recording

  - **Edit in Camtasia Studio when finished** — toggles opening the Editor after saving the recording

  - **At the end of the presentation** — options for end of recording action including to continue or stop the recording or be prompted to decide at the time

  - **Include watermark** — burns a permanent watermark into the video during the recording unlike adding an adjustable watermark within the Editor

- **Video and Audio** — includes additional settings for input source, video format, and system sounds

  - **Video frame rate** — lists the video frames per second with more frames equaling higher quality and file size

  - **Capture layered windows** — preserves unusually shaped or transparent dialog windows

  - **Record audio** — toggles the recording of audio input device

  - **Audio source** — a dropdown menu to select the audio device to capture the audio

  - **Volume** — slider control and preview of audio volume

  - **Capture system audio** — activates the collection of system sounds

  - **Advanced** — the advanced settings controls the advanced audio and video compression and formats similar to the **Tools Options > Input** dialog boxes within the Recorder

- **Picture-In-Picture** — when enabled, additional setting for camera input

  - **Record from camera** – toggles the recording of video input device

■ **Record hotkey** — change key strokes for Hotkey commands for Record/Pause and Stop

- **Record/Pause** — starts and pauses the recording

- **Stop** — ends the recording

Menus and Options After the Recording Starts

The default setting is for the **Recorder** to start paused and for the **Camtasia Studio Recording Paused** dialog box to show in the lower right hand side of the presentation screen. The pause before recording option can be turned off in the **Recording Options** dialog box. It is recommended to keep this action for a final audio check before the recording starts.

This dialog box has an **audio volume slider** and preview check. Press the **Click to begin recording button to start the recording** (See Figure 3.38).

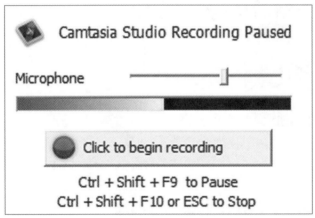

FIGURE 3.38 — Camtasia Studio Recording Paused box.

3.6 — Production Wizard

For the **Recorder**, **PowerPoint Add-in**, and the **Editor**, the **production wizard** will walk through all the saving and producing options (See Figure 3.39).

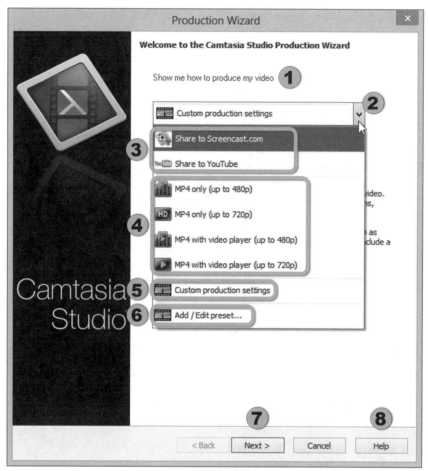

FIGURE 3.39 — Production Wizard used to render video projects for final use

Overview Review — The Production Wizard

1. **Help Link** — a link to the TechSmith Website opened to a tutorial page

2. **Option dropdown** — a dropdown menu that holds the type of production

3. **Preset site production** — preset to produce and upload to Screencast. com and YouTube

4. **Preset video production** — preset to produce videos with additional sharing files

5. **Custom production** — a selection to produce with custom settings

6. **Add/Edit preset** — an option to add or edit a preset or create a new one

7. **Next** — the Next button will navigate through the Production Wizard windows

8. **Help** — launches the help documents

Selected Interface Highlights: The Production Wizard

3.6a — Production Presets

A list of preset rendering and sharing options are available in the dropdown menu (See Figure 3.40). These selections have preset rendering and sharing settings and will have less wizard walkthrough dialog boxes because most of the settings are already chosen.

FIGURE 3.40 — The Production Wizard dropdown menu with six preset settings to choose from.

- **Share to Screencast.com** — ideal settings for Screencast.com including upload walkthrough

- **Share to YouTube** — ideal settings for YouTube including upload walkthrough

- **MP4 only (up to 480p)** — 480 pixels of vertical resolution, progressive scan, video file only

- **MP4 only (up to 720p)** — 720 pixels of vertical resolution, progressive scan, video file only

- **MP4 with video player (up to 480p)** — 480 pixels of vertical resolution, progressive scan, video file with accompanying support files

- **MP4 with video player (up to 720p)** — 720 pixels of vertical resolution, progressive scan, video file with accompanying support files

3.6b — Custom Settings

The Production Wizard will change the series of selected dialog boxes depending on the type of file rendering selected. The Production Wizard will only show the related settings and tools available to the type of file render (See Figure 3.41).

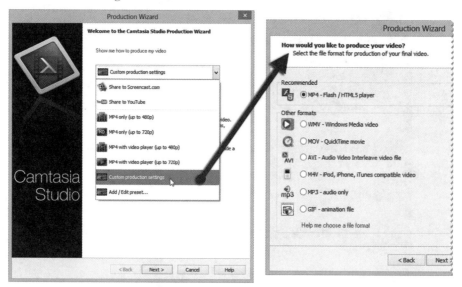

FIGURE 3.41 — Production Wizard with the Custom production setting highlighted and other types of file formats available.

- **MP4 — Flash/HTML5 Player** — .mp4 — Motion Picture expert group 4

- **WMV — Windows Media Video** — .wmv — Window Media Video

- **MOV — QuickTime movie** — .mov — Quick Time Movie

- **AVI — Audio Video Interleave video file** — .avi — audio video interleave video file

- **M4V — iPod, iPhone, iTunes compatible video** — .m4v — MPEG-4 Video file from iTunes

- **MP3 — audio only** — .mp3 — MPEG 1 or MPEG 2 audio Layer 3

- **GIF — animation file** — .gif — Graphics Interchange Format

Each of these selections might have a different series of dialog boxes but all will walk you through the production process.

3.6c — Production Results

After the video render, the Production Results dialog will pop up showing the data for the project (See Figure 3.42).

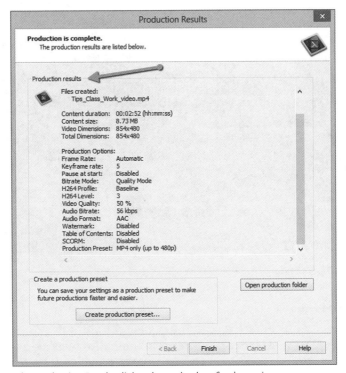

FIGURE 3.42 — The Production Results dialog shows the data for the project.

You can use this menu to review the project rendering, navigation, and create a new custom preset setting.

3.7 — Configuring and Customizing

There will be time when your project has many tracks, or you need to magnify on an area of the tracks, or want to increase the size of the production window or media bin and task tabs. The Camtasia Editor is a flexible interface and will allow for resizing of the timeline, tracks, preview window, and tool and asset preview. The boundary of these sections will have a slight line dividing the sections. Hover your mouse over these lines and the cursor will change to a double arrow indicating the directions the interface area can be moved. On the timeline, the sliders control the track height and magnification (See Figure 3.43).

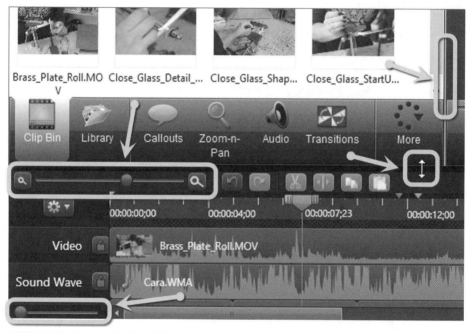

FIGURE 3.43 — The interface is flexible and can be moved.

Expanded Menus

Some menus have the option to extend or add tools to the menu bar. For example, the **Application menu** in the **Editor** has a dropdown menu with a selection to add **New**, **Open**, and **Save** icons to the menu bar (See Figure 3.44).

FIGURE 3.44 — The Application can be expanded.

Custom Settings

By creating custom settings and presets, you can streamline your workflow for optimal use. For example, within the Recorder, selected Hotkey commands can be changed to fit your workflow by using the **Hotkeys tab** in the **Tools Option** dialog box (See Figure 3.45). The path to the dialog box is **Camtasia Recorder > Tools > Options > Hotkey tab**.

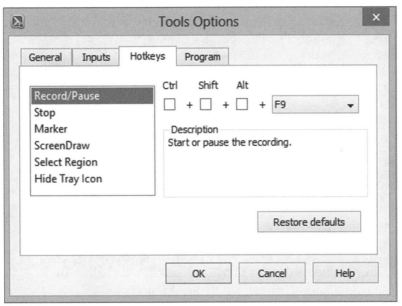

FIGURE 3.45 — The Tool Options shows the Hotkey commands.

It is best to keep the default Camtasia Studio setting until you learn more about the program and the workflow before you create custom settings.

CHAPTER SUMMARY

In Chapter 3, we looked at an overview of the Camtasia Recorder and Editor interfaces and terminology to navigate through Camtasia Studio. Some of the menus are embedded within each other and can be complex in its structure. We also explored how to start PowerPoint Plug-in and some of its features. We showed an overview of selected Production Wizard's interface highlights and some of the possibilities of presets, custom settings, and production results. In later chapters in this book, we will focus on a deeper understanding and provide a step-by-step guide to a variety of action tasks to develop your projects.

CHAPTER PROJECTS

1. Discuss or write about the importance of the Timeline and its toolbar.

2. Define ten technical terms in this book in your own words and where you would find them or how you would use them.

3. Explore the hotkey commands and customize two commands.

4. Describe some of the features of the recording section.

5. Use some Effects in a project and share them.

6. Why are the preview window and the watermark important? Give examples.

7. Start your own project using a variety of options from each area and share it.

8. Watch at least four tutorials or help documents from TechSmith (www.techsmith.com) and write a summary about them.

9. Download five items from the TechSmith (www.techsmith.com) library and explain ways you can use them in projects.

CHAPTER 4

RECORDING: SCREEN CAPTURING

IN THIS CHAPTER

In previous chapters, we discussed preparation and what steps to take to create a professional looking project. We also took an in-depth look and explanation of the tools and interfaces of Camtasia Studio. In this chapter, we will go step-by-step over many different features and types of recording. These actions will read as a checklist or how-to guide for the individual tasks. If at any time you want to have more of an explanation of a feature or location of menu item, remember Chapter 3 is your roadmap to Camtasia Studio.

Many of these tasks are similar in nature and the checklist will have many of the same steps with only one or more variation. These variations will point out different selected type of recording methods. The tasks are as individual as possible for quick reference and to clarify the steps to complete the individual tasks. As an additional resource, the **Quick Clips** will show each task as a short video that is located on the DVD.

The same technical writing method that was used in Chapter 3 will be used throughout this chapter. Menu items, programs, and file extensions will be in bold lettering while the mouse navigation and keystrokes action will be displayed with a ">" symbol.

Once you've completed this chapter, you will be able to:

- Record screencasts and narration efficiently and prepared for editing
- Understand camera recording
- Understand audio recording
- Save the raw recording for sharing or editing

Files: All figures in this chapter are in color located in the chapter folder on the DVD.

4.1 — The Camtasia Studio Recorder

The **Camtasia Recorder** can capture the entire screen or a section of the screen, specific dimensions, a selected window, or an application. The **Recorder** is designed to be user friendly and is easy to use. Basically, just click the **Record button** and you will start recording the screen.

The Recorder automatically captures:

- **Cursor data** — allows customization of cursor effects in the **Editor**

- **Keyboard commands** — allows automatic generation of commands as callouts in the Editor

- **Microphone audio recording** — if a microphone is activated, the recorder will capture the sound

- **SmartFocus data** — automatically inserts zoom and pan information into the **timeline**

- **System audio recording** — sounds your computer system creates

4.1a — Launching the Camtasia Studio Recorder

Before we can capture the screen, we need to open the Recorder. There are multiple ways to open the Recorder and start recording (See Figure 4.1).

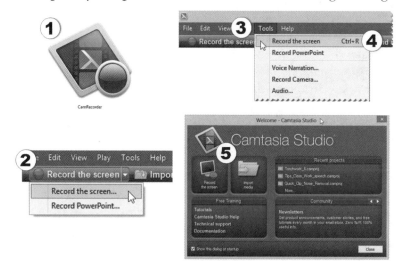

FIGURE 4.1 — A selection of possible ways to launch the Camtasia Recorder.

1. **Shortcut icon** — an icon located on your computer

2. **Record the Screen** — a button that opens a dropdown menu option within the **Editor**

3. **Menu options** — a Menu option dropdown within the **Editor**

4. **Hotkey Command** —a key stroke within the **Editor**

5. **Welcome Window** — a dialog box that opens once the **Editor** is launched

4.1b — Overview Review: Camtasia Studio Recorder

The Camtasia Studio Recorder toolbars, menus, and options were outlined in Chapter 3; however, an outline review is listed here for easy reference. The following recording steps will use all three phases of the Recorder, custom screen area selection, and the expanded menu options.

Overview Review — The Recording Phases

Camtasia Studio Recorder includes three phases of the recording process. The recording interface changes during each phase (See Figure 4.2).

FIGURE 4.2 — Screenshots of the three recording phases (pre-recording, recording, and post-recording).

1. **Pre-recording phase interface** — tool selection and settings before recording

2. **Recording phase interface** — expanded tools during the recording phase

3. **Post-recording phase interface** — preview of the recording with sharing and saving options

The pre-recording interface will overlay the screen once the **Recorder** is launched (See Figure 4.3).

Overview Review — Pre-recording Interface

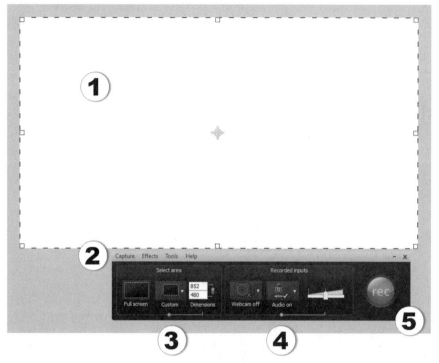

FIGURE 4.3 — Screenshot of the Camtasia Recorder interface overlaid over a white desktop background showing the selection box, menu options, selection area, recorded inputs, and record button.

1. **Recording Area Selection Box** — overlay selection of the interface to set and adjust the dimensions of the recording

   The Recording Toolbar

2. **Menu Options** — application pull-down menu for options features as well as additional tools

3. **Selection Area** — full screen, preset, and custom recording dimensions linked to the recording area selection box

4. **Recorded Inputs** — controls for input devices such as cameras and microphones

5. **Record Button** — button to starts the recordings

The **Recorder** interface during a recording (See Figure 4.4).

Overview Review – Recording Interface

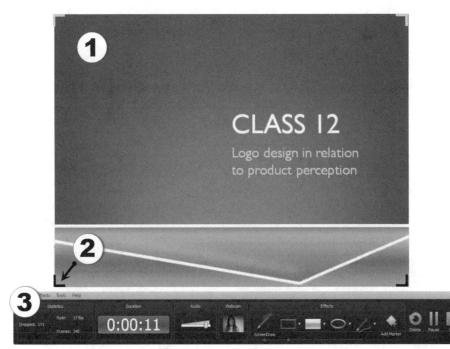

FIGURE 4.4 — Overview of the Recording phase interface shows the recording area, corners, and recording toolbar.

1. **Recording Area** — everything within the area outlined by the corners will be captured in the recording

2. **Corners** —indicate the edge of the recording area and will change color and blink once the recording has started

3. **Recording Toolbar** — expanded menu that contain statistics, duration, audio, Webcam preview, drawing effects, markers, delete, pause, play and stop buttons, and information

The **Post-Recorder** interface after a recording (See Figure 4.5).

Overview — Post-recording Interface

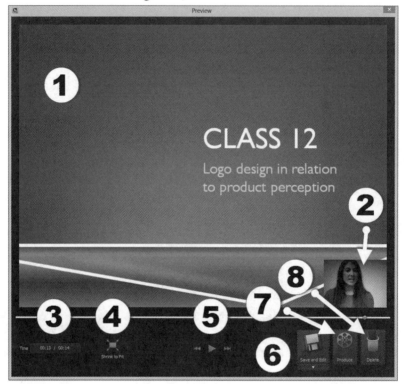

FIGURE 4.5 – Recorder Preview window opens automatically once the recording is stopped.

1. **Video preview** —a preview of the recording

2. **Webcam input preview** —a live feed of what the camera is capturing

3. **Time** — the time the play head is located and the overall duration and the recording

4. **Shrink to fit/View at 100%** — toggles the video from full size to fitting within the **Video Preview**

5. **Player controls** — buttons for **Restart**, **Jump to End**, and **Start/ Pause**

6. **Save and edit icon** — open the recording in the **Editor**

7. **Produce icon** —the **Production Wizard** opens to create a shareable video

8. **Delete** — deletes the recording without saving

4.2 — Recording Step-by-Step: Screen Capturing

Once you've prepared your project and checked your settings, you are ready to record your screen. Think of Camtasia Recorder as a video camera that is recording the full or selected area of your screen. Every action within the recording area will be captured with the Recorder while everything outside will not be recorded.

NOTE
The Step-by-Steps lists used in this chapter are based on the General Recording list. Each topic list will add the steps needed to complete the topic task to the base general list. This makes the Step-by-Step lists very similar but also self-contained.

NOTE
*The **Optional** tasks that are listed in the Step-by-Step lists are covered throughout the chapter.*

4.2a — Step-by-Step: General Recording

Before we go step-by-step through different types, functions, and settings of the **Recorder**, we need to take a look at some general functions. This first **Quick List** runs us through a general recording showing all the steps, along with a closer look at some general functions and tips that will be used in most recordings.

Quick List: Recording the Screen — General Recording

1. Open **Camtasia Studio Recorder**

2. Select the area of the screen to capture (Full or Custom)

3. *Optional:* Click the **Custom** button. Enter or select size once custom options is expanded

4. *Optional:* Click the **Webcam** button to activate camera recording

5. *Optional:* Click the **Audio** button to activate audio recording

6. *Optional:* Click **Tools > Recording Toolbars** to add recording tool options

7. Hit the **F9** (*default*) hotkey or the **Record** button to start recording

8. Watch the 3-2-1 countdown and get ready for the recording to start

9. Record your screen project

10. *Optional:* Add effects to the recording

11. Hit **F10** *(default)* hotkey or the **Stop** button to end recording

12. Preview the recording in the **Recorder Preview Window**

13. Click the **Save and edit** button to save the file as a **.camrec** file and open the recording within the **Editor** for editing

14. Click the **Produce** button to open the **Production Wizard** to create the video without editing

QUICK CLIP | Recording a screen capture

4.2b — A Closer Look: General Recording

Camtasia Recorder is designed to be simple to use. With just a few steps you can record a general recording and produce your project. For the best results, still follow through the preparation list, know the end use of your project, and check equipment input.

Open the Recorder

Open the **Recorder** when you are ready to capture the screen by clicking the **record the screen** button from the **welcome** dialog box or from launch options.

Open and Check Materials and Equipment

Before you start your recording, it is best to run through a quick checklist for a smooth recording.

1. Check the equipment that you will be using to make sure everything is working properly

2. Check camera and audio inputs and levels

3. Preform a full run-through of the project and what you are going to record

4. Make sure any video or slideshow is set to where you want to begin recording

5. Check the computer system alerts and sounds

6. Check placement of windows and applications used in the recording

Select a Recording Area

For most recordings, full screen will work well, or you can select an area of the screen to capture. Try and match the size to the end use of your project. If you are unsure, use one of the presets. There are a few different ways to select a screen area, including full, custom, and lock to application selections (See Figure 4.6).

Start the Recording

FIGURE 4.6 — Select a recording area from the left side of the recording tool bar before you start recording.

Key commands can be used to start and stop recording. **F9** to start recording and **F10** stop recording.

NOTE *A list of hotkey commands lists are in Appendix A. Some are unchangeable while others are customizable.*

Once you are ready to start recording, click the **F9** key or the **REC** button (See Figure 4.7).

FIGURE 4.7 — One way to start the recording is to click on the REC button on the right.

The **Recorder** interface will change to the recording phase. The new interface **recording bar** will overlay your screen. This bar will have all the **Recording Tools** that were selected before the recording. These include audio, Webcam, statistics, effects, and duration.

Countdown

A **3-2-1 countdown window** pops up once you start recording (See Figure 4.8). Use this countdown to prepare to start your project. If narrating, take a deep breath and let it out while speaking the numbers, pushing your voice lower, and speaking at a slower pace. Remember to use the voice tips from Chapter 2 like articulation, using pauses, and changing tones.

FIGURE 4.8 — The Recorder interface with the 3-2-1 countdown window.

Use the countdown timer to get your voice ready to record. Speak the numbers out loud with decreasing pitch with a slight pause after the number one. This is an old trick news reporters use to prepare their voice for recording.

Recording the Screen

When the recording starts, an indicator corner on the edge of the recording area will change from green to red. You can pause your recording by hitting **F9** and start it again by hitting **F9** a second time.

You should see the audio indicator moving as you talk while you are recording (See Figure 4.9). If it is not moving, stop the recording and preform a test. You might need to check the microphone or volume levels. The volume levels should be in the middle of the bar when talking.

FIGURE 4.9 — The audio bar should be moving while you are narrating during the recording.

Previewing the Recording

Once you are done with the capture, hit **F10** to end the recording. The **Preview Window** will open to review the capture (See Figure 4.10). Use the play/pause, fast forward, rewind, or play head to move through the recording.

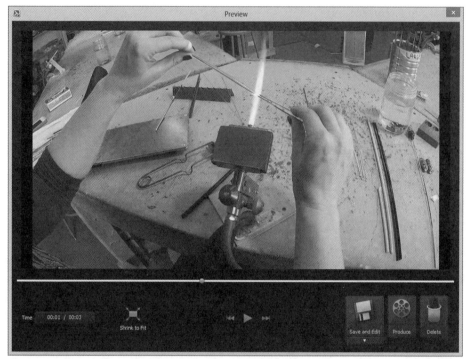

FIGURE 4.10 — The recording Preview Window will playback the capture for review.

The **Time** bar will show the full duration and the place of the play head within the recording. The button to **Shrink to fit** or **View at 100%** will adjust the window size of the playback.

Save, Produce, or Delete the Recording

After you are done reviewing the capture, you have the options to **Save and Edit**, **Save as**, **Produce**, or **Delete** your recording (See Figure 4.11).

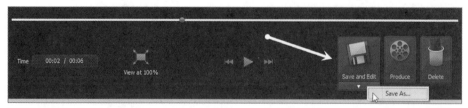

FIGURE 4.11 — Save and producing options in the recorder Preview Window.

Once one of the **Save and Edit**, **Save as**, or **Produce** buttons is selected, a navigation dialog box will pop up and there you will choose a location for the file to be saved (See Figure 4.12).

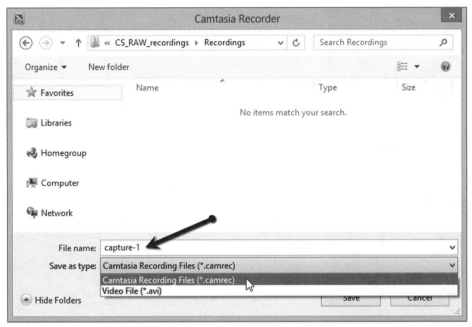

FIGURE 4.12 — Save file navigation dialog box.

The **Save and Edit** and **Save as** options will save the recording as a **.camrec** or **.avi** file. **Save and Edit** will open the file into the **Camtasia Editor** program for editing.

The **Produce** button will open the **Production Wizard** to produce the recording (See Figure 4.13). The wizard will walk you through the different types of production options including file formats, timestamps, watermarks, and captions.

The last option is **Delete** that will delete the recording without saving. This option will also bring you back to the pre-recording interface.

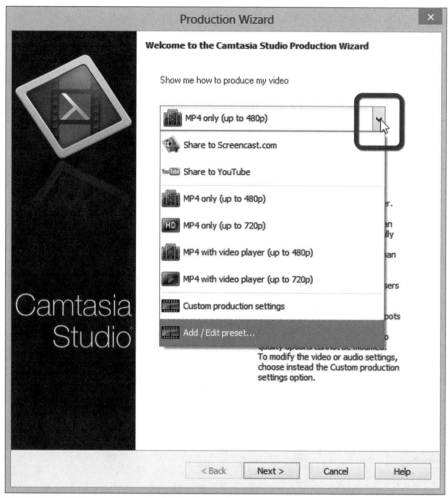

FIGURE 4.13 — The Production Wizard will take you through step-by-step on producing your project.

4.3 — Step-by-Step to Record: Screen Area Selections

Before recording, you can select the area of the screen to capture. The options include full screen, preset aspect ratio, lock to application, selected window, or custom sizes. The recording area is represented by a green dotted line that can be adjusted and moved to fit the recording (See Figure 4.14).

Overview Review — Screen Recording Area

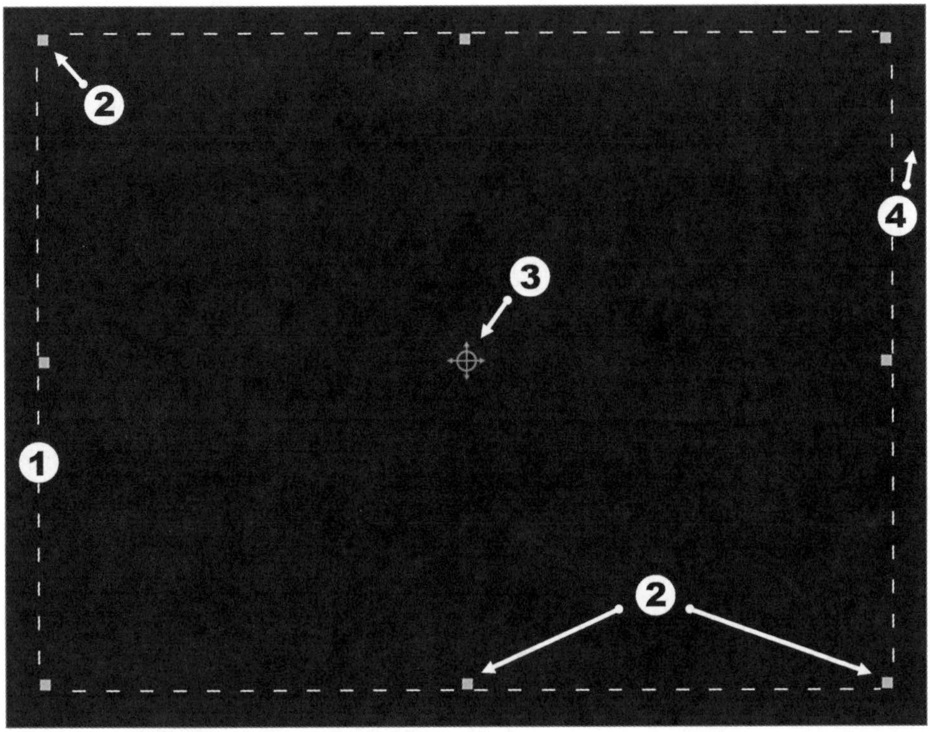

FIGURE 4.14 — Selection area outline and adjustments showing recording area, adjustment handles, moving compass, and the outside of the capture area.

1. **Recording Area Selection box** — a dotted green box that outlines the area of the screen to be recorded

2. **Adjustment handles** —can be clicked on with the mouse and dragged to adjust the recording area selection box to the desired dimension on both the sides and the corners of the selection area box

3. **Moving compass** — an icon that when clicked allows you to fully move and reposition the selection area while keeping the dimensions

4. **Outside the Capture Area** — any portion of the screen outside the dotted box that will not be included in the capture

4.3a — Step-by-Step: Full Screen Recording

Recording with the full screen option will capture everything that shows on your screen. This setting works for most projects that encompass the majority or a large portion of the screen. To capture the full screen, maximize the applications, windows, or activities you will be using to encompass your computer desktop. Or you can setup your files that you will be using in your screencast knowing that everything will be captured in the recorder.

Quick List: Recording the Screen — Full Screen Recording

1. Open **Camtasia Studio Recorder**

2. Click the **Fill screen** button located in the **Selection area**

3. *Optional:* Click the **Webcam** button to activate camera recording

4. *Optional:* Click the **Audio** button to activate audio recording

5. *Optional:* Click **Tools > Recording Toolbars** to add recording tool options

6. Hit the **F9** *(default)* hotkey or the **Record** button to start recording

7. Watch the 3-2-1 countdown and get ready for the recording to start

8. Record your screen project

9. *Optional:* Add effects to the recording

10. Hit the **F10** *(default)* hotkey or the **Stop** button to end recording

11. Preview the recording in the **Recorder Preview Window**

12. Click the **Save and edit** button to save the file as a **.camrec** file and open the recording within the **Editor** for editing

13. Click the **Produce** button to open the **Production Wizard** to create the video without editing

Once selected and the **Full screen** button is activated, a small blue dot will appear under the button and the green dotted line will expand to fit the entire screen (See Figure 4.15).

FIGURE 4.15 — The Full screen button in the Selection area will select the entire screen for capture.

When recording using the full screen selection, the recording toolbar minimizes to the **system tray** or **task bar**. To access the toolbar during the recording, click on the icon in the system tray. Click the **system tray** icon again or the minimize button to minimize the toolbar. However, if you open the recording toolbar during a full screen selection recording, the toolbar will be included in the final recording. To avoid this, use the hotkey commands to pause or end the recording. Once the recording is paused you can make any adjustments needed.

Change when the toolbar minimizes:
Tools > Options > Program tab > Minimize

NOTE

*There could be situations when recording full screen that you will need to open the **Recording toolbar** and cannot pause. Leave time before and after the action to leave footage to edit out the toolbar when editing.*

4.3b — Step-by-Step: Custom Adjustable Area Selection

Camtasia Studio allows you to select any part of your screen to record by moving the adjustment handles. This is useful if the project you are recording is not a common aspect ratio or size. Another good use of this type of screen area selection is to capture objects on your screen to be crafted with additional clips using the **Editor**.

Quick List: Recording the Screen — Custom Adjustable Area Selection

1. Open **Camtasia Studio Recorder**.
2. Click the **Custom** button in the **Selection area** to expand the menu.

3. To select an area to record, click and drag the adjustment handles to encompass the area of the screen you want to capture. Release mouse button when done.

4. *Optional:* Click the **Webcam** button to activate camera recording.

5. *Optional:* Click the **Audio** button to activate audio recording.

6. *Optional:* Click **Tools > Recording Toolbars** to add recording tool options.

7. Hit the **F9** *(default)* hotkey or the **Record** button to start recording.

8. Watch the 3-2-1 countdown and get ready for the recording to start.

9. Record your screen project.

10. *Optional:* Add effects to the recording.

11. Hit the **F10** *(default)* hotkey or the **Stop** button to end recording.

12. Preview the recording in the **Recorder Preview Window**.

13. Click the **Save and edit** button to save the file as a **.camrec** file and open the recording within the **Editor** for editing.

14. Click the **Produce** button to open the **Production Wizard** to create the video without editing.

QUICK CLIP | Recording a custom selection.

Moving and Adjusting the Area Selection

You can move or resize the recording area by clicking and dragging the adjustment handles at the corners and side edges of the **Recording Area Selection** box. The handles can be moved in any direction. When you hover over the **adjustment handles** or the **moving compass**, your mouse cursor will change. This shift indicates that if the left mouse button is clicked and held, you can drag that point to a new location (See Figure 4.16).

 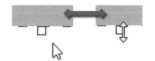 

FIGURE 4.16 — Samples of how the cursor changes shape when it hovers over an adjustment handle or moving compass.

If you select the middle compass of the recording box, you can move it around your screen to a new location while keeping the dimensions set. Moving the compass to a new location works for all custom sizes but not for the full screen selection.

The dotted green line shows the boundary of the recording area. Everything inside the dotted box will be recorded while everything outside will not be part of the capture. The grayed out portion that is outside of the **Recording Area Selection** box overlay will not be captured in the screen recording (See Figure 4.17).

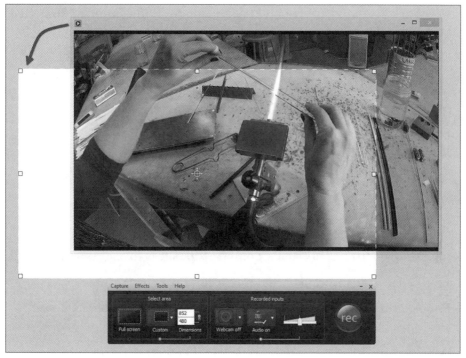

FIGURE 4.17 — An example of bad alignment of the recording selection area and the subject to be recorded.

If you are only recording a portion of your screen, you can use the area outside the recording area to have objects or other dialog boxes ready to bring into the recording area for a smooth transition for your project.

4.3c — Step-by-Step: Using Preset Size Selections

To select preset recording dimensions based on both widescreen and standard aspect ratios; click the dropdown menu represented by the down arrow next to the **Custom** button (See Figure 4.18).

> *Quick List:* Recording the Screen — Using Preset Sizes

1. Open **Camtasia Studio Recorder**

2. Click the **Custom** button in the **Selection area**

3. Click the dropdown button to select a preset **Widescreen** or **Standard** dimension

4. *Optional:* Click the **Webcam** button to activate camera recording

5. *Optional:* Click the **Audio** button to activate audio recording

6. *Optional:* Click **Tools > Recording Toolbars** to add recording tool options

7. Hit the **F9** *(default)* hotkey or the **Record** button to start recording

8. Watch the 3-2-1 countdown and get ready for the recording to start

9. Record your screen project

10. *Optional:* Add effects to the recording

11. Hit the **F10** *(default)* hotkey or the **Stop** button to end recording

12. Preview the recording in the **Recorder Preview Window**

13. Click the **Save and edit** button to save the file as a .camrec file and open the recording within the **Editor** for editing

14. Click the **Produce** button to open the **Production Wizard** to create the video without editing

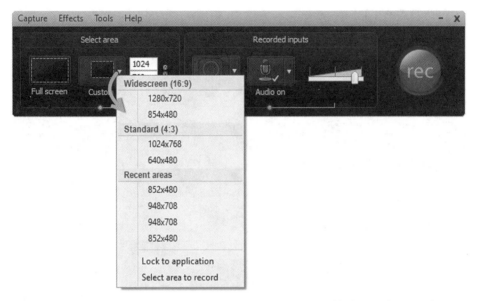

FIGURE 4.18 — The open dropdown menu for preset sizes, recent areas, and lock to application selections.

Selecting the Correct Aspect Ratio

The aspect ratio is the ratio of the width to the height. Your recording selection on the screen should proportionally match the video frame or the video playback ratio that you want for your project. Otherwise, you will see black bars at the top and bottom or sides of your video.

The end use of your video project and destination might affect the aspect ratio you pick during the recording stage. Try and match the recording aspect ratio with the end use. For example, if your video will be played on a widescreen device, select a widescreen aspect ratio. Selecting a standard size will leave unused space at the sides of the recording. The standard aspect ratio is shaped more like a square (See Figure 4.19) while the wide screen ratio is more like a rectangle (See Figure 4.20).

In this photo of a fish, we can see that more of the fish is shown in the widescreen format. If you do not know the end use of your project, then it is recommended to pick a preset size that fits your recording needs.

For best results, use dimensions with the same aspect ratio to edit and produce the final video when recording at a custom size.

FIGURE 4.19 — Sample of a standard aspect ratio.

FIGURE 4.20 — Sample of a widescreen aspect ratio.

Common Aspect Ratios

- **Standard** — 4:3 with resolutions — 640x480, 800x600, 1024x768

  Traditional television and computer monitor standard

- **Widescreen** — 16:9 with resolutions — 854x480, 1280x720, 1366x768, 1600x900

  Video widescreen standard, used in high-definition television

Cameras and other devices might have a different aspect ratio. For example, a classic 35mm or digital equivalent may use a 3:2 (or 24mmx36mm) aspect ratio. Other cameras might use a 1:1 or square ratio.

When recording, pick a video aspect ratio that you will be displaying your video. If you do know or you might be sharing the video in multiple locations, select one of the common standard or widescreen aspect ratios. When editing, you might have to crop or enlarge your photographs. For quality, use the largest size photographs you have to manipulate within the editor.

4.3d — Step-by-Step: Text Field Dimensions

The open text field allows you to type in a custom pixel amount. The option is good if you know one or both of the sides of the end product that your project needs to fit. For example, if you are making a recording for a Website at 500 pixels wide, you can type in this number to the width field. You can record your project to size and have a better idea of how this size looks on the screen.

> *Quick List:* Recording the Screen — Custom Text Field Dimensions

1. Open **Camtasia Studio Recorder**

2. Click the **Custom** button in the **Selection area**

3. Type in a pixel size in the height and width text fields

4. *Optional:* Click the **Lock** icon to keep the height and width locked to each other

5. *Optional:* Click the **Webcam** button to activate camera recording

6. *Optional:* Click the **Audio** button to activate audio recording

7. *Optional:* Click **Tools > Recording Toolbars** to add recording tool options

8. Hit the **F9** *(default)* hotkey or the Record button to start recording

9. Watch the 3-2-1 countdown and get ready for the recording to start

10. Record your screen project

11. *Optional:* Add effects to the recording

12. Hit the **F10** *(default)* hotkey or the **Stop** button to end recording

13. Preview the recording in the **Recorder Preview Window**

14. Click the **Save and edit** button to save the file as a .camrec file and open the recording within the Editor for editing

15. Click the **Produce** button to open the **Production Wizard** to create the video without editing

Lock the Recording Aspect Ratio

Even if you type in a size within the text field, you still might want to keep a widescreen or standard aspect ratio. After selecting an aspect ratio, you can still change the size of the recording selection area. The lock icon can chain the aspect ratio to the width and height. When one dimension is changed, the other is changed the same amount keeping the correct ratio (See Figure 4.21).

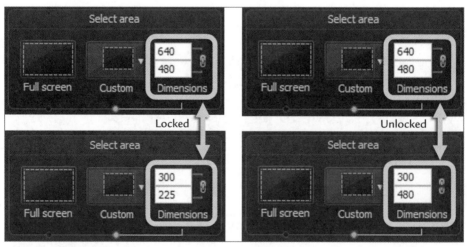

FIGURE 4.21 — Examples of locked and unlocked dimensions.

Camtasia remembers the last size you selected for the recording including the custom size so if you are recording multiple projects you can keep them consistent.

When entering dimensions into the width and height fields, click the Lock icon to maintain the aspect ratio of the selection area.

4.3e — Step-by-Step: Lock Selection Area to an Application

There are times when you want to record everything inside an application window. This window might be a custom size or you might be changing the size of the window between recordings. Instead of constantly adjusting the recording selection area, you can lock the area to an application window. The **Lock to Application** option will automatically resize the selection area if the application window is changed. The same is true in reverse. When locked, any change in the selection area will change the application window to match. If used in conjunction with selecting an **aspect ratio** and the **Lock** icon, the proper aspect ratio can be maintained during any resizing of the window or application.

Quick List: Recording the Screen — Lock Selection Area to an Application

1. Open **Camtasia Studio Recorder**.

2. Click on the application or window to be locked.

3. Click the **Custom** button. Enter or select size once custom options is expanded.

4. Select the **Lock to application** selection from the **Custom** dropdown menu within the **Select area**.

5. Click on the window or application.

6. *Optional:* Click and select an aspect ratio and the **Lock** icon to fix ratio.

7. *Optional:* Click the **Webcam** button to activate camera recording.

8. *Optional:* Click the **Audio** button to activate audio recording.

9. *Optional:* Click **Tools > Recording Toolbars** to add recording tool options.

10. Hit the **F9** *(default)* hotkey or the Record button to start recording.

11. Watch the 3-2-1 countdown and get ready for the recording to start.

12. Record your screen project.

13. *Optional:* Add effects to the recording.

14. Hit the **F10** *(default)* hotkey or the **Stop** button to end recording.

15. Preview the recording in the **Recorder Preview Window**.

16. Click the **Save and edit** button to save the file as a **.camrec** file and open the recording within the **Editor** for editing.

17. Click the **Produce** button to open the **Production Wizard** to create the video without editing.

Another way to **Lock to application** is through the **Capture** menu option. Click **Capture > Lock to application** (See Figure 4.22).

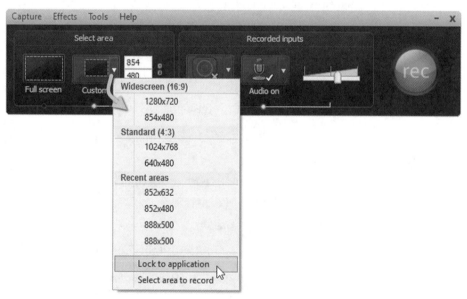

FIGURE 4.22 — The dropdown menu within the Selection area is one way to lock the area to a selected application.

4.3f — Step-by-Step: Select Specific Window or Area within a Window

Record a specific area on the screen, a window, or an application. This option quickly snaps the selection to the selected area and magnifies guides for pinpoint control.

Quick List: Recording the Screen — Select Specific Window or Area within a Window

1. Open **Camtasia Studio Recorder**.

2. Click on the application or window to be locked.

3. Click the **Custom** button. Enter or select size once custom options is expanded.

4. Select the **Select area to Record** selection from the **Custom** dropdown menu within the **Select area**.

5. Select the window, application, or area of the screen to capture.

6. Move the cursor until the area or window is highlighted. Click to select.

7. *Optional:* Click and select an aspect ratio and the **Lock** icon to fix ratio.

8. *Optional:* Click the **Webcam** button to activate camera recording.

9. *Optional:* Click the **Audio** button to activate audio recording.

10. *Optional:* Click **Tools > Recording Toolbars** to add recording tool options.

11. Hit the **F9** *(default)* hotkey or the **Record** button to start recording.

12. Watch the 3-2-1 countdown and get ready for the recording to start.

13. Record your screen project.

14. *Optional:* Add effects to the recording.

15. Hit the **F10** *(default)* hotkey or the **Stop** button to end recording.

16. Preview the recording in the **Recorder Preview Window**.

17. Click the **Save and edit** button to save the file as a **.camrec** file and open the recording within the **Editor** for editing.

18. Click the **Produce** button to open the **Production Wizard** to create the video without editing.

The **Select area to Record** menu option will bring up a crosshair and magnifying box for more precise control over the recording area. A light blue box will highlight open desktop windows including internal windows (See Figure 4.23).

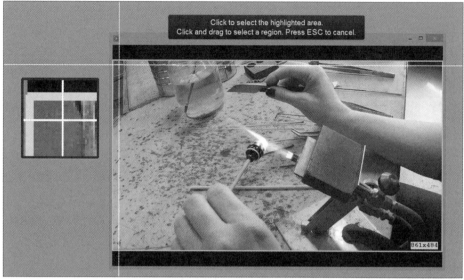

Click to select the highlighted area.
Click and drag to select a region. Press ESC to cancel.

861x484

FIGURE 4.23 — The light blue line represents the selected recording area. It snaps to windows or areas within the windows.

The smaller box to the side of the recording area is a magnified view to check the edges of the recording box to make sure the edges include everything you want to include. This is helpful in checking that the edges of a dialog box are lined up with the recording box.

4.4 — Step-by-Step: Recording Audio

Camtasia Recorder captures audio through the computer system and external microphones. The microphone and system audio are recorded by default, and both can be turned off. Background sounds can also be captured in your recording. If you are recording a narration, try and find the quietest location for your project. See Chapter 2 for tips on recording good audio tracks.

Quick List: Recording with Audio

1. Open **Camtasia Studio Recorder**.

2. Select the area of the screen to capture (Full or Custom).

3. *Optional:* Click the **Custom** button. Enter or select size once custom options is expanded.

4. *Optional:* Click the **Webcam** button to activate camera recording.

5. Click the **Audio** button to activate audio recording.

6. Click on the audio dropdown menu to select input the device from possible sources.

7. Check audio volume input (volume should be within the middle range).

8. *Optional:* Click **Tools > Recording Toolbars** to add recording tool options.

9. Hit the **F9** *(default)* hotkey or the Record button to start recording.

10. Watch the 3-2-1 countdown and get ready for the recording to start.

11. Record your screen project.

12. *Optional:* Add effects to the recording.

13. Hit the **F10** *(default)* hotkey or the **Stop** button to end recording.

14. Preview the recording in the **Recorder Preview Window**.

15. Click the **Save and edit** button to save the file as a **.camrec** file and open the recording within the **Editor** for editing.

16. Click the **Produce** button to open the **Production Wizard** to create the video without editing.

QUICK CLIP Recording with audio

NOTE *You can record an audio only track without the screen capture by using the Voice Narration tab in the Editor (See Chapter 8).*

4.4a — Selecting Microphones

If the audio recording is not activated within the recording toolbar, click on the **Audio off** icon button. This will turn the red **X** to a **green checkmark** and change the name to **Audio on**. This activates and deactivates the audio recording (See Figure 4.24).

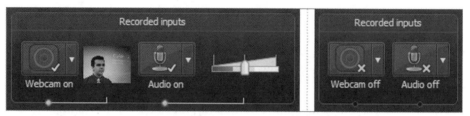

FIGURE 4.24 — Example screenshot of turning the audio input on and off.

To select an audio source, click on the **Audio dropdown** menu to open and select an audio input source (See Figure 4.25). Activated devices will show in the list. Because different devices might be plugged into the computer at different times, this list will change.

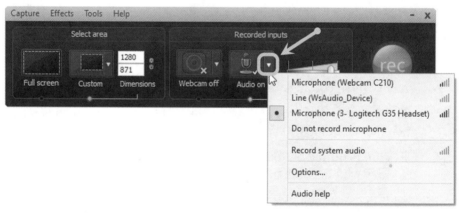

FIGURE 4.25 — Select the Audio dropdown menu to select an input device or turn it off.

You can also select and activate the audio and source using the **Menu Options** by clicking **Tools > Options > Inputs tab** (See Figure 4.26).

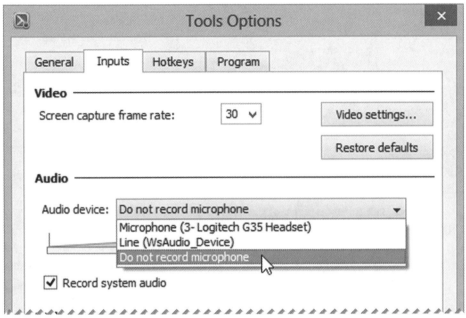

FIGURE 4.26 — Audio options to turn on and off audio device or system sounds.

A secondary handheld audio device recording during the screen capture can serve as a backup to the initial recording. Audio can also be recorded with the **Voice Narration** option within **Editor** to recapture or add audio that was not captured during the initial recording.

4.4b — System Sounds

System sounds are any kind of sound the computer operating system might create. This includes any audio playback that might occur during the capture. For example, if your project involves capturing a video, its audio will be captured during your screencast. You might have to adjust the volume of your computer speakers or turn them off during narration recording.

Examples of System Sounds

- Navigation sounds (maximizing or minimizing windows)
- Program alarms

- Video playback

- Mouse clicks

- Recycle bin

Even if the system sounds are turned off, the recorder will capture cursor data and you will be able to add the mouse click sounds later using the editor.

To turn on and off the system sounds:
Tools > Options > Inputs tab or Audio dropdown > Options > Inputs tab

4.4c — Checking Audio Levels

Even if you checked your audio levels earlier, it is good practice to double check just before recording to avoid any mishaps. A bad audio recording can ruin a perfect recording session.

Live audio meters are available in the **Audio** button dropdown (See Figure 4.27). When the **audio sources** are set up properly, the source audio meter, next to the source name are active. The meters are active for all sources that are activated and receiving sound. You should see green bars representing the strength of the input.

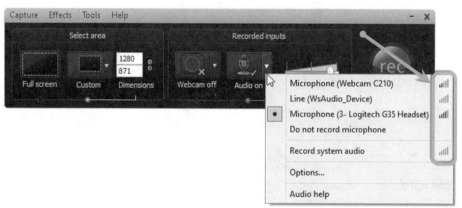

FIGURE 4.27 — The dropdown menu in the Audio button show active sources of audio and their input strength.

Speak into your microphone or turn up the speaker and play a system audio to check audio volume levels. You should see the audio meters respond (See Figure 4.28). If there are any problems, take the time to make adjustments to your setup before recording. It is better to take the time now to get the setting right because it will save time later in the editing process or having to re-do recordings because your audio is unusable.

FIGURE 4.28 — Screenshot of a good audio volume bar.

Use the volume slider bar to get a middle of the bar level. The highest volume should be in the green to yellow range. The orange to red range might cause audio clipping (See Figure 4.29 and Figure 4.30).

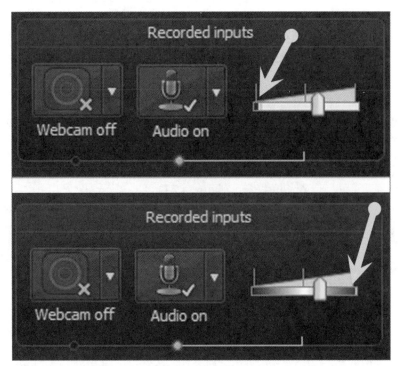

FIGURE 4.29 — Samples of audio that is too low (top) and too high (bottom).

Audio Clipping — A distortion that happens when the audio wave overloads the audio output clipping part of the sound.

Range of the Audio	State or Problem	Action
None	no range is showing	Check source: connected and activated, unmuted, the correct source selected
Low Green	high point only hits a low green	Drag the volume slider to the right
Green to Yellow	high point does not pass middle	Drag the volume slider to the right
Yellow	high point just past middle	No change needed
Yellow to Orange	clipping might occur	Drag the volume slider to the left
Orange to Red	clipping occurs	Drag the volume slider to the left

FIGURE 4.30 — Audio Meter Ranges

Always test your microphone levels before recording. You can check the audio levels without saving the recording, however, a playback or checking the clip within the **Editor** can reveal more information. For example, the waves of an audio within the timeline should stay within 1/4 to 3/4 from the top and bottom of the clip. Dotted horizontal lines will show the safety zone lines. If the highs or lows of the wave surpass the safety zone, the audio will either be too soft or loud (See Figure 4.31).

FIGURE 4.31 — Screenshot of an audio wave clip inside Camtasia Editor shows the highs and lows of the waves.

!
TIP

*Do a quick audio levels test with your microphone by performing a quick recording. For an extra audio check, playback the recording within the **Editor** and check that the audio wave highs and lows are within the middle portion safety zone of the clip within the timeline.*

Advance Settings

Audio settings can be changed from the **Menu Options** by selecting **Tools > Options > Input tab > Audio Settings** (See Figure 4.32).

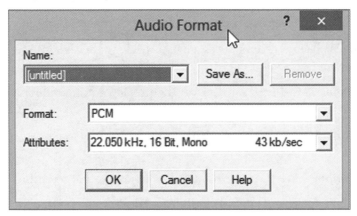

FIGURE 4.32 — Screenshot of advanced audio settings dialog box (name, format, and attributes).

The **audio format** dialog box can adjust the format and attributes of the recorded audio. The default settings work for most occasions and it is not recommended to change the settings unless you have understanding on the types and differences of audio formats.

4.5 — Step-by-Step: Recording with a Camera

The Recorder has the ability to record additional camera input using a Web camera. This feature can be used to capture your screen while also recording a lecturer, yourself, or anything that you want to record at the same time as your screencast. The camera input will be recorded on a separate video track within Editor.

Quick List – Recording with a Camera

1. Open **Camtasia Studio Recorder**.

2. Select the area of the screen to capture *(Full or Custom)*.

3. *Optional:* Click the **Custom** button. Enter or select size once custom options is expanded.

4. Click the **Webcam** icon button to activate camera recording.

5. Click the **Webcam dropdown** to select the camera source.

6. The Web camera appears as a live preview to the right of the **Webcam** icon button.

7. *Optional:* Hover the cursor over the preview thumbnail for a larger view.

8. *Optional:* Click **Webcam dropdown > Options** to change the camera options.

9. *Optional:* Click the **Audio** button to activate audio recording.

10. *Optional:* Click **Tools > Recording Toolbars** to add recording tool options.

11. Hit the **F9** *(default)* hotkey or the **Record** button to start recording.

12. Watch the 3-2-1 countdown and get ready for the recording to start.

13. Record your screen project.

14. *Optional:* Add effects to the recording.

15. Hit the **F10** *(default)* hotkey or the **Stop** button to end recording.

16. Preview the recording in the **Recorder Preview Window**.

17. Check to make sure the camera input was recorded.

18. Click the **Save and edit** button to save the file as a .camrec file and open the recording within the **Editor** for editing.

19. Click the **Produce** button to open the **Production Wizard** to create the video without editing.

QUICK
CLIP   Recording with a camera.

A closer look — Recording with a Camera

4.5a — Webcam Activation and Recording

Activation

To activate the camera to use in conjunction with the screencast recording, click the **Webcam** icon button to enable the camera. The red **X** on the button will change to a **green checkmark** and a small live preview of the camera input will appear (See Figure 4.33).

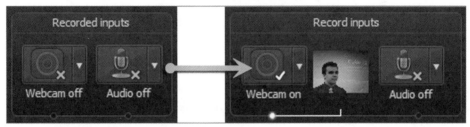

FIGURE 4.33 — A screenshot of the Webcam icon button activation expansion.

Another way to activate the camera is using the **Menu Options** by clicking **Capture > Record Webcam**.

Selection and Options

Click on the **Webcam dropdown** arrow to select the camera device and options menu (See Figure 4.34). The dropdown menu also holds the **Tools Options** dialog box and Webcam help.

FIGURE 4.34 — Click the Webcam dropdown to select the camera input and other options.

To change the camera options, bring up the **Tools Options** dialog box by clicking **Webcam dropdown > Options > Inputs tab** (See Figure 4.35). The **Input tab** holds the camera preview, selection, device properties, and format settings. The **Device** properties dialog box will change depending on your camera device.

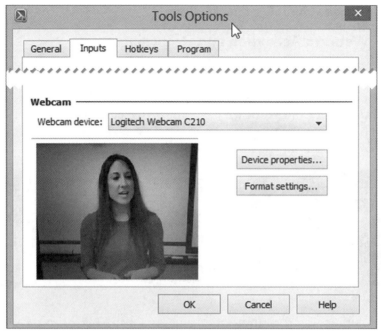

FIGURE 4.35 — The Tools Options dialog box with camera input preview and selections.

Camera Positioning

Hovering the cursor over the small camera preview thumbnail in the **Recorder Toolbar** will expand the preview image for a larger view (See Figure 4.36). The larger view will assist in positioning the camera and subject for optimal view.

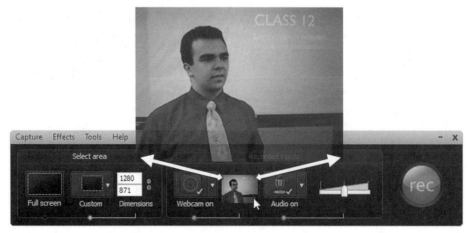

FIGURE 4.36 — A screenshot of a larger camera preview and the record bar.

If the subject will be moving during the recording, mark the floor or plan an area to keep the subject within the camera view (See Figure 4.37). Camera blocking is important to find any issues with camera or subject movements.

Blocking — To plan or rehearse in order to work out the movement of the camera and placement of the cast and crew for a shot or scene.

FIGURE 4.37 — An example of good blocking where you can see everything.

Bad blocking will ruin your capture. It is recommended to perform a full run-through of the project to map out any movements or problem areas (See Figure 4.38). If you cannot perform a test run-through, test what you can and keep an eye on the camera preview. Some editing can fix bad blocking but it will take extra time and might not work.

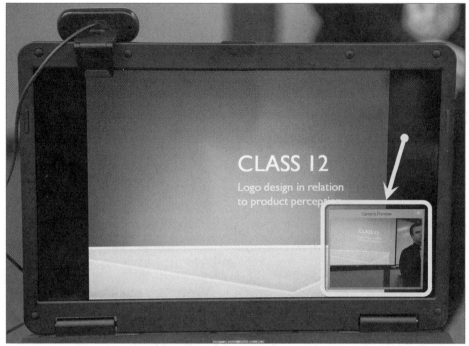

FIGURE 4.38 — An example of bad camera positioning and blocking where you only see part of the person.

Recording Preview

During the recording phase, the **camera preview** will be in the **Recording Toolbar** (See Figure 4.39). It is a live preview and the action that the camera is recording can be viewed and monitored.

FIGURE 4.39 — The Recording toolbar during the recording phase with the camera preview.

In the post-recording, the camera preview will be located in the lower right hand side of the preview window (See Figure 4.40). The **camera preview** is an overlay that is recorded as a second video track and not burned into the recording.

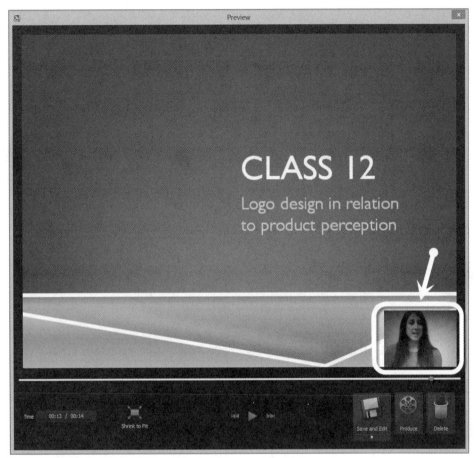

FIGURE 4.40 — The recording preview window with camera preview overlay.

4.5b — Picture-in-Picture

When recording with a Web camera, the camera picture will be captured and overlaid over your recording during playback with the preview window, a picture-in-picture preview. After the recording is saved and opened within the Editor, the camera track is placed onto its own track within the timeline (See Figure 4.41).

Because the camera and screencast recordings are on separate tracks, they can be edited independently. If a fix needs to be made to one track, you do not need to rerecord both tracks over. You can just import the new recording into your project and edit the tracks.

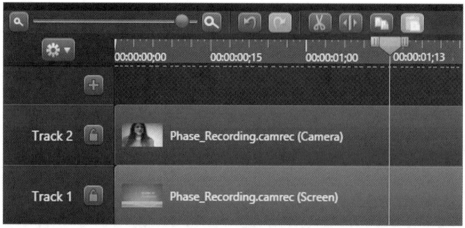

FIGURE 4.41 — A screenshot of the picture-in-picture dual tracks in the Timeline.

NOTE *There is an option to record video with a Web camera with the* ***Record camera*** *option in* ***Camtasia Studio Editor****.*

Because the Webcam input is being saved as a separate track, the .camrec file format will be the only format available when saving your recording.

4.6 — Recording Screen Special Effects

During the recording phase, you can add special effects to your screen capture including drawing lines, arrows, boxes, adding timestamps. Many of these features are available when using the editor, however, there might be times where you need a quick response or do not have time to edit the recording.

NOTE **Warning** *— adding the effects in the recording phase will permanently burn them into the recording. They cannot be removed. It is recommended, when possible to add any effects when using the* ***Editor*** *where they can be changed, moved, or deleted.*

4.6a — Displaying Recording Toolbars

To add any effects, the tool or corresponding toolbars need to be activated during the pre-recording phase. To activate the tools, go to the Recorder Menu Options bar and click **Tools > Recording Toolbars** and select the tools you want to show or use during the recording phase (See Figure 4.42).

FIGURE 4.42 — The Recording Toolbars dialog box with selections for an expanded tool selection during recording.

NOTE *The Webcam and Audio options in the Recording Toolbars dialog box are only available if the Webcam or Audio input area activated and set to record.*

Activating the tools will expand the **Recording Toolbar** during the recording phase to show the settings for the effects (See Figure 4.43). By default, only the basic toolbars will show until changed.

The statistics and duration tools are informational toolbars showing the data about the video recording including the frame rate, dropped frames, and overall length. The audio and camera toolbars will show the live input previews; while the effects option will activate the drawing tools and marker button.

FIGURE 4.43 — Full expansion of the Recording Toolbar with all tools and information.

4.6b — Drawing on the Screen

The **ScreenDraw** feature will add drawing effects over your selected screen area when you are recording.

Quick List — Drawing on the Screen (Custom Screen Selection)

1. Open **Camtasia Studio Recorder**.

2. Click the **Custom** button. Enter or select size once custom options is expanded.

3. *Optional:* Click the **Webcam** button to activate camera recording.

4. *Optional:* Click the **Audio** button to activate audio recording.

5. Click **Tools > Recording Toolbars** to add recording tool options.

6. Activate the **Effects** toolbar.

7. Hit the **F9** *(default)* hotkey or the **Record** button to start recording.

8. Watch the 3-2-1 countdown and get ready for the recording to start.

9. Record your screen project.

10. *Optional:* Pause the recording by clicking **F9** to draw in a paused state.

11. Click the **ScreenDraw** icon button to expand the effects toolbar.

12. With ScreenDraw tools expand, select a tool to draw with.

13. Click and drag the mouse on the screen to draw.

14. *Optional:* Change the default tools and attributes by selecting the dropdown menus next to the drawing icon buttons.

15. *Optional:* Press **CTRL+Z** to undo the last ScreenDraw action.

16. To exit ScreenDraw mode and clear the screen from drawing effects, press **ESC** or **CTRL+SHIFT+D**.

17. Hit the **F10** *(default)* hotkey or the **Stop** button to end recording.

18. Preview the recording in the **Recorder Preview Window**.

19. Click the **Save and edit** button to save the file as a **.camrec** file and open the recording within the **Editor** for editing.

20. Click the **Produce** button to open the **Production Wizard** to create the video without editing.

QUICK CLIP   Drawing on the Screen

A closer look – Drawing on the screen

Before you can draw on your screen, you need to activate the Effects Toolbar. (See figure 4.44) To open the **Recording Toolbars** dialog box click: **Tools > Recording Toolbars**.

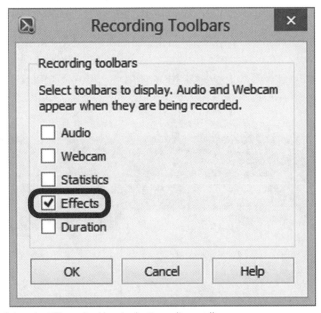

FIGURE 4.44 — Select the Effects checkbox in the Recording toolbar.

Once the **Effects toolbar** is activated, the collapsed toolbar will show during the recording phase. To expand the toolbar, click on the **ScreenDraw** icon button (See Figure 4.45).

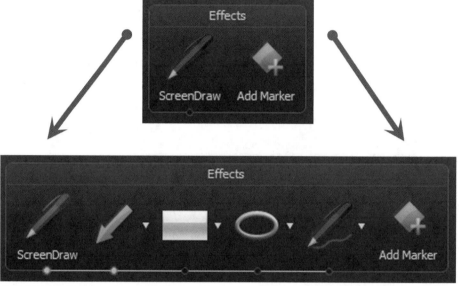

FIGURE 4.45 — The expansion of the Effects toolbar to show the ScreenDraw options.

The effects toolbar expansion will show four slots to interchange selected drawing tools. You can mix and match different drawing tools, colors, and stroke widths. Click on any of the tools dropdown menus to select and change any of drawing pen, highlight, or shapes (See Figure 4.46).

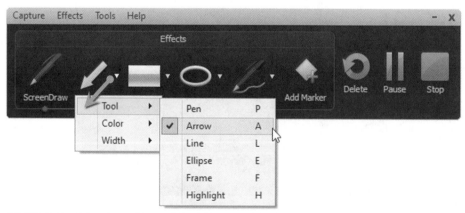

FIGURE 4.46 — Select the attributes of the different tools by clicking on the dropdown menu next to the icon buttons.

Drawing

Once you select a tool, click on your screen and hold the mouse button down. With the mouse button still held down, drag the mouse over the screen to draw. Release the mouse button when you are finished.

Use the **Pause** button during the recording to draw on the screen when the video stopped. This will allow you more time to make accurate drawings. There are times when you will not be able to pause the recording. During these times try and practice screen drawing before you click record to give you a familiarity with the drawing tools with your project.

Clearing or Ending the ScreenDraw Effect

When you are finished with the ScreenDraw, or if you like to clear the screen to set up another drawing session, click the **ScreenDraw icon button** again or press the **ESC** or **CTRL+SHIFT+D** key commands.

ScreenDraw During Full Screen Selection

The full screen selection minimizes the **Recording toolbar** so it will not be seen in the recording. This makes using the ScreenDraw feature a little more difficult. Pause the recording or use the **hotkey** commands to activate and draw on the screen without showing the **Recording Toolbar**.

ScreenDraw Hotkeys (not customizable)

Enable/Disable ScreenDraw	CTRL + SHIFT + D
Exit ScreenDraw	ESC
Redo	CTRL + Y
Tool Width	1 - 8
Undo	CTRL + Z

Shape

Arrow	A
Ellipse	E
Frame	F
Highlight	H
Line	L
Pen	P

Color

Black	K
Blue	B
Cyan	C
Green	G
Magenta	M
Red	R
White	W
Yellow	Y

4.6c — Adding Markers

Think of markers as sticky notes that are added during the recording or in the timeline. These marks can be used to pinpoint parts of the recording to edit or to include enhanced features during the editing and producing stages.

When you are recording, press **CTRL+M** or click the **Add Marker** icon on the Recording toolbar to add a marker to that point in the recording (See Figure 4.47).

FIGURE 4.47 — During the recording phase, if the Effects toolbar is activated the Add Marker icon will show in the Recording toolbar.

Reasons to add makers:

- **Edits** — if you made a mistake, place a marker to find and fix it when editing

- **Callouts** — pinpoints an area to add callouts or other special effects

- **Split tracks** — highlights a point to split or cut the recording track for insert tracks

- **Navigation points** — key commands can be used to jump from marker to marker making them a fast and effective tool for navigating around your timeline

- **Table of contents** —markers can function as title entries and navigation points in the table of contents

QUICK CLIP | Adding Markers to Your Recording

You will not see these markers during the video preview playback. The location data of the markers are saved using the **.camrec** file format for use in the **Editor** or **Production Wizard**. Marker locations can be viewed, moved, and deleted when you open or import the **.camrec** file into **Camtasia Editor**. The **markers** appear on the timeline (See Figure 4.48).

FIGURE 4.48 — The timeline with the Marker view activated showing the locations of the markers.

4.6d — Cursor Effects and Mouse Clicks

Depending on the size of your recording, or how complicated your mouse movements are, the viewer might have difficulty following your mouse. To highlight or bring attention to your cursor during a screencast recording, you can add special effects and sounds to the cursor actions. The effects can highlight the mouse from the background, make the cursor larger, and select a custom cursor or sound to draw attention to the screen action. This will help the viewer to follow along with the mouse and what you are trying to show.

The default setting is to record cursor data in the background for use with the **Editor**. There are options to show these effects during the recording, however, the effects will be added to the recording permanently. Because of this destructive nature, it is advisable to use the default settings and add the cursor effects within the **Editor**.

NOTE
The cursor effects will not show during the recording, however you will be able to review the cursor effects during the video preview playback after the recording ends.

Quick List — Recording Cursor Effects During the Recording

1. Open **Camtasia Studio Recorder**.

2. Select the area of the screen to capture *(Full or Custom)*.

3. *Optional:* Click the **Custom** button. Enter or select size once custom options is expanded.

4. *Optional:* Click the **Webcam** button to activate camera recording.

5. *Optional:* Click the **Audio** button to activate audio recording.

6. *Optional:* Click **Tools > Recording Toolbars** to add recording tool options.

7. Select **Effects > Options > Cursor tab**.

8. Uncheck the **Make cursor effects editable in Camtasia Studio** option.

9. Adjust cursor effects and click **OK**.

10. *Optional:* Select **Effects > Options > Sound tab**.

11. *Optional:* Adjust mouse click sounds and click **OK**.

12. Hit the **F9** *(default)* hotkey or the Record button to start recording.

13. Watch the 3-2-1 countdown and get ready for the recording to start.

14. Record your screen project.

15. *Optional:* Add effects to the recording.

16. Hit the **F10** *(default)* hotkey or the **Stop** button to end recording.

17. Preview the recording in the **Recorder Preview Window**.

18. Click the **Save and edit** button to save the file as a **.camrec** file and open the recording within the **Editor** for editing.

19. Click the **Produce** button to open the **Production Wizard** to create the video without editing.

QUICK
CLIP | Adding Cursor Effects

A Closer Look — Adding Cursor Effects

Collecting Cursor Data for Use Within the Editor

To confirm that the **Recorder** is collecting cursor data for use within the **Editor**, the **Make cursor effects editable in Camtasia Studio** option needs to be checked and enabled within the **Effects Options Cursor tab**. To open the Cursor tab, click **Recorder > Effects > Options > Cursor tab** (See Figure 4.49).

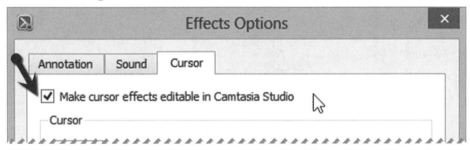

FIGURE 4.49 — Cursor effect option dialog box located: Recorder > Effects > Options > Cursor tab.

Adding Cursor Effects While Recording

In order to enable cursor effects, the **Make cursor effects editable in Camtasia Studio** option needs to be unchecked. This will toggle the **Recorder** to use the cursor data during the recording instead of saving the data for use within the Editor. If the checkbox is checked, then the remaining dialog box will be grayed out and unable to be selected. With the checkbox unchecked, the settings for the effects can be adjusted (See Figure 4.50).

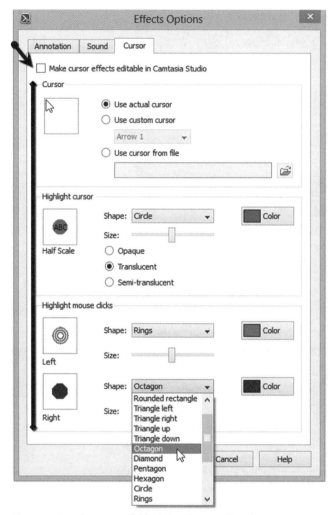

FIGURE 4.50 – Cursor options that are available during the recording phase.

The **Cursor tab** holds options for changing the cursor to a custom cursor, highlight the cursor, and highlight both right and left mouse clicks.

Selecting a Custom Cursor

There are preset cursors or you can select one from a file on your computer when selecting a custom cursor. During the recording phase, the cursor will be the default cursor, however, the custom cursor will show when previewing the recording.

Adding Cursor Highlights

The highlight settings can change the shape, size, opacity, and color of the effect. There are a number of available sections to customize the effect to fix your project. The highlight cursor and highlight mouse clicks work independently of each other. These effects can be turned on and off independently during the recording using the expanded **Recording Toolbar** options.

Adding Mouse Click Sound Effects

Mouse clicks are sound effects that play when you click the right or left mouse buttons. You can use the default sounds or select new sounds from a **.wav** file. Select **Effects > Options > Sound tab** to pick a new mouse sound to use (See Figure 4.51). Once the tab is open, use the navigation tools to find and select the new sound file.

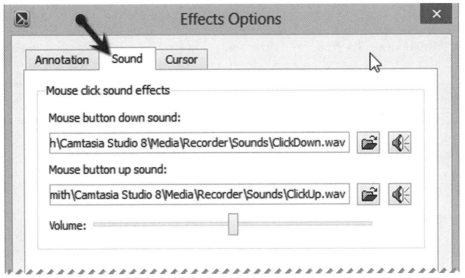

FIGURE 4.51 — Effects Options — Sound (mouse click sound effects).

The speaker icon will play the sound back to you as it will sound during the recording. The volume slider bar can adjust the sound if it is too loud or soft.

Activating Cursor Effects While Recording

After you have adjusted the effect settings for the cursor and mouse sounds, you need to activate the effects for use during the recording. The activation toggles are located under the **Effects Menu Option**. The black dot or checkmark next to the option will indicated that the option is activated (See Figure 4.52).

FIGURE 4.52 – Selecting any of the highlight options will enable the effects during the recording.

There are options to activate only the highlight clicks, cursor, or both. These options are available during the recording phase in the expanded **Recording Toolbar**. After the sounds are selected, you need to check to make sure that the mouse sound data collection is activated. From the **Recorder toolbar Menu Option**, select **Effects > Sound > Use Mouse Click Sounds**. The checkmark indicates that the feature is activated. The mouse sounds appear until you deactivate the feature.

NOTE

If the Web Camera option is activated, you will not be able to record mouse sounds during the recording (See Figure 4.53). In these instances, use the **Make cursor effects editable in Camtasia Studio** *option enabled within the* **Recorder > Effects > Options > Cursor tab**. *This will save the mouse data to use inside the* **Editor** *while still recording the camera input.*

FIGURE 4.53 – Camtasia Recorder showing it will not record mouse click sounds and why.

Show or Hide the Cursor

The cursor can be set to not record and will not show in the final video. During the recording, the cursor will still appear, however during the recording preview and the final production, the cursor will not show. This option is good when your cursor action is not needed in the project and you do not want to draw attention away from the action. To toggle on and off the cursor showing in the final recording, select **Effects > Cursor > Hide cursor or Effects > Cursor > Show cursor**.

Cursor Effects During the Recording

Once you start recording, the expanded **Recording toolbar** will show the **Cursor Effects** within the Effects portion. Click on the **Highlight Cursor** or **Highlight Clicks** icons to toggle on and off the effects (See Figure 4.54).

FIGURE 4.54 — The expanded Recording Toolbar with the cursor effects enabled.

You will not see the effect during the recording phase; however, you will see them when you preview the recording in the **Preview Window**. When previewing the recording, closely check the effects as they are final and cannot be edited once you save the file.

4.6e — Recording for SmartFocus

SmartFocus™ is a feature that focuses on cursor movement during the recording. This data is collected and stored with the file. Once saved in the **.camrec** file format and opened within the **Editor**, SmartFocus can be activated to automatically add zooms and pan effects. These effects will center on the cursor data recording during the screen capture.

SmartFocus During Recording

The main concept to remember, when creating a screencast recording and planning to use SmartFocus, is that the cursor action is the enter point. For example, if you want to show a Web page and need to scroll the page down, use the scroll wheel on the mouse (if the mouse has one) instead of the program navigation scroll sliders. If you use the program sliders, you will be moving your mouse to the side or bottom of the screen to click on the slider. This will shift focus away from the action and to your cursor preforming a navigation move. When planning to use SmartFocus, try and keep the mouse movements to a minimal amount and centered only on the action you want to highlight.

Tips for effective SmartFocus data collection

- **Hover or pause the cursor close to or on action areas** — Give SmartFocus time to gather data; keep the cursor still next to or on any action when possible

- **Recordings should be longer than 30 seconds** — SmartFocus is designed for recording longer than 30 seconds; if your project is shorter, add the effects using the Zoom-n-Pan manually

- **Use minimal mouse movements** — Do not move the mouse without purpose, every movement is giving data to SmartFocus

- **Use slower mouse movements** — Give time for the SmartFocus to gather data; use slower mouse movements without moving the cursor around the screen too fast

- **Use the mouse scroll wheel** — If possible, use the mouse scroll wheel instead of using the program navigation scroll bar

- **When entering text, keep the cursor close** — Even if you click a textbox to enter text, you should keep the mouse close to the box to keep the focus close to the textbox

SmartFocus During Editing

Once in the **Editor**, apply the **SmartFocus** by clicking on the **Zoom-n-Pan** task tab and clicking on the **SmartFocus** selection buttons (See Figure 4.55). You can apply the options to one clip or the full timeline.

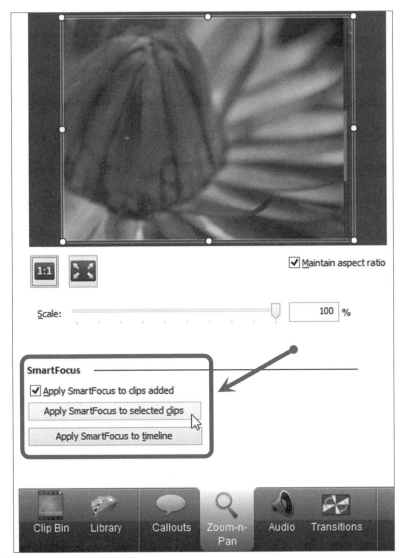

FIGURE 4.55 — The Zoom-n-Pan task tab with SmartFocus options.

SmartFocus is designed to work at a smaller production size video than the size of the initial recording. If the dimensions used within the Editor are the same as the recording dimensions of the clip, a dialog box will pop up (See Figure 4.56) alerting you about the discrepancy.

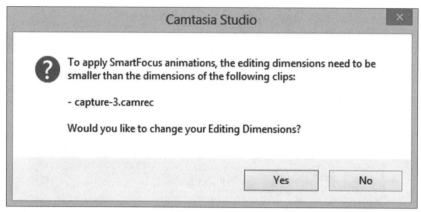

FIGURE 4.56 — A dialog box alerting the user of a size discrepancy.

SmartFocus works best if you record at a larger size setting then producing the video at a smaller setting. An example would be to record in full screen mode and produce the video at a smaller size for a Website or a mobile device. The automated Zoom-n-Pan will keep the center of the video focused on the action being showed.

Moving, deleting, and editing

Any automated zooms and pans that were added by the SmartFocus function can be moved, deleted, or edited within the **Editor**. Many times the SmartFocus will not successfully add every zoom and pan to ideally showcase all the action recorded on the screen and some editing will need to be done. Even though you still might need adjustments after using SmartFocus, it is a very good jumping off point to start with. It is a time saver to adjust zooms and pans than to create them all from scratch.

4.6f — Add Captions and System Stamps

Text can be added to the video during recording as a caption or a system stamp. As with other effects enabled during the recording phase, the effect is burned into the video and cannot be removed or adjusted. When activated, the caption and system stamps will not show during the recording phase but will show when previewing the recording.

Quick List — Adding a System Stamp and Caption

1. Open **Camtasia Studio Recorder**.

2. Select the area of the screen to capture *(Full or Custom)*.

3. Turn on the caption and stamp options by selecting **Effects > Annotation > Caption** and/or **Effects > Annotation > Add System Stamp**.

4. Select **Effects > Options > Annotation tab**.

5. Select System Stamp to add the time and date.

6. Click the **Time/Date Format** button to change the order and layout of the stamp then click **OK**.

7. Click the **System Stamp Options** to adjust the text style, background, and position of the stamp then click **OK**.

8. To add a caption, enter text in the caption text box.

9. Select the **Prompt before capture** option to show the caption text in a dialog box before the recording starts.

10. Click the **Caption Options** button to adjust the text style, background, and position of the caption then click **OK**.

11. In the **Annotation tab**, click **OK**.

12. *Optional:* Click the **Custom** button. Enter or select size once custom options is expanded.

13. *Optional:* Click the **Webcam** button to activate camera recording.

14. *Optional:* Click the **Audio** button to activate audio recording.

15. *Optional:* Click **Tools > Recording Toolbars** to add recording tool options.

16. Hit the **F9** *(default)* hotkey or the **Record** button to start recording.

17. Watch the 3-2-1 countdown and get ready for the recording to start.

18. Record your screen project.

19. *Optional:* Add effects to the recording.

20. Hit the **F10** *(default)* hotkey or the **Stop** button to end recording.

21. Preview the recording in the **Recorder Preview Window**.

22. Click the **Save and edit** button to save the file as a **.camrec** file and open the recording within the **Editor** for editing.

23. Click the **Produce** button to open the **Production Wizard** to create the video without editing.

Captions While Recording

The caption added during the recording phase will be the same throughout the recording. It is best used when adding copyright information, instructions, or other important information that should be displayed throughout the video. The customization selections can move or change the caption to stand out or blend in the background of your project (See Figure 4.57). The caption will stay active until the feature is toggled off by selecting **Effects > Annotation> Caption**. The Annotation activation is indicated by a checkmark next to the menu listing.

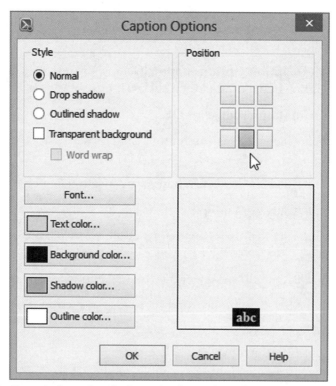

FIGURE 4.57 — Customization options for the caption feature during the recording phase.

System Stamps While Recording

A system stamp adds information such as the time and date of the capture along with the elapsed time of the recording. The **Time/Date Format** button opens the options to adjust the order, style, and information displayed in the stamp (See Figure 4.58). The system stamp feature has similar customization options as the captions with being able to move or change the caption to stand out or blend in the background of your project. The system stamp will stay active until the feature is toggled off by selecting **Effects > Annotation > Add System Stamp**.

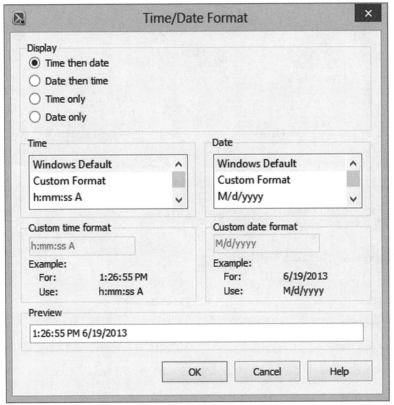

FIGURE 4.58 — The Time/Stamp Format dialog box with options to adjust information displayed within the stamp.

This feature is not recommended if you plan to edit your video project as the time will appear to jump depending on the edit.

4.6g — Recorder Hotkey Commands

Hotkeys are keyboard shortcuts that use keystrokes to activate menus or task actions. Using hotkeys can streamline your workflow and prevent unwanted mouse movements. They can later be automatically added as a callout when editing (See Figure 4.59).

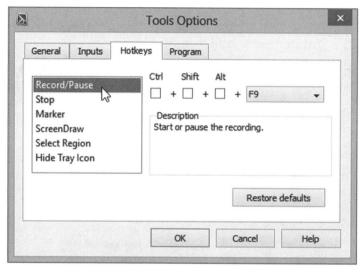

FIGURE 4.59 — Tools Options — Hotkeys (Record/Pause, Stop, Marker, ScreenDraw, Select Region, and Hide Tray Icon).

The Recorder Default Hotkeys

Hide Tray Icon	None Assigned
Marker	CTRL + M
Record/Pause	F9
ScreenDraw	CTRL + SHIFT + D
Select Region	None Assigned
Stop	F10

Quick List — Changing the Hotkey Commands

1. Open **Camtasia Recorder**

2. Select **Tools > Options > Hotkeys tab**

3. Select the recording function you wish to change

4. Choose a keystroke for the hotkey

5. *Optional:* **Restore defaults** button will reset commands to the default settings

6. Click **OK** when finished

Keyboard keystrokes data is collected as default during the recording. These can be added as callouts featured when editing. If you are going to use this data, try and use the default keys for consistency for the viewer.

NOTE

Right click on a selected clip within the Editor to automatically generate the hotkey shortcuts into callout. The callout will be added every time a key command was used during the recording (See Figure 4.60).

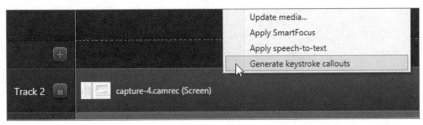

FIGURE 4.60 — Right click on a clip within Editor to automatically generate key commands.

QUICK CLIP | Adding Automatic Keystroke Callouts

4.7 — Previewing and Saving the Recording

After the recording stops, the **Recorder Preview Window** will appear for a final check before saving, producing, or deleting the file. Use the preview to check the audio, camera, and mouse movements. If you added a recording effect, this is the last time you can view its effectiveness as it cannot be edited (See Figure 4.61).

FIGURE 4.61 — Recording Preview Window that displays after the recording is stopped.

Preview Playback Size

The preview window does not have to be the same size as the actual recording dimensions. The **Recorder Preview Window** size is adjustable and does not affect the size of the recording. You can shrink the video to the size of the **Recorder Preview Window** or view the recording at the actual recording size. If the recording size is larger than the **Preview Window**, then navigation sliders will appear at the bottom and sides of the window. You can also adjust the size of the window to fit the recording size. Click the **Shrink to Fit or View at 100%** icon buttons to quickly adjust the playback view (See Figure 4.62).

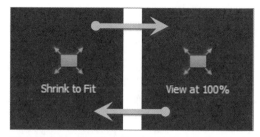

FIGURE 4.62 — Shrink to Fit on the left and View at 100% on the right can be quickly adjusted.

Save and Edit, Produce, or Delete the Recording

From the Recorder Preview Window there are options to Save and Edit, Save as, Produce, or Delete your recording (See Figure 4.63). Other than delete, each icon button will bring up the save navigation dialog box to select a save location.

FIGURE 4.63 – The Record preview window shows where to Save As.

Saving icon button functions:

- **Save and Edit** — Saves the file and launches Camtasia Editor

- **Save As** — Saves the file with a possibility to change file format

- **Produce** — Saves the file and launches the Production Wizard

- **Delete** — Deletes the file without saving

4.7a — File Formats

The **.camrec** and **.avi** are two file formats you can save your screen capture as after you stop recording. By default, the **Recorder** will save in the **.camrec** file format. The **.camrec** file format is a format constructed to be used within the **Editor**. It saves the collected system sounds, mouse use, Web camera input, and SmartFocus data but is not sharable until the file is produced. An .avi file is produced and can be shared right away, but does not carry over any system sounds, camera input, or other collected data (See Figure 4.64).

FIGURE 4.64 – A dialog box warning that the .avi file format will not save the system audio.

It is recommended to save the file as a **.camrec** file first because it will give you more options when you edit and produce you project.

.camrec — Camtasia Recording File

This is the default recording file format used by the **Recorder**. It can only be used by the **Editor**, but saves a wide range of data that is collected during the recording.

.avi — Audio Video Interleave

This format can be used with multiple playback programs and is not bound to the **Editor**. When saved as an .avi, the project can be shared or viewed instantly. However, it does not save recording data to be used with the **Editor**.

> **NOTE**
>
> *When selecting the **.avi** format some testing might need to be performed. The default codex for the **.avi** format is **tsc2** that might not play on some media players (See Figure 4.65). To change the codex, click in the Recorder toolbar **Tools > Options > Inputs > Video Settings**.*

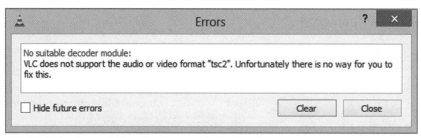

FIGURE 4.65 — Errors window showing: No suitable decoder module.

To change the recording file format, in the **Recording Toolbar** click on **Tools > Options > General tab > saving > Record to option**.

4.7b — Saving for Editing

There are a lot of advantages to saving your recordings as a **.camrec** file format and it is the recommended format to use. If you plan to edit your video, use the **.camrec** format.

The .camrec file may contain:

- Audio input

- Cursor data

- Keyboard shortcut data

- Marker data

- SmartFocus data

- System audio

- Webcam input

Even if you are not planning to edit the recording, save your recording as a **.camrec** file format. This will keep the possibility of being able to edit the collected data if you decide to later.

CHAPTER SUMMARY

In Chapter 4, we developed a deeper understanding of recording using screen capture and recording with audio. Both have step-by-step directions and examples for general use and how to customize each area for more advance users such as using cursor effects, mouse clicks, captions, drawing on screen, and using SmartFocus and markers. Remember to always check the TechSmith site for updates, downloads, and tutorials before you start recording. In the next chapter, we will learn how to record Microsoft PowerPoint® using the Camtasia Studio PowerPoint Add-in and we will import the makers and notes from our presentations into the Editor Timeline.

CHAPTER PROJECTS

1. When recording, how would you preview an area with a Webcam and show time?

2. How and when would you use shrink to fit, save, edit, produce, and delete?

3. Explain in your own words how and when to use the options in ScreenDraw while recording.

4. Explain the differences and why it is important knowing the settings of different media before you start recording.

5. What audio tips did you find most useful and why?

6. How do you draw on the screen (ScreenDraw) while recording?

7. Make up three customized hotkeys of your own and explain how you would use them.

8. If you are having trouble with the volume level, what are some things you can do to troubleshoot the problem?

9. What five recording tips are most helpful to you and why?

10. How do you save raw recordings and why would you want to save them?

11. Explain four reasons why you would review your recording and sound.

12. What is the difference between Standard and Widescreen Aspect Ratio? Include in your answer when you would use each.

13. Describe two situations in detail in which you would use a Webcam.

14. How would you position your Web camera and preview it?

15. In detail, give two examples of when you should add captions during the recording phase.

16. Give two examples of why and when markers are necessary.

CHAPTER 5

RECORDING: POWERPOINT

IN THIS CHAPTER

In this chapter, we will record our Microsoft PowerPoint® presentation using the Camtasia Studio PowerPoint Add-in. We will import the markers and notes from our presentations into the Editor Timeline. In Chapter 3, we reviewed the menus and features for the PowerPoint Add-in. In this chapter, we will start to record the presentations.

Many of these tasks are similar in nature and the checklist will have the same steps with only one or more variation. The lists serve as a quick reference before explaining in more detail on the steps to complete the tasks. The **Quick Clips** will show each task as a short video that is located on the DVD.

NOTE

As with the previous chapters, the same technical writing method will be used throughout this chapter. Menu items, programs, and file extensions will be in bold lettering while the mouse navigation and keystrokes action will be displayed with a ">" symbol.

Once you've completed this chapter, you will be able to:

• Locate and use the PowerPoint plug-in
• Check audio input levels
• Check camera placement
• Record picture-in-picture
• Add notes and markers to your presentation

Files: All figures in this chapter are in color located in the chapter folder on the DVD.

5.1 — The PowerPoint Add-in and Menus

Camtasia Studio includes a **PowerPoint Add-in** that enables the ability to record audio, video, and camera **Picture-in-Picture** included within the presentations. **Markers** can be added for each slide during the recording process to help with streamlining the editing workflow or adding to a video table of contents. These recordings are saved in the **.camrec** file format that can be opened in the **Camtasia Editor** for editing and sharing or produced for immediate sharing.

NOTE

*Although Camtasia Studio includes the PowerPoint Add-in for presentation recording, the Camtasia Recorder can also be used to record PowerPoint presentations. There are slight differences between using the Add-in and the Recorder. For example, when using the **Add-in** your presentation notes can be carried over as **Captions** to the Editor, while using the **Recorder** data is stored in the .camrec file to create **SmartFocus** and **Cursor Effects**. Both recording methods have advantages and disadvantages. It is recommended to try both styles to see which fits your workflow and the needs of your presentation more effectively.*

5.1a — Start Recording with PowerPoint

As with the Recorder, there are a few different ways to start recording using the PowerPoint Add-in (See Figure 5.1).

1. **Camtasia Studio Menu Option** — A dropdown option to launch or maximize PowerPoint

2. **Record Toolbar** — within the **Record the screen** button is a dropdown option to launch or maximize **PowerPoint**

3. **PowerPoint Recording Toolbar** — under the **Add-ins** menu tab option within PowerPoint is a Record button in the **Recording Toolbar**

If you select the **Record PowerPoint** option through the **Editor**, **PowerPoint** will launch if the program is not already running or it will maximize the window if the program is already running. Clicking the **Record** button within **PowerPoint** will automatically start recording the presentation.

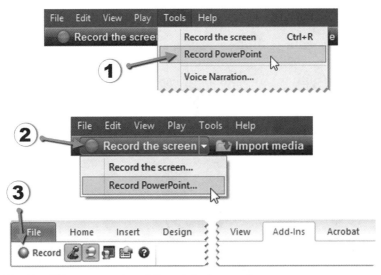

FIGURE 5.1 — Two different ways to launch PowerPoint for recording.

Configuring and Installing the Add-in

When you first install **Camtasia Studio**, the **Add-in** will also be installed and enabled if you have **PowerPoint** already installed on the computer you are using. The **Add-in** can be activated at a later time by selecting:

Camtasia Studio Editor > Tools > Options > PowerPoint tab > Enable PowerPoint Add-in

The checkmark indicates that the option is selected (See Figure 5.2). Uncheck the box to disable.

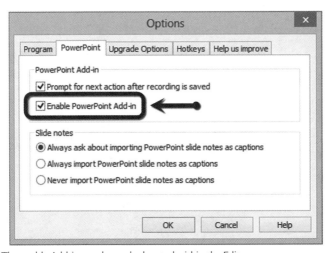

FIGURE 5.2 — The enable Add-in toggle can be located within the Editor.

5.1b — Add-in Recording Toolbar Menu and Options

The **Recording Toolbar** holds all of the tools and settings for the recording **Add-in** (See Figure 5.3). Here is a quick overview of the **Recording Toolbar**. For more information on the toolbar, Chapter 3 goes in-depth on all the tools and settings.

Overview Review — PowerPoint Add-in Menus and Features

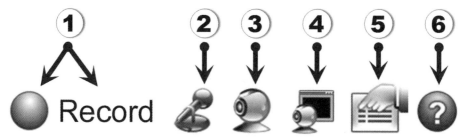

FIGURE 5.3 — Breakdown of the Add-in recording toolbar.

1. **Record icon button** — Starts the recording and your presentation
2. **Record Audio** — Toggles recording audio input
3. **Record Camera** — Toggles recording camera input
4. **Camera Preview** — launches a window showing what the camera will be recording
5. **Recording Options** — launches **Options** dialog box
6. **Help Topic** — launches the **Help Topic** guide

NOTE

*The **Record** icon button will change to **Stop Recording** icon button if you are still recording after the end of the presentation (See Figure 5.4).*

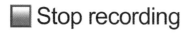

FIGURE 5.4 — The Recording Toolbar after the presentation ended but not the recording.

Hotkey Commands Used with the PowerPoint Add-in

Try and use the key commands when recording to limit the mouse movements.

PowerPoint Hotkey Commands

- **Record/Pause** — CTRL+SHIFT+F9

- **Stop** — CTRL+SHIFT+F10

The default hotkey can be changed in the **Recording Options** dialog box. Unlike the **Recorder**, the key command data will not be collected for automated callouts generation (See Figure 5.5).

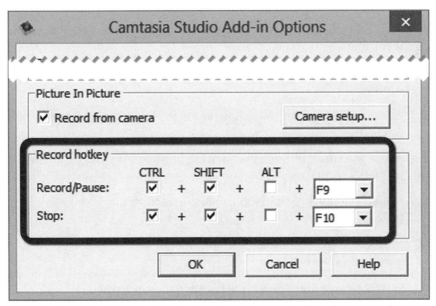

FIGURE 5.5 — PowerPoint Add-in Options displaying box with customizable hotkey commands.

5.2 — Recording Your PowerPoint Presentation

Recording your presentation only takes a few steps. Depending on the type of recording, you can adjust the recording settings for optimal results. The Add-in will record input from a Web camera, microphone, system sounds, cursor data, and effects.

5.2a — Step-by-Step: Recording the PowerPoint Presentation

The overview is a step-by-step list before we take a closer look at each step in the process.

Quick List: Recording the PowerPoint Presentation

1. Open PowerPoint and the presentation that will be recorded

2. Click on the **Add-in** menu tab to show the **Recording Toolbar**

3. *Optional:* Click the **Record Audio** button to record voice narration

4. *Optional:* Check the audio levels by opening the **Recording Options** dialog box

5. *Optional:* Click the **Record Camera** button to enable camera recording

6. *Optional:* Check camera placement by opening the **Camera Preview** window

7. Click the **Record** button to launch the slideshow presentation in full screen mode

8. Select the **Click to begin recording** button or use the hotkeys to begin the recording

9. Run through the presentation while the recorder is recording in the background

10. Press the **ESC** key or hotkey to stop recording at any time or let the presentation end

11. Save the recording by entering the filename and location

12. File is saved as a **.camrec** file format and is opened within the **Editor** for sharing or editing

QUICK
CLIP
PowerPoint Recording

A Closer Look — Recording the Presentation

5.2b — Pre-Recording Preparation

When you are first learning, it is best to use the default settings before making adjustments to the recording settings. The **Recording Options** has a number of advanced and customizable settings. For the most part, the default settings will work for most end users and it is best to start with these settings before tailoring of optimal use.

Open and Check Your Presentation and Equipment

Before you start your presentation, run through a production checklist. Chapter 2 holds additional list and tips.

- Check equipment, including audio and video settings

- Check Internet connection, if needed

- Check your files and media start points including that you are on your first slide

After the **PowerPoint** presentation is open and ready to be recorded, select the **Add-ins** tab to show the **Recording Toolbar** (See Figure 5.6).

FIGURE 5.6 — PowerPoint Add-in and Recording toolbar.

Select Recording Devices

Select **Record Audio** or **Record Camera** depending on your presentation. If either is selected, click on the **Camera Preview** and **Recording Options** buttons to check settings and select input devices.

Recording

After clicking on the **Record** button, the **PowerPoint** presentation will launch in a paused state with a settings dialog box (See Figure 5.7). This is the last time you will be able to check your presentation or settings before you start recording. If you are recording audio, preform a last audio check by speaking into the microphone. The audio volume median should be in the middle of the volume bar. Move the volume slider to adjust the setting.

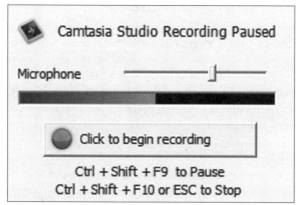

FIGURE 5.7 – A screenshot of the recording settings dialog box that overlays your presentation before the recording starts.

Click on the **Click to begin recording** button to start recording your presentation. Run through your project as you normally would. If you make a mistake, pause, and then restart from before the mistake. This will help when you edit your presentation. Chapter 2 lists additional presentation tips.

Stopping the Recording

There are a few actions that can take place once you are finished with a recording. These options can be selected before the recording in the **Camtasia Studio Add-in Options** dialog box (See Figure 5.8).

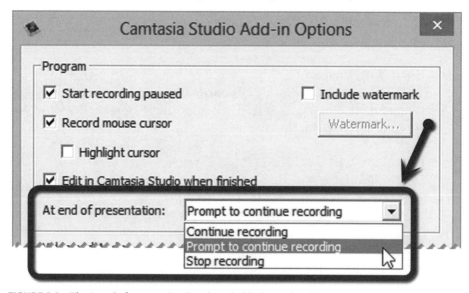

FIGURE 5.8 – The At end of presentation dropdown holds three selectable actions when the recording ends.

Depending on your ending selection, let the presentation end or hit the ESC key to end the recording and save your recording.

Saving the Project

After the end of the recording, a navigation dialog box will pop up to assign a location for the save file. The file is saved in the .camrec file format. Data is recorded within the **.camrec** file format; however, there are fewer options when using the **Add-in**. For example, SmartFocus data can be collected. The nature of a slide presentation does not have as much mouse movements or screen action information to gather. Another example is the cursor effects are limited to highlighting.

After selecting a location for the saved file, a dialog box will pop up asking if you want to produce or edit your recording. Producing will launch the **Production Wizard** while the edit option will launch the **Editor**.

Project: Use the files in the project folder to assemble a PowerPoint presentation and record it.

5.2c — Step-by-Step: Recording Narration and Audio

You can narrate an audio track along with the PowerPoint screen presentation. By clicking on the **Microphone icon** within the **Add-in Recording Toolbar**, you enable the audio input to record sound.

Quick List: Recording Narration and Audio

1. Open PowerPoint and the presentation that will be recorded

2. Click on the **Add-in** menu tab to show the **Recording Toolbar**

3. Click the **Record Audio** button to record voice narration

4. Check the audio levels by opening the **Recording Options** dialog box

5. *Optional:* Click the **Record Camera** button to enable camera recording

6. *Optional:* Check camera placement by opening the **Camera Preview** window

7. Click the **Record** button to launch the slideshow presentation in full screen mode

8. Check the audio volume level

9. Select the **Click to begin recording** button or use the hotkeys to begin the recording

10. Run through the presentation while the recorder is recording in the background

11. Press the **ESC** key or hotkey to stop recording at any time or let the presentation end

12. Save the recording by entering the filename and location

13. File is saved as a **.camrec** file format and is opened within the **Editor** for sharing or editing

A Closer Look — Recording Narration and Audio

Toggle the **Record Audio** button to enable or disable audio input depending on the type of presentation you are recording. Once activated, check the audio input levels and audio source for sound input by selecting

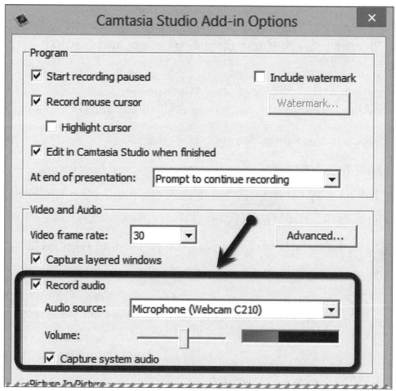

FIGURE 5.9 — Audio setting within the Add-in Options showing record audio and capture system audio highlighted.

the **Camtasia Studio Add-in Options** from the **Add-in Recording Toolbar**. The audio input levels ideally should be in the near middle of the volume bar (See Figure 5.9).

Audio Settings

The video and audio area within the **Camtasia Studio Add-in Options** contains settings similar to the **Tools Options Input tab** when using the Camtasia Recorder.

- **Record audio** — toggles the recording of audio input device

- **Audio source** — a dropdown menu to select the audio device to capture the audio

- **Volume** — slider control and preview of audio volume

- **Capture system audio** — activates the collection of system sounds

When recording any audio, it is recommended that you open the **Camtasia Studio Add-in Options** and test the audio source and volume level.

5.2d — Step-by-Step: Recording Camera Input

During your PowerPoint presentation, you can record input from a Web camera. The input will be recorded on a separate movable layer in a picture-in-picture. You can record yourself, a lecturer, an audience, or a location to enhance the slide presentation.

Quick List: Recording Camera Input and Picture-in-Picture

1. Open PowerPoint and the presentation that will be recorded

2. Click on the **Add-in** menu tab to show the **Recording Toolbar**

3. *Optional:* Click the **Record Audio** button to record voice narration

4. *Optional:* Check the audio levels by opening the **Recording Options** dialog box

5. Click the **Record Camera** button to enable camera recording

6. Check camera placement by opening the **Camera Preview** window

7. Click the **Record** button to launch the slideshow presentation in full screen mode

8. Select the **Click to begin recording** button or use the hotkeys to begin the recording

9. Run through the presentation while the recorder is recording in the background

10. Press the **ESC** key or hotkey to stop recording at any time or let the presentation end

11. Save the recording by entering the filename and location

12. File is saved in the **.camrec** file format and is opened within the **Editor** for sharing or editing

A Closer Look — Recording Camera Input and Picture-in-Picture

Enable the video for a camera to record a picture-in-picture during your presentation. Select the **Camera Preview** to check camera input and subject placement or blocking. Once enabled, a **Camera Preview** window will appear with a view of what the camera is seeing. Check to make sure your subject is within the camera's view. It is easy for the subject to move outside the camera's view (See Figure 5.10).

FIGURE 5.10 — Example of improper blocking in the Camera Preview window.

The **Camera Preview** window can be moved around the screen both before and during the recording phase (See Figure 5.11). During the recording phase, the **Camera Preview** will only show if it is selected before the recording starts.

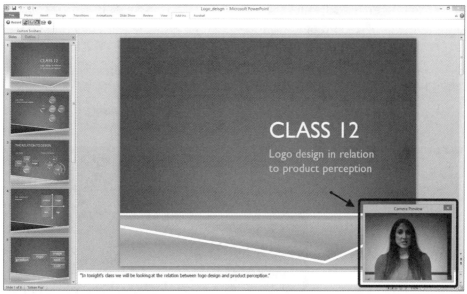

FIGURE 5.11 — Screenshot of PowerPoint presentation with the Camera Preview enabled.

The camera preview will be captured during the recording. The advantage is seeing the live camera input for placement. The downside is that the preview will be burned into the recording and will not be able to be edited (See Figure 5.12).

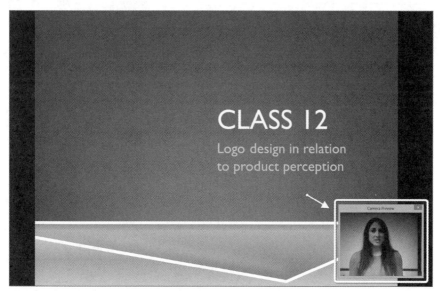

FIGURE 5.12 — A screenshot of the PowerPoint presentation with the Camera preview overlay during the recording phase.

The camera will still capture video if the preview is disabled. Camera input will be recording during the recording of the presentation and will have its own timeline track within the **Editor**.

After the presentation has ended and the recording is saved, open the file inside the **Editor** to view and edit the separate camera input and presentation tracks (See Figure 5.13). The camera track can be moved, cut, or sized over the screen recording.

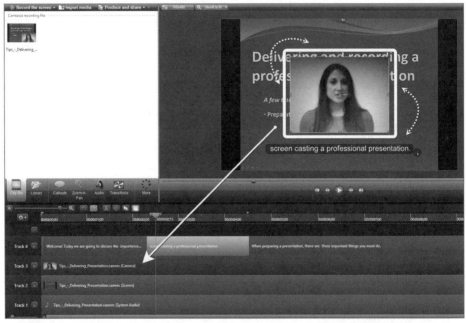

FIGURE 5.13 — The Editor with the picture-in-picture presentation recording within the timeline.

Video Settings

The **Video and Audio** area within the **Camtasia Studio Add-in Options** contains a few video settings. Unless it is necessary, leave the advance settings to the default, they will work for most settings (See Figure 5.14).

- **Video frame rate** — Lists the video frames per second with the more frames equaling higher quality and file size

- **Capture layered windows** — Preserves unusually shaped or transparent dialog windows

- **Advanced** — Advanced audio and video compression and formats
- **Picture-in-Picture** — Toggle for camera activation
- **Camera setup** — Individual device and video format settings

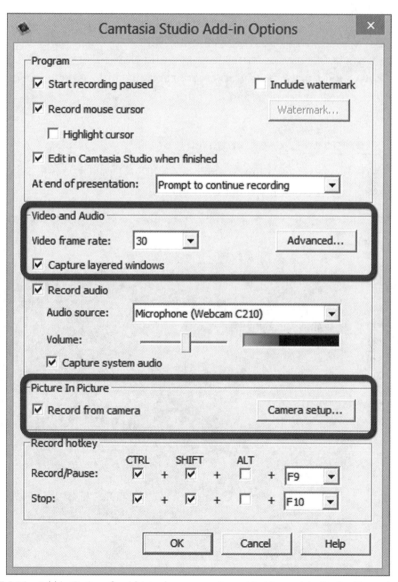

FIGURE 5.14 — Add-in Options for video and camera settings with video and audio plus Picture-in-Picture highlighted.

5.3 — Advanced Features and Special Effects

There are a few features and special effects that can be added to your presentation. There are not as many as the **Recorder**, but with the use of the **Editor** you can add any of the features. Creating notes and giving titles to slides for markers will be a workflow time saver after the recording.

Project: Add text to notes field and add slide titles in a PowerPoint presentation to create captions and markers when the recording is opened in the Editor.

5.3a — Notes and Close Captions

In PowerPoint, the notes field can be filled in with your script (See Figure 5.15). You can fill in notes for each slide.

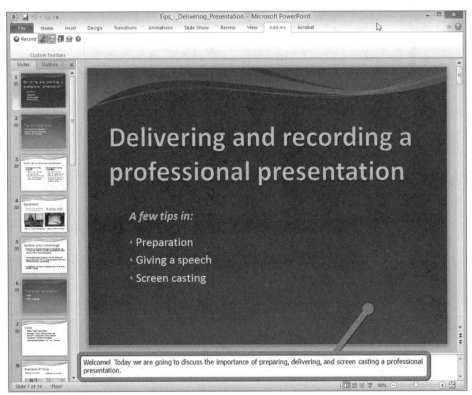

FIGURE 5.15 — A screenshot of the notes field within PowerPoint.

PowerPoint Notes and Captions

If your PowerPoint presentation has notes within the notes field, those notes can be imported into the **Editor**. After you save the recording and open the file in the **Editor,** an **Import PowerPoint Slide Notes** dialog box will open asking if you want the notes imported (See Figure 5.16).

FIGURE 5.16 — The Import PowerPoint Side Notes dialog box will appear if you have notes in your presentation.

The imported notes are set as captions on a separate track on your editing timeline. This is very useful for creating captions for your project. You still might have to edit, split, or cut the captions in the timeline to make them ADA compliant, but, importing the notes is often faster than starting from scratch (See Figure 5.17).

Save the file as an **.mp4** file to include the captions in the final produced video file. These captions can be opened or closed when first playing the video. If the video has closed captions to start, the captions can be opened during playback (See Figure 5.18).

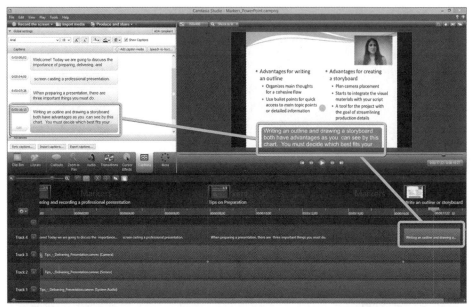

FIGURE 5.17 — Captions in the task tab, timeline, and canvas within Editor that were imported from PowerPoint.

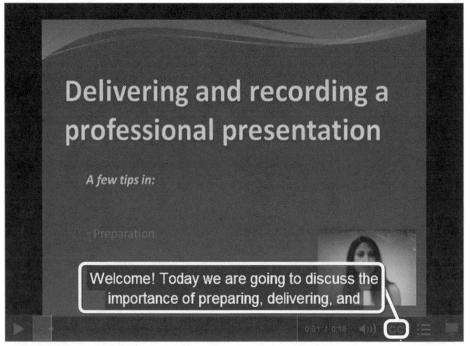

FIGURE 5.18 — Caption toggle button with caption overlay during playback

5.3b — Adding Markers and a Table of Contents

Markers are a very useful tool in the editing process and for creating a table of contents for your video. The titles of the presentation slides will be the titles of the markers. If the title is in multiple boxes on the slide, the title might not be complete once it is brought into the **Editor**. These can be adjusted by renaming the markers in the timeline (See Figure 5.19).

NOTE *The importance of creating and using markers during a screencast is covered in Chapter 4 and during the Editing stage in Chapter 7.*

QUICK CLIP PowerPoint Markers and Table of Contents

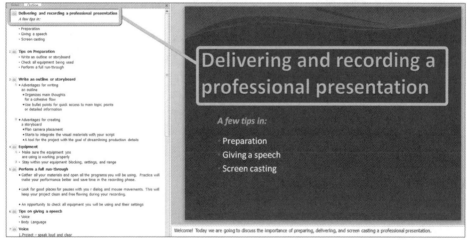

FIGURE 5.19 — Titles of PowerPoint slides that will be converted into markers in the timeline.

The marker will appear at the start of each slide within the timeline. These can be moved, renamed, and deleted to match any editing of the project (See Figure 5.20).

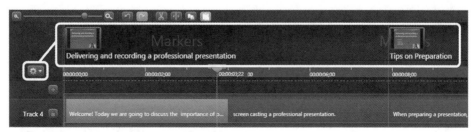

FIGURE 5.20 — Marker view within the Editor timeline.

NOTE *To view the markers within the timeline, click the Show Marker View to open the Marker bar.*

The marker names will also be the names of the table of contents listings. Select your produce file as an **.mp4** file format. During video production, the table of contents listings can be turned on, off, add numbers, and renamed (See Figure 5.21).

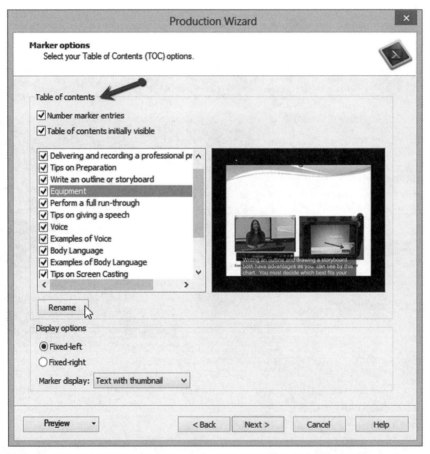

FIGURE 5.21 — The Table of Contents options in the Production Wizard's Marker Options.

After the video production, the table of contents panel can be open or closed depending on if the **Table of contents initially visible** click box is selected. Once the panel is opened, you can navigate throughout the video by selecting a listing in the table of contents (See Figure 5.22).

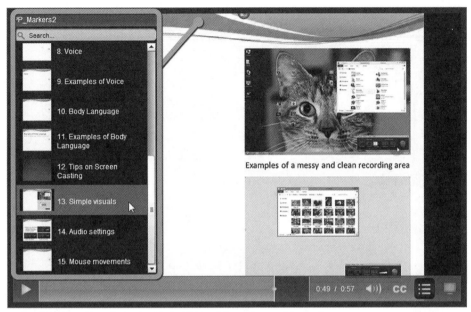

FIGURE 5.22 — Video playback with the Table of Contents panel opened.

5.3c — Adding a Watermark

Watermarks added during the recording phase are permanently burned into the video, adding an adjustable watermark within the **Editor** is recommended. This will allow for maximum customization and ease in editing.

To select a watermark, click open the **Camtasia Studio Add-in Options** dialog box and check the **Include Watermark** box. This will enable the **Watermark** button. Click on the button to open the **Watermark Options** dialog box (See Figure 5.23).

Within the **Watermark Options** dialog box, you can select a custom image for the watermark from a file on your computer. The scale, position, and transparency can all be adjusted. The watermark will not show during the recording but will be burned into the recording and showed in the **Editor** and final video production.

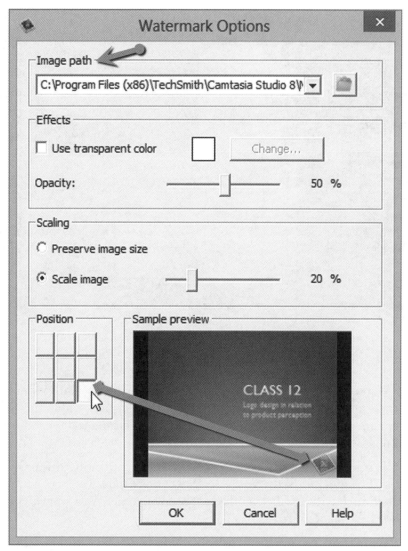

FIGURE 5.23 — The Watermark Options dialog box with customizable options.

5.3d — Adding Cursor Effects

The highlight cursor option is available during the recording, but it does not have as many adjustments as using Cursor Effects within the **Recorder** or **Editor**. Click open the **Camtasia Studio Add-in Options** dialog box to toggle recording or highlighting the cursor (See Figure 5.24).

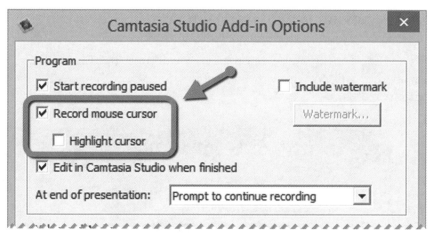

FIGURE 5.24 — Options to record, hide, or highlight cursor effect during recording.

The cursor effects will not show during the presentation but will show when the file is opened onto the **Editor**. The cursor effect cannot be changed after the presentation recording. However, unlike the **Recorder**, the cursor data is not stored and can be added in the **Editor** (See Figure 5.25).

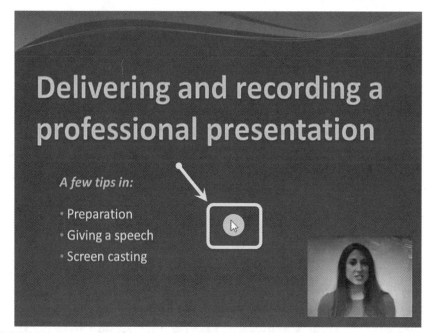

FIGURE 5.25 — A screenshot of the video playback with a highlighted cursor.

5.4 – Saving the PowerPoint Add-in Recordings

As soon as the presentation ends or you press the **Esc** button, a save dialog box will pop up with a selection stop or continue recording (See Figure 5.26).

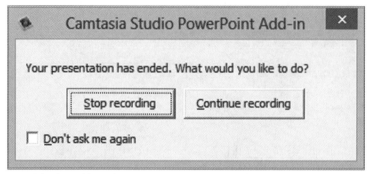

FIGURE 5.26 – Dialog box with a selection or continue recording after the end of the presentation.

Continue Recording

Selecting the **Continue recording** button will keep the capture recording. This can be used to continue recording camera or audio input after the slideshow. If you choose **Continue recording**, a **Stop recording** button will now show in the **Recording Toolbar** to end the recording (See Figure 5.27).

FIGURE 5.27 – The Recording Toolbar changes if you select to continue recording after the end of the presentation.

Stop Recording

Selecting the **Stop recording** button will stop the recording and save the file. After the recording is stopped the **Save Camtasia Recording As** dialog box will appear for file naming and save location (See Figure 5.28).

The **Save as type** is the **.camrec** file format used by the **Editor**. Once the file is saved the **Camtasia Studio for PowerPoint** will appear. This

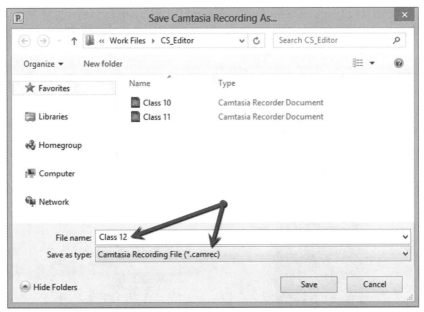

FIGURE 5.28 — Save navigation dialog box after the recording stops.

dialog box has options for entering the **Production Wizard** or editing the recording with the **Editor** (See Figure 5.29).

FIGURE 5.29 — A save action dialog box after navigating and saving the file.

Both of these selections will bring up the **Editor**; however, the **Produce your recording** selection will automatically launch the Production Wizard (See Figure 5.30). The recording is still saved and is able to be edited even if you use the **Production Wizard** first.

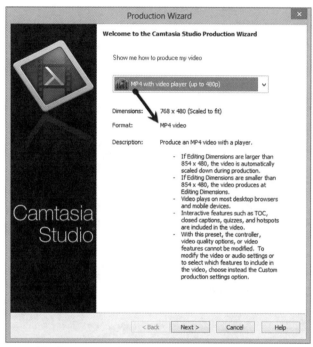

FIGURE 5.30 – Universal Production Wizard that will launch once the file is saved.

Cancelling the Recording

To cancel a presentation recording, press the **Esc** key to stop and exit the presentation. Click **Stop recording** and then click **Cancel** when the **Save Camtasia Recording As** dialog pops up. Selecting the **Yes** button will end the recording unsaved and ready to start the recording process over (See Figure 5.31).

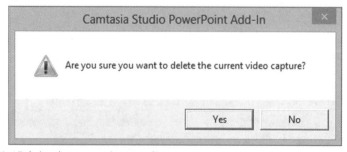

FIGURE 5.31 – Deleting the presentation recording.

Saving Slides as Images

You can save individual images of your PowerPoint presentation for additional use or to fix a mistake. For example, after you record your presentation you notice an error in one of your slides. You can correct the error by making an image of the correct slide and overlaying the new image over the video track within Camtasia editor. This will save you the time in having to rerecord your presentation.

To create an image file

1. Select **File > Save As**

2. When the **Save As** dialog box appears, select the type of file from the dropdown menu

3. Select an image format from .bmp, .gif, .jpg, .png

4. Click **Save**

5. Select **Every Slide** or **Current Slide Only**

To save a slide as an image, navigate your version of PowerPoint to the **File > Save As** and select an image file format from the dialog box. Then select **Every Slide** or **Current Slide Only** from the next dialog box (See Figure 5.32).

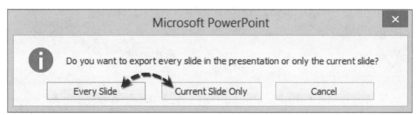

FIGURE 5.32 — Save slides as individual images.

Using PowerPoint Slides Without the Add-in

If you do not have access to the PowerPoint program Add-in, you can use the individual slide images to create the presentation using the **Editor**. Save each slide as an independent image. Import the images into the clip bin and arrange them on your timeline. Use the **transition task tab** to create a transition between images. Use the **voice narration task tab** to add any audio narration to the presentation. You can also import your notes as captions.

CHAPTER SUMMARY

In this chapter, we learned pre-recording preparations, how to record and set narration, audio, and camera input, and how to save in Microsoft PowerPoint® using the Camtasia Studio PowerPoint Add-in. We also learned advanced features and special effects such as adding notes, close captions, markers, table of contents, watermarks, picture-in-picture, and cursor effects to PowerPoint. The PowerPoint Add-in features and effects provide a professional appearance to your presentation.

CHAPTER PROJECTS

1. What are four PowerPoint Recording tips and why did you pick them?

2. Which advanced features or special effects do you want to use in your Power Point presentation and why?

3. Describe ways to start recording aPowerPoint presentation. Try using all of them. Which do you like the best and why?

4. Describe all of the equipment, connections, and files you need to check before recording your PowerPoint presentation.

5. Discuss the ways to save your PowerPoint project.

6. Give two reasons, with examples, of why the camera preview is important.

7. Describe the steps of importing notes into your PowerPoint presentation and try them.

8. Why are markers important and how do you use them in your PowerPoint project?

9. What is a watermark and how would you add it to your PowerPoint presentation?

10. Develop a PowerPoint presentation using at least four different features of PowerPoint Add-in.

CHAPTER **6**

EDITING:
CLIP BIN *AND* LIBRARY

IN THIS CHAPTER

In this chapter, we will be shown how to import media files into both the clip bin and the library in your current project. We will also take an in-depth look at how to view, organize, and remove files from both the library and clip bin. Managing your media files and assets are very important for both present and future use.

NOTE

The same technical writing method that was used in Chapter 3 will be used throughout this chapter. Menu items, programs, and file extensions will be in bold lettering while the mouse navigation and keystrokes action will be displayed with a ">" symbol.

Once you've completed this chapter, you will be able to:

- Import media into the clip bin and library
- Preview selected media
- View, organize, and remove files from the clip bin and library
- Manage media files and assets

Files: All figures in this chapter are in color located in the chapter folder on the DVD.

6.1 — Camtasia Studio Editor Overview

The **Camtasia Studio Editor** is the centerpiece program in the studio. It works as a stand-alone program or in conjunction with the **Camtasia Recorder** and **PowerPoint Add-in**. When using the **Editor**, you can combine, cut, arrange, and add special effects, and other features to video, audio, and image clips. By combining them together, you can produce your own video project.

Like the **Recorder**, the **Editor** uses its own file format to save files. The **.camproj** format is a native editor format that can only be opened and used with the **Camtasia Editor**. The recorder's **.camrec** files are used within the **Editor**.

6.1a — Launching the Camtasia Studio Editor

There are two main ways to launch the **Camtasia Studio Editor** (See Figure 6.1). You can click on the desktop shortcut or use the Save and Edit selection at the end of a screen or presentation recording.

FIGURE 6.1 — Camtasia Studio shortcut icon (Save and Edit).

1. Click on the desktop or shortcut icon to launch the **Editor**

2. After a recording ends, click the **Save and Edit** button

When launching Camtasia Studio from the desktop short cut, the **Editor** will launch with options to open the Recorder and PowerPoint Add-in. You can also launch the **Editor** using your computer operating system and navigating to the saved files or pinning the program to your taskbar.

The Camtasia Studio Editor Interface

The editor interface is split into three main sections. They are the **media** and **task tabs**, **preview area**, and the **timeline**. The preview area and timeline work in direct correlation with each other (See Figure 6.2).

Chapter 3 talks about interface, tools, and settings. In this chapter, we will show a quick overview of the three main sections before focusing on the clip bin and library media tabs.

Overview Review —The Editor Interface

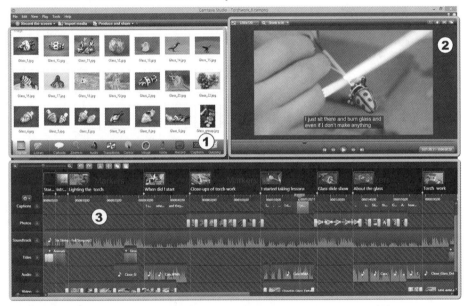

FIGURE 6.2 – The Camtasia Studio Editor interface (Media and Task tab, Preview window, and Timeline).

1. **Media and Task Tabs** — tabs that hold media and tools to create and perform selected features

2. **Preview Window** —previews the selected area of the timeline where the playhead is positioned

3. **Timeline** — shows all of the frames, tracks, and features of your project including videos, images, audio, special effects, and other features

The **Editor** interface is adjustable and the sides of the tool and asset preview, preview window, and timeline can all be increased or decreased to show more of the desired section. This makes the interface dynamic and customizable to your project's needs.

6.2 — The Clip Bin

The clip bin lists all media that was imported into the current project. It is like a catalog of selectable media that organizes media files to make it easy to find and to select the files you would like to use in your project (See Figure 6.3).

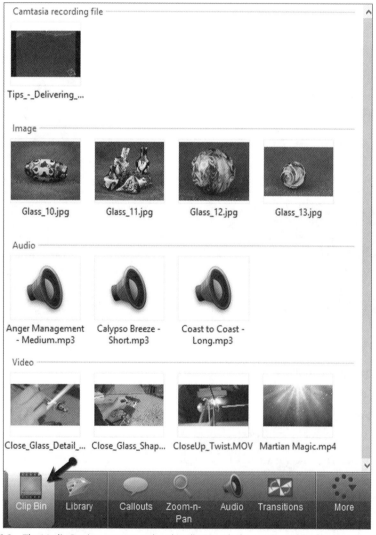

FIGURE 6.3 — The Media Preview area opened to the Clip Bin tab showcasing media files that were imported into the current project.

The media is not embedded into the project but there's a link to that media where it is located on your computer. If you move the files on your computer, the **Editor** will ask for you to navigate to the new location of the file to re-link the media. Backing up your project will collect all of the media in your clip bin in one place. We will go step-by-step on how to backup your project later in this chapter.

Because the media files are a link rather than the full file, using and editing the media will not alter the files on your computer. You can use the same media clip multiple times throughout the timeline and cut, slip, or add effects to them individually.

6.2a — Importing Files

All imported media files are imported into the **Clip Bin**. A screen recording is automatically imported into the clip bin if the **Save and Edit** option is selected when saving the recording.

The clip bin organizes the files by the type of media they contain, such as Camtasia recording, image, audio, or video files. You can constantly add and delete media to the clip bin.

Quick List: Importing Media Files into the Clip Bin

1. Open the **Editor**

2. Click in the **Import Media** icon button in the Application menu

3. An open file navigation dialog box will pop up

4. From the dialog box, select the files to be imported

5. *Optional:* Hold the **CTRL** or **SHIFT** keys to select multiple files

6. Click **Open** once the files are selected

7. The media files appear in the **Clip Bin**

NOTE | *To preview the file without adding it to the timeline, double click or right click on the media file in the clip bin.*

A Closer Look: Importing Media Files into the Clip Bin

After the **Editor** is opened, you are ready to start your video project. First, you will need to import the media files you wish to use in the project. To import files, select the **Import media** from the application menu at the top left portion of the interface (See Figure 6.4).

FIGURE 6.4 – The Application menus with the Import media icon button.

Once selected, an **Open file** navigation dialog box will pop up. Navigate the window to the location on your computer that stores the files. Select a file or group of files to import (See Figure 6.5).

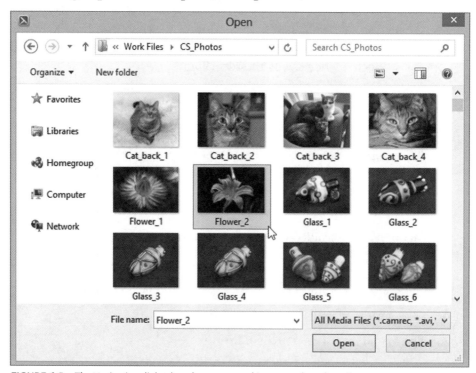

FIGURE 6.5 – The Navigation dialog box that opens and imports selected media.

The **All Media Files** dropdown menu will list all supported file formats. If the file you are looking for does not appear in the window, it might not be supported as an importable media file. You might have to convert the file into a supported format.

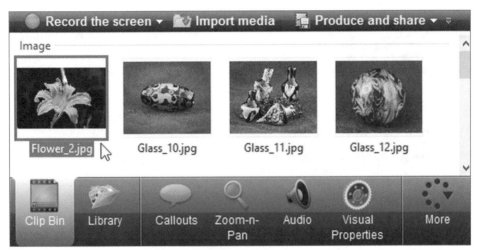

FIGURE 6.6 — A highlight of the imported image file that was imported into the clip bin.

Once a file or a group of files are selected, click the **Open** button to import the files into the **Clip Bin.** From the **Clip Bin**, the media is ready to be used in your project (See Figure 6.6).

Double click on the media file to see a working preview of the clip within the **Preview window.** The preview will play any video, animation, or sound without interfering with or modifying your project.

NOTE

*As with most Camtasia Studio tools, there are more than one way to perform functions within the program. You can also import media by right-clicking on an empty space within the **Clip Bin** tab and selecting **Import Media** from the context menu or from the **Menu Options** select **File > Import Files**. You can also use the hotkey command **Ctrl + I** to import the media. In this book, only one possible way to perform an action might be highlighted although there might be others. Use the style that best fits your workflow.*

6.2b — Types of Importable Media and File Formats

The **Editor** can support many types of audio, image, and video file formats. When importing media, the dropdown menu within the **Open** dialog box will show all the media files the **Editor** supports (See Figure 6.7).

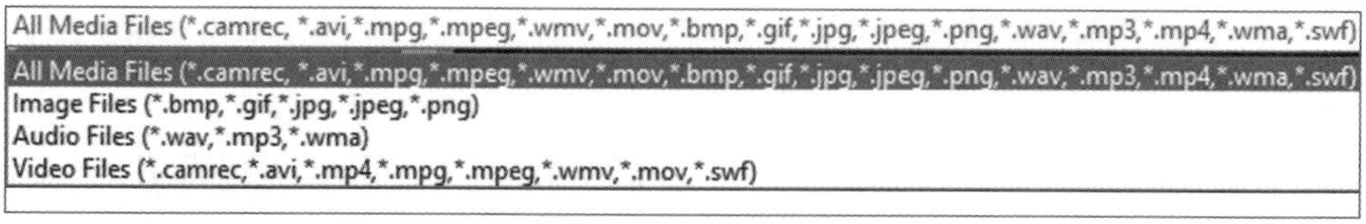

All Media Files (*.camrec, *.avi,*.mpg,*.mpeg,*.wmv,*.mov,*.bmp,*.gif,*.jpg,*.jpeg,*.png,*.wav,*.mp3,*.mp4,*.wma,*.swf)
All Media Files (*.camrec, *.avi,*.mpg,*.mpeg,*.wmv,*.mov,*.bmp,*.gif,*.jpg,*.jpeg,*.png,*.wav,*.mp3,*.mp4,*.wma,*.swf)
Image Files (*.bmp,*.gif,*.jpg,*.jpeg,*.png)
Audio Files (*.wav,*.mp3,*.wma)
Video Files (*.camrec,*.avi,*.mp4,*.mpg,*.mpeg,*.wmv,*.mov,*.swf)

FIGURE 6.7 – The file format selection in the Import Media dropdown menu.

Types of Importable Media

Camtasia Recording files

- **.camrec** — Camtasia Recording File

Image files

- **.bmp** — Bitmap image file
- **.gif** — Graphics Interchange Format
- **.jpg/.jpeg** — Joint Photographic Experts Group
- **.png** — Portable Network Graphics

Audio files

- **.wav** — Waveform Audio File Format
- **.mp3** — MPEG 1 or MPEG 2 audio layer 3
- **.wma** — Windows Media Audio

Video files

- **.avi** — Audio Video Interleave
- **.mp4** — Motion Picture Expert Group 4
- **.mpg/.mpeg** — Motion Picture Expert Group 1
- **.wmv** — Window Media Video
- **.mov** — Quick Time Movie
- **.swf** — Adobe Flash

Net Search **File Formats** — Perform a file format search including types of formats used by Camtasia Studio. Compare the type of audio, image, and video formats and how they store information.

Previewing any imported media is recommended. Some files like a **.mov** file carry more than one track contained within them, and importing the media might only bring one of the tracks. Others like **.swf** might need to be created from a particular program like **Jing**. If you are having trouble with importing a file, check the **Help manual** or TechSmith Website for the latest technical information and help.

 Project: Import the selection of files in the project folder to the Clip Bin.

QUICK CLIP | Importing and adding media from the Clip Bin to the Timeline.

6.2c — Adding Clip Bin Media to Timeline

The imported media in your **Clip Bin** is ready to be used in your project; however, it is not added to your project until you add the media into the **Timeline** to be part of your video. The final produced video will only show media that is placed into the **Timeline**. There are a few ways to add a media file that is in the **Clip Bin** to your **Timeline**.

Click and Drag

The easiest way to add a media file to the **Timeline** is to click on the file in the **Clip Bin** and while holding down the mouse button, drag the file to the desired location in your **Timeline** (See Figure 6.8).

Pick an open spot on the **Timeline** to drag the media file. You will only be allowed to place new clips in open spaces on your **Timeline**. If the duration of the new clip is longer than the space provided, it will push the clips after the entry point farther down the **Timeline** to make room. If this is not the desired effect, drag and drop the new clip to an empty track. Once it is placed, you can adjust the media file as needed.

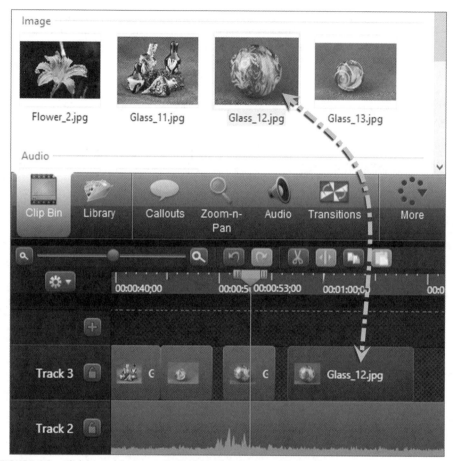

FIGURE 6.8 — Click on and drag a media file from the Clip Bin to the Timeline.

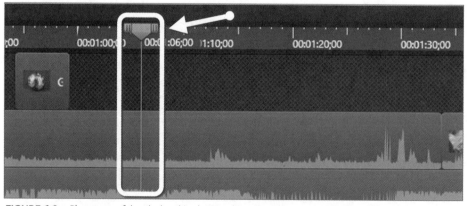

FIGURE 6.9 — Placement of the playhead in the Timeline where the new media file will be added.

Right Click

To add media using the right click option, place the playhead to the location of the **Timeline** where you want to add the file (See Figure 6.9).

After the playhead is set, right-click on the media file in the **Clip Bin** and select the **Add to Timeline at Playhead** from the menu (See Figure 6.10).

FIGURE 6.10 — Right-click on a file in the Clip Bin to add the clip to the Timeline.

The selected media will now appear in the **Timeline** at the location of the playhead on the first available track (See Figure 6.11).

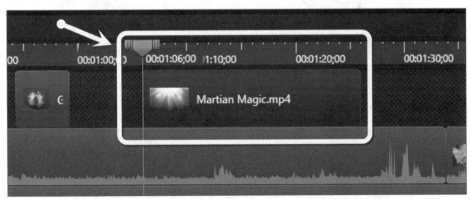

FIGURE 6.11 — The selected media file from the Clip Bin had been added to the Timeline.

Both the **click and drag** and **right click** methods of adding media files from the Clip Bin to the Timeline work when multiple files are selected.

Track Availability

When adding a media file from the **Clip Bin** to the **Timeline**, the space you are dragging the file or where the playhead is needs to be available to receive the media.

A layer might be unavailable if the layer is locked, is fill with a clip, has clips that are too close together to fit the incoming media, or there is another open track before it in the track layers. If all the tracks at the playhead are locked or unavailable, a new track will be created.

For example, when adding a clip with the right-click **Add to Timeline at Playhead** option, the clip will be placed at the first available track layer on the **Timeline** (See Figure 6.12).

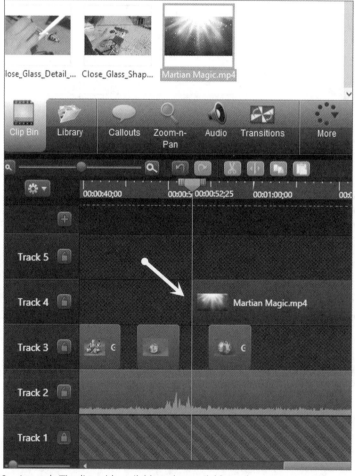

FIGURE 6.12 — A sample Timeline with available and unavailable tracks.

Track availability in Figure 12

- **Track 1** — is locked and cannot be modified

- **Track 2** — is full were the playhead is located

- **Track 3** — the two clips are too close to fit the incoming media

- **Track 4** — is eligible and has received the incoming media

- **Track 5** — is eligible but will not receive the media because Track 4 is the first available

When using the drag and drop method to add media files to the **Clip Bin**, the mouse cursor will change shape to represent track availability. Eligible tracks and locations will be represented by a **plus sign**. Ineligible tracks are represented by a **cross-out** symbol (See Figure 6.13).

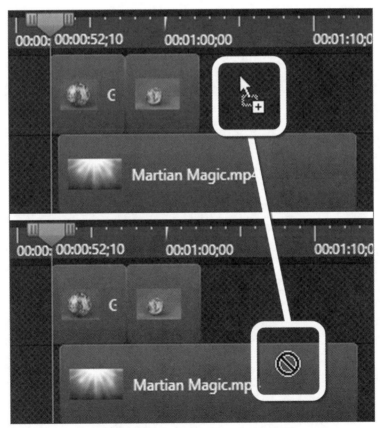

FIGURE 6.13 — The mouse cursor changes indicating track location availability.

If you want to add the media files to a location that is not available, place the files on a new track or open space. After the media files are placed, they can be adjusted to fit in previously unavailable places within the timeline.

If you want to force a track to be next in the placement order, you can temporarily lock preceding tracks making them ineligible. Locking tracks you are not working on will also minimize adding media to the wrong location.

6.2d — Viewing Media in the Clip Bin

The default setting to view the media file within the **Clip Bin** is a thumbnail view sorted in media type groups. Depending on the type of project you are creating or your workflow, a more detailed view of the media file might be necessary.

To change the media preview to the detailed view, right-click on an empty space within the **Clip Bin**. A context menu will open with options to change the file view and grouping (See Figure 6.14).

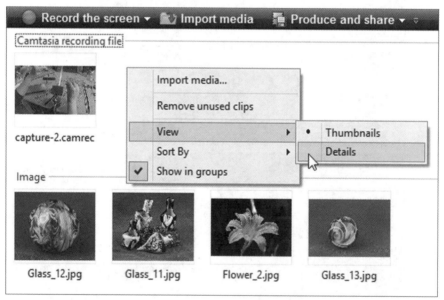

FIGURE 6.14 — The right-click context menu when clicking on an empty space in the Clip Bin.

The **Show in groups** selection toggles organizing the clip files within their media types. The detailed view will display information about the clips in one clear list (See Figure 6.15).

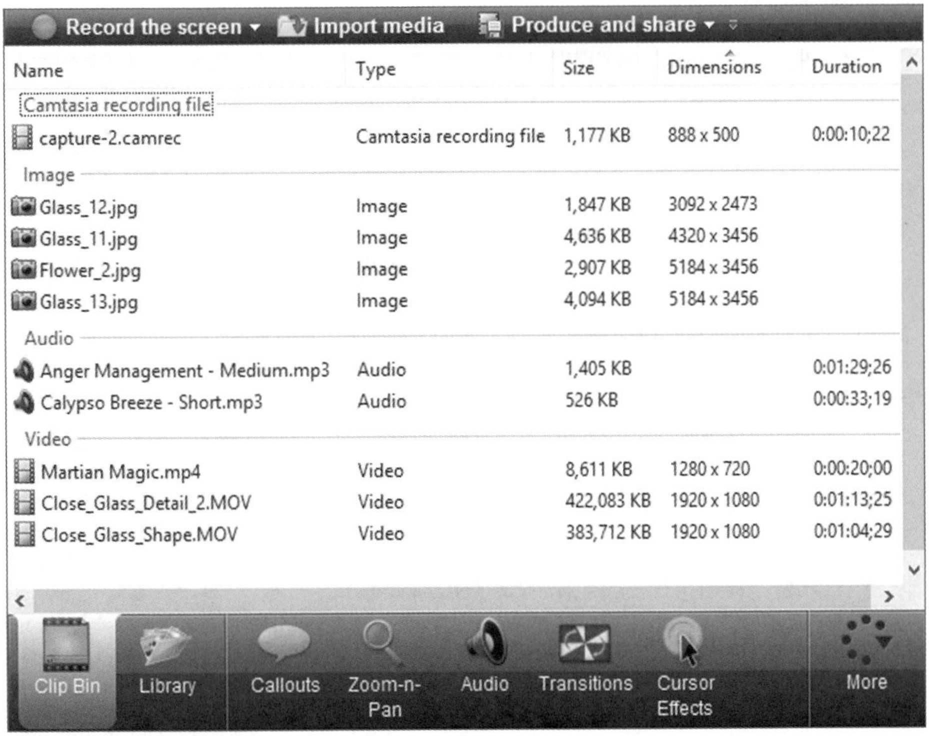

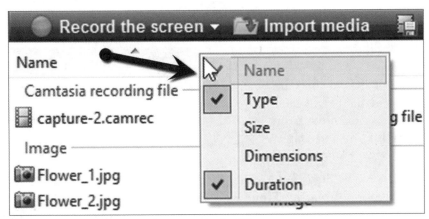

Record the screen
Import media
Produce and share
Name
Type
Size
Dimensions
Duration
Camtasia recording file
capture-2.camrec
Camtasia recording file
1,177 KB
888 x 500
0:00:10;22
Image
Glass_12.jpg
Image
1,847 KB
3092 x 2473
Glass_11.jpg
Image
4,636 KB
4320 x 3456
Flower_2.jpg
Image
2,907 KB
5184 x 3456
Glass_13.jpg
Image
4,094 KB
5184 x 3456
Audio
Anger Management - Medium.mp3
Audio
1,405 KB
0:01:29;26
Calypso Breeze - Short.mp3
Audio
526 KB
0:00:33;19
Video
Martian Magic.mp4
Video
8,611 KB
1280 x 720
0:00:20;00
Close_Glass_Detail_2.MOV
Video
422,083 KB
1920 x 1080
0:01:13;25
Close_Glass_Shape.MOV
Video
383,712 KB
1920 x 1080
0:01:04;29
Clip Bin
Library
Callouts
Zoom-n-Pan
Audio
Transitions
Cursor Effects
More

FIGURE 6.15 — A detailed view of the media files within the Clip Bin.

To add categories to the detailed view, right click on the top portion of the **Clip Bin**. This will launch a context menu to toggle showing name, type, size, dimensions, and duration details (See Figure 6.16).

Record the screen
Import media
Name
Camtasia recording file
capture-2.camrec
Image
Flower_1.jpg
Flower_2.jpg
Name
Type
Size
Dimensions
Duration

FIGURE 6.16 — A context menu to add entries to the detail list.

Additional file organizational options can be added by selecting the **Sort by** option in the right-click menu. Select to sort the files by name or file type. This can be especially useful in projects with a large amount of files in the **Clip Bin**.

View Media Properties

Additional file information can be viewed by selecting a file, right-clicking on the file, then selecting **Properties** from the menu. A pop-up window with file location, size, modified date, width, height, colors, and file format pops up.

Previewing Media

Double click on a media file to view the file in the **Preview Window**. If the media file is an audio or video file, the media will play in the **Preview Window** without modifying your project in the timeline.

6.2e — Removing Media in the Clip Bin

If you decide you no longer need a file that you imported into the **Clip Bin**, you can delete individual or multiple files as long as they are not placed within the **Timeline**.

One way to remove the selected files is to click on the file or files in the **Clip Bin** and then click, **Menu Options > Edit > Remove from Clip Bin**.

Another way to remove files is to select a file or files in the **Clip Bin** and then right click and select **Remove from Clip Bin** from the context menu (See Figure 6.17).

FIGURE 6.17 — To remove media from the Clip Bin, select the media and right-click and select Remove from Clip Bin.

If a media file is used within the **Timeline**, it cannot be deleted until it is removed from the **Timeline**. If you select a file in the **Clip Bin** to delete and it's being used in the **Timeline**, a **warning** pop-up will appear indicating that the action cannot be performed (See Figure 6.18).

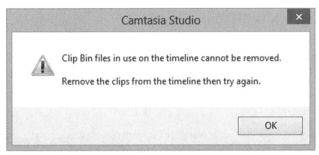

FIGURE 6.18 — A warning pop-up informing the user that a selected file to be deleted is in use in the Timeline.

Because the **Clip Bin** is a link to the original file, deleting the media from the **Clip Bin** will not delete the file from your computer. Removing the file from the **Clip Bin** only erases the viewed link to the original file.

Unused Media in Clip Bin

To remove media files from the **Clip Bin** that are not being used on the **Timeline**, right-click in an open space in the **Clip Bin** and select **Remove unused clips** from the context menu. This is useful for projects with a large number of original imported files that were not used or files that might have a large file size. Every file is collected in creating a backup so it is recommended to remove any unused files before backing up the project (See Figure 6.19).

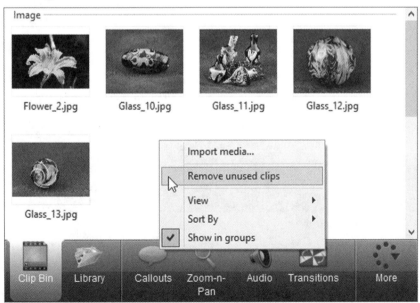

FIGURE 6.19 — Right-click on an empty space of the Clip Bin to remove unused clips

6.3 — The Library

The **Library tab** has most of the same functions and works very similar to the **Clip Bin tab**. One of the major differences is that the media added to the clip bin is only for the current project, media added to the library will be available for all projects using the **Editor**. (See Figure 6.20)

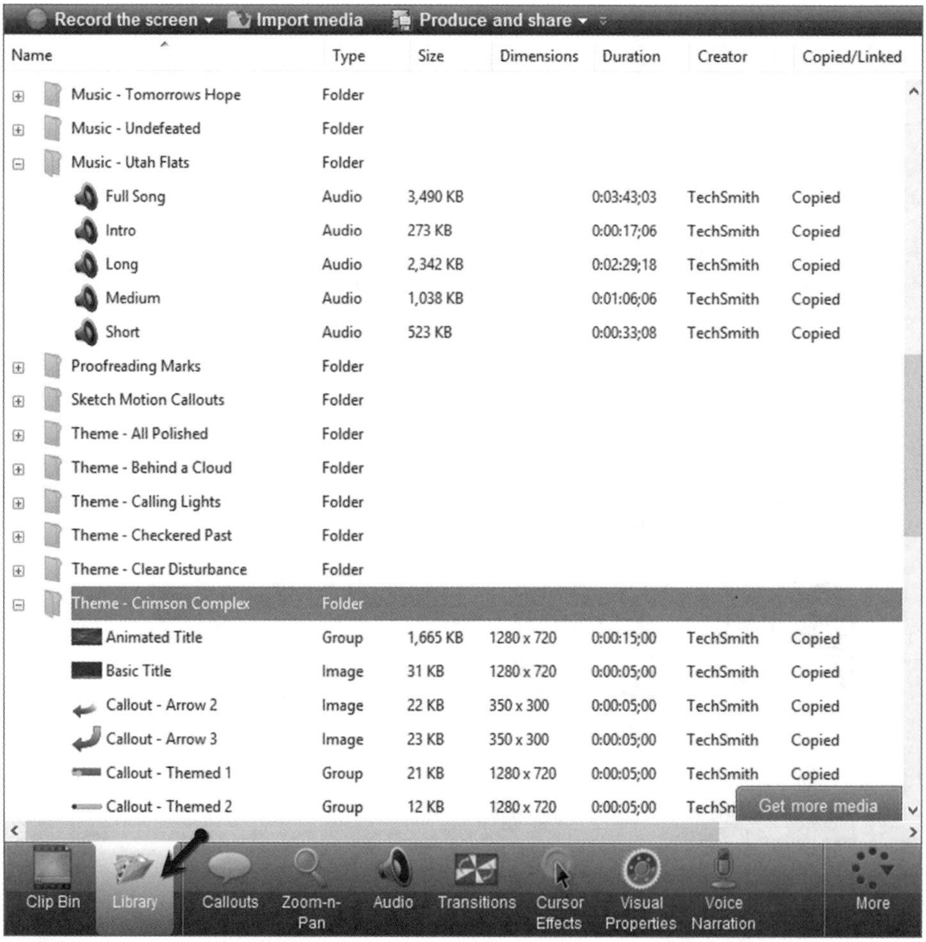

Name	Type	Size	Dimensions	Duration	Creator	Copied/Linked
Music - Tomorrows Hope	Folder					
Music - Undefeated	Folder					
Music - Utah Flats	Folder					
Full Song	Audio	3,490 KB		0:03:43;03	TechSmith	Copied
Intro	Audio	273 KB		0:00:17;06	TechSmith	Copied
Long	Audio	2,342 KB		0:02:29;18	TechSmith	Copied
Medium	Audio	1,038 KB		0:01:06;06	TechSmith	Copied
Short	Audio	523 KB		0:00:33;08	TechSmith	Copied
Proofreading Marks	Folder					
Sketch Motion Callouts	Folder					
Theme - All Polished	Folder					
Theme - Behind a Cloud	Folder					
Theme - Calling Lights	Folder					
Theme - Checkered Past	Folder					
Theme - Clear Disturbance	Folder					
Theme - Crimson Complex	Folder					
Animated Title	Group	1,665 KB	1280 x 720	0:00:15;00	TechSmith	Copied
Basic Title	Image	31 KB	1280 x 720	0:00:05;00	TechSmith	Copied
Callout - Arrow 2	Image	22 KB	350 x 300	0:00:05;00	TechSmith	Copied
Callout - Arrow 3	Image	23 KB	350 x 300	0:00:05;00	TechSmith	Copied
Callout - Themed 1	Group	21 KB	1280 x 720	0:00:05;00	TechSmith	Copied
Callout - Themed 2	Group	12 KB	1280 x 720	0:00:05;00	TechSm	

FIGURE 6.20 — The Library tab with media files and folders.

Even if you never imported media, the **Library** starts loaded with royalty free media from TechSmith that are available to use in your projects. These files are also useful as test media for practice projects.

The **Library** can store an array of media including video, image, audio, effects, and timeline groups. Double click on a file listed in the **Library** to preview the media in the **Preview Window**.

| QUICK CLIP | Previewing and Using the Library Media |

6.3a — Adding Library Files to the Timeline

Adding media files from the **Library** to the **Timeline** uses the same methods used for **Clip Bin**. The track availability also is the same.

Click and drag

Click on a selected file or group of files in the Library and hold the mouse button down while dragging the files to an available area in the timeline.

Right Click

Move the playhead to the point in the timeline that you want to place the incoming files. Select the file or files in the Library and right-click. Select Add to Timeline at Playhead option from the context menu.

6.3b – Adding to the Library Content

The **library** can import the same file formats types as available with the **Clip Bin**. Unlike the **clip bin**, the library can also import timeline segments and groups. You can import media files from outside sources and from the timeline.

Adding media files from outside source

■ Right-click on an empty space inside the Library to open the context menu with the **Import media to Library** selection

■ Click on **Menu Options > File > Library > Import media to Library** (See Figure 6.21)

FIGURE 6.21 — Importing media files to the Library using the Menu Options.

Adding Media Files from the Timeline

The **Library** saves assets to be used in multiple projects. Timeline selections, groups, features, and effects can be added to the library. This feature is very useful to keep a consistent look between projects. For example, once you create a title intro with text, sound, animation, and transition, you can group these clips and add them to the library. Then instead of recreating the title intro, you can drop and drag the clip from the library onto your timeline. Some adjustments might still need to be made, however, this saves a lot of time in your workflow as you are not starting from scratch each time.

Timeline group or selection assets available to be imported to Library:

- Animations

- Audio

- Callouts

- Captions

- Clip selections

- Images

- Quizzes

- Transitions

- Video

NOTE
The term Media File generally refers to the video, audio, and images within the project. The term Media Assets or Assets includes the Media Files and additional project features such as captions, quizzes, and callouts.

Adding Individual, Multiple, or Grouped Clips

The process for adding individual clips, multiple selected clips, or grouped clips is the same. To add the assets, right-click on the selected assets in the **Timeline** and click **Add asset to Library** option from the context menu (See Figure 6.22). The same option is located by clicking on **Menu Options > File > Library > Import media to Library**.

Assets in the **Timeline** that are grouped can contain several clips or feature inside the group casing. For clips and effects that you use often or work as a set can be grouped to easy use including importing the group to the Library. With a group, multiple assets act as one.

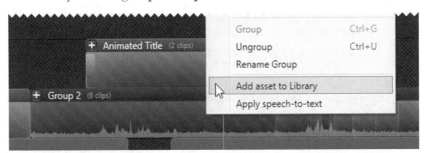

FIGURE 6.22 — Add Library assets by right-clicking on a clip or group from the Timeline

Adding a Playhead Selection to the Library

There might be times where a selection of the overall project is what you would like to add to the **Library**. Use the playhead to select the portion of the **Timeline** (See Figure 6.23).

1. Move the **green** and **red playhead points** to the start and end of the selection

2. Then right-click within the highlighted blue area

3. Select **Add playhead selection to Library** to add the selection

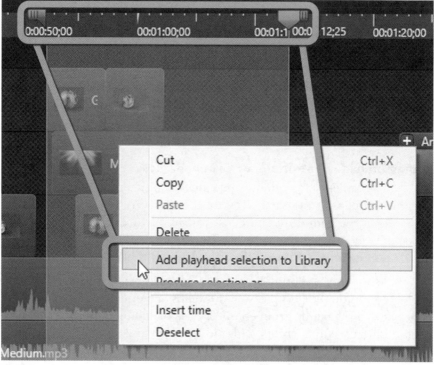

FIGURE 6.23 — Adding Timeline playhead selection to the Library.

When using the playhead selection, the whole media clip will be added to the library and stored. This will increase file size but include the possibility to reuse. Assets retrieved from the library can be modified in the timeline without changing the stored information.

QUICK CLIP   Adding Clips to the Library Media

Project: Open project file and add clips to the Library.

Get More media

In the lower right hand corner of the **Library tab** is a **Get more media** button. This button will launch the TechSmith Website opened to the **Library Media section**. You can download new media files to add to your library (See Figure 6.24).

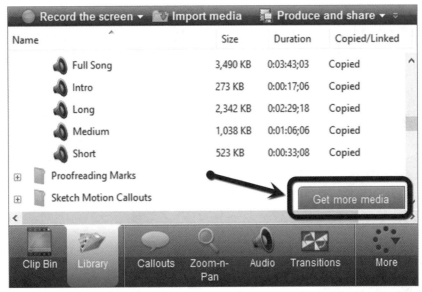

FIGURE 6.24 – The Get more media button will launch the TechSmith Website to download new media.

You can also launch the TechSmith Website from the **Library Media section** by clicking on the **Menu Options > File > Library > Import media to the Library**.

6.3c – Organizing Library Assets

The assets that were already installed in the **Library** are stored in folders. These folders organize the assets in manageable group. There can be a lot of files that you would like to share with other projects such as company logos, title page, images, or animation group. Use folders and a naming convention to group and organize your library assets. Sorting and changing the view will add another layer of organization.

Managing the Assets

Creating Folders

To create a new folder, click on **Menu Options > File > Library > New Folder** to add a new folder. You can also right-click on an empty space to the far left in the **Library tab**. Then click on **New Folder** in the context menu and give the new folder a name. Subfolders are not supported within the library.

Adding and Removing Assets to Folders

To add assets to the folders, click and drag the asset on top of folder and then let the mouse button go and drop. To remove an asset, click and drag the asset in the folder outside of the folder to a new location in the **Library Tab** and drop.

Changing Asset and Folder Names

Changing the names of the assets sounds simple, however using a unified file or folder naming convention will enhance the view and sort options. To change names, click on the asset or folder, then pause, the click again. This will highlight the name enabling it to be renamed.

Sort Assets

To sort assets within the **Library**, right-click on an empty area of the library, and use the context menu to select the sort options. You can also right-click on the top of the tab to select the detail entries. A new detail entry of **Copied/Linked** is in the context menu list.

Asset Properties

To view more data on a particular asset, right-click on the selected file, then select Properties from the context menu. A pop-up window with file location, size, modified date, width, height, colors, and file format.

Delete Assets or Folders from the Library

One important concept to remember is that the library holds files that can be used in all projects and not just the current project. Removing assets from the **Library** might affect other projects that used the assets and was not backed up properly. It is recommended to check and backup previous files before deleting any assets from the **Library**.

To remove files, select a file or files in the **Library** and then right click and select **Delete from Library** from the context menu.

NOTE

*Deleting a linked media file from the **Library** or **Clip Bin** deletes the link to the file not the original file. However, because media assets are fully copied into the Library and not linked, deleting an asset will delete that copy from the Library. The asset is deleted from use in any project unless a copy is saved within a library or project backup and is restored.*

6.4 — Managing Your Media Files and Assets

Between the **Clip Bin** and the **Library**, a project can have a long list of media that is being used. Managing the media files and assets can save you from missing or modified media links that will prevent you from using and editing the clips. Losing track of media files can be costly. It is always recommended to save and backup your files.

6.4a — Linked Assets

The **Clip Bin** media files are visible links to file that exist on your computer. If that file is moved or deleted, the link to the file will be broken and will not be able to be opened inside the **Editor**. The **Library** has an option to link or copy the assets when added.

Copy or Link Library Assets

The library has a few extra options for managing its stored files. To open these settings click **Tools > Options > Program tab** (See Figure 6.25).

Copy Content into Library

This selection copies the whole asset onto the **Library**. This function will increases the file size of the projects. However, there is less worry over missing or broken links. Use the **Clip Bin** for media only used in individual projects and the **Library** for assets used over multiple projects.

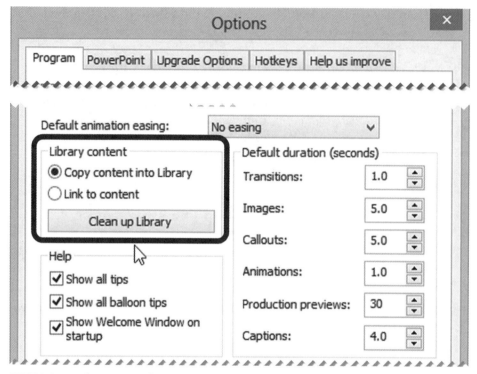

FIGURE 6.25 — Library options for managing assets under Program.

Link to Content

This option will create a link to the file on the computer and will not import the file into the program. This will decrease the file size but will run the risk of missing, modified, or deleted media files. It is recommended to place any media files that will be linked into a semi-permanent location on the computer where they will not be accidently moved or deleted.

Clean Up Library

The **Clean-Up Library** function will try and fix any problems within the **Library** that might happen when assets are frequently added, deleted, or moved. The action will remove any broken links and updates the folders. Once performed, the previous version of the **Library** cannot be restored.

6.4b — Backing Up Your Files

Backup your project by clicking **Menu Options > Export project as .zip** to ensure the used media files and assets are collected with the project in one place. This will prevent any missing or deleted links that create issues with your project. It is recommended to keep the **Include all files from the Clip Bin in .zip** checked (See Figure 6.26). If file size is an issue, delete all unused or unneeded media files from the **Clip Bin** before backing up the project.

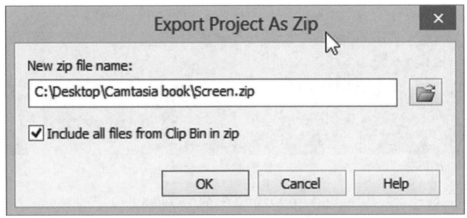

FIGURE 6.26 — The pop-up dialog box to export the project as a .zip file.

The **.zip** project files are easily moved or transferred without the fear of breaking links. All the files needs within the projects are included inside the **.zip** files. Select **Menu options > File > Import Zipped Project** to open a project from a **.zip** file.

If a link does break, a missing media thumbnail will show instead of a thumbnail representing the media. The file location will have to be updated in order to use the missing link and for the clip to be included in the final project rendering (See Figure 6.27).

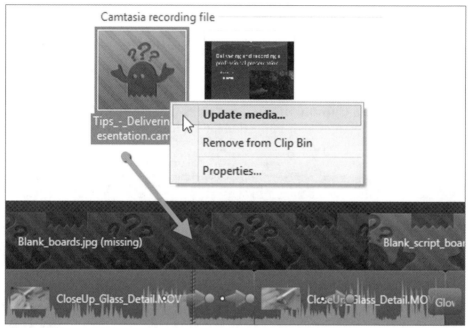

FIGURE 6.27 — A screenshot of a broken link because of a missing file.

6.4c — Exporting and Importing Archive Files

Exporting your project as a **.zip** will not only back up the project but also allow the project to be shared with coworkers or friends. If you do not want to share the project but just the assets, you can export files in the **Library** or the full **Library**. The file format for the **Library** is the **.libzip**.

Export Library Assets

1. Open the **Library tab**

2. *Optional:* Click on an asset file or multiple assets

3. Right-click on an open area of the **Library**

4. Select **Export Library** from the context menu

5. Navigate to a save file location and click **OK**

The saved **.libzip** file from the individual file and full library export will look the same, be sure to name them appropriately.

Import a Zipped Library File

1. Open the **Editor**

2. Select **Menu options > File >Library > Import zipped Library**

3. A navigation dialog appear

4. Browse to and select a **.libzip** file

5. Click **OK** to begin the import

 Project: Import .libzip file in the project folder into the Library.

It is recommended to periodically to backup all projects and the **Library** and archive them. Files, computers, and hard drives can change; it is safer to always backup your work.

CHAPTER SUMMARY

This chapter has shown you some very exciting ways of using both the Clip Bin and Library in both your current project and in future projects. You now have the ability to import, organize, view, and remove any files from the Clip Bin and Library. You also have a better understanding of how to manage your media files and assets. This ability is very important for both your present project but also for future projects.

CHAPTER PROJECTS

1. How do you research and download files from TechSmith?

2. Describe how to import and export **.zip** files.

3. Describe how you would manage the library content such as changing an asset's name, creating a folder, adding assets to a folder, and deleting a library folder?

4. Explain what happens to **Clip Bin** and what you need to do if you move your files on your computer.

5. Search File Formats and compare the type of audio image and video formats and how would you would store them to Camtasia Studio.

6. In your own words, explain how to add to a video clip or media to a timeline when space is not available.

7. Why would you remove media files from a **Clip Bin** and the **Library** and how would you do it?

8. Name two differences between the **Clip Bin** and **Library** and why they are important.

9. Discuss and give examples of why you should organize your folders in the **Library**.

10. Write about a personal experience or an experience a friend had that happened when files were not backed up.

11. Import five images into both the **Clip Bin** and **Library** and share them. Why did you select them?

CHAPTER 7

EDITING: PREVIEW WINDOW AND TIMELINE

IN THIS CHAPTER

In this chapter, we will edit the screen or PowerPoint recording. Linking the Timeline and Preview Window will be shown and the many ways you can use the Preview Window to edit your clips will also be shown. We will take an in depth look at using the timeline tracks and playhead. Adding, moving, arranging, cutting, splitting, trimming, clip speed, and duration of clips will be covered. How to use markers and hotkeys in **Editor** will be revealed.

> **NOTE**
>
> *The same technical writing method that was used in Chapter 3 will be used throughout this chapter. Menu items, programs, and file extensions will be in bold lettering while the mouse navigation and keystrokes action will be displayed with a ">" symbol.*

Once you've completed this chapter, you will be able to:

- Edit your project
- Understand how to link the **Timeline** and **Preview Window**
- Work with the **Preview Window, Canvas,** and **Timeline**
- Use clips and markers
- Know the hotkeys within the **Editor**

Files: All figures in this chapter are in color located in the chapter folder on the DVD.

Camtasia Studio Editor Interface Review

I n this chapter, we will be discussing the connection between the **Timeline** and the **Preview Window**.

Media will be dragged and added to the **Timeline** and arrange, rotate, resize, and move the media in the **Preview Window**. The **Editor** interface has three main work areas, **Media** and **Task Tabs**, **Preview Window**, and **Timeline** (See Figure 7.1). The preview area and timeline work will be in direct correlation with each other.

Overview Review — The Editor Interface

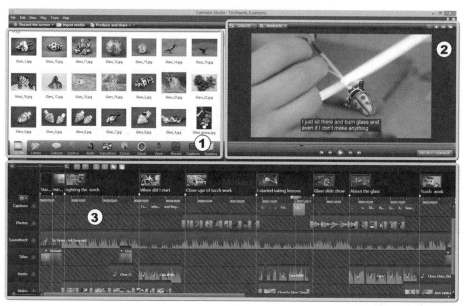

FIGURE 7.1 — The Camtasia Studio Editor interface showing three areas (media and task tabs, preview window, and timeline).

1. **Media and Task Tabs** — tabs that hold media and tools to create and perform selected features

2. **Preview Window** — will show for preview the selected area of the timeline where the playhead is positioned

3. **Timeline** — shows all of the frames, tracks, and features of your project including videos, images, audio, special effects, and other features

7.1 — Editing Your Project

Camtasia Editor can arrange and edit media on the **Timeline** to create your video project. The **Clip Bin** holds the media, the **Timeline** will arrange and edit the media, the **task tabs** will add effects and graphic elements, and the **Preview Window** will show the live playback at the spot of the **playhead** in the timeline. All the media types that can be imported into the clip bin can be adjusted in the timeline and the preview window. Using all these items together will edit your project into your final video project.

This quick list is a step-by-step of the editing process in a general project.

Quick List: Edit Your Project — General Editing

1. Open **Camtasia Studio Recorder**

2. **Import** record files, images, and video and audio clips

3. Edit and arrange clips on the **timeline**

4. Cut and split clips, move clips

5. Add **markers**

6. Add **voice narration** and **record camera**

7. Edit **audio** tracks

8. Add **title clips** and **transitions**

9. Add **callouts**, **captions**, and **quiz effects**

10. Apply **SmartFocus, zoom-n-pan,** and **animations**

11. **Save** and **produce** the video project

7.2 — Linked: The Timeline and the Preview Window

The **Timeline** and **Preview Window** are linked to each other. Anytime you move or add media to the timeline this change also takes place in the preview window. If you select a clip in the timeline, the clip is also selected on the canvas (See Figure 7.2).

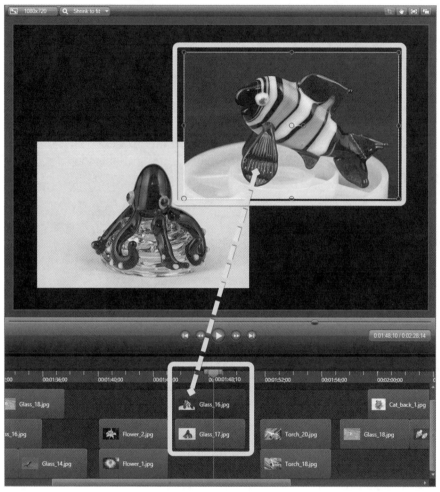

FIGURE 7.2 — Clip is selected on both the timeline and canvas.

As you move the playhead through the timeline, the preview window will show the current frame. Everything that happens in the timeline will show in the preview window. If you select a clip in the timeline, it will be selected on the canvas, and if you select a clip in the preview window, it will be selected in the timeline.

If you are editing clips away from the location of the playhead, then the action might not show in the preview window, because the preview window will only show the current frame where the playhead is located on the timeline. If you move the playhead to the clips you were editing, then the actions will show in the preview window.

7.3 — Working with the Preview Window

The preview window has four main parts, however, most of the work you will be doing will take place on the **Canvas** area. This area is not just a playback window, but a work area where you can select clips and adjust them to fit your project needs (See Figure 7.3).

Overview Review — The Preview Window

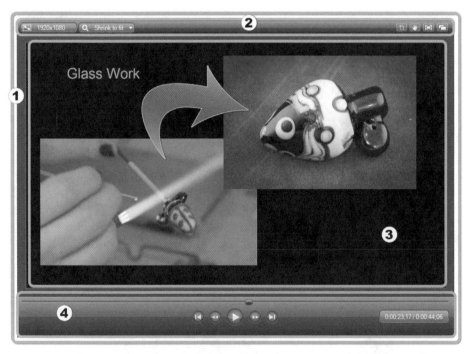

FIGURE 7.3 — This screen shows the preview window, view options, canvas, and playback controls.

1. **Preview Window** — overall area containing the playback controls, canvas, and view options

2. **View Options** — editing dimensions, view options, and video dimensions

3. **Canvas** — video playback with the ability to arrange, rotate, resize, and order the content linked to the timeline

4. **Playback Controls** — controls the video playback with play, pause, fast forward, fast rewind, and shows the time and current frame

A Closer Look — The Preview Window

7.3a — Working with the Canvas

After the media is placed into the timeline, the **Canvas** will be the work area to arrange, rotate, resize, and move the media.

Selecting Media

There are two main ways to select media on canvas. You can select media on the canvas itself or in the timeline. Multiple clips can be selected on multiple tracks to move or arrange at the same time. These multiple selections can be grouped together to be saved to the library, copied, arranged, or moved as a one.

Selecting Single Media

Click on a media clip with the mouse button in the timeline or on the canvas. The media box will highlight in the canvas and the clip will turn blue in the timeline (See Figure 7.4).

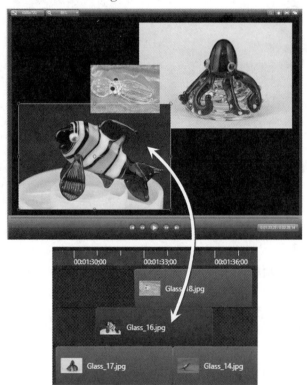

FIGURE 7.4 — The highlighted media clip on the canvas turns blue in the timeline.

Selecting Multiple Media Objects

Click on the first clip, then press and hold the **Shift** key down while clicking on additional clips. This will highlight the multiple clips in the timeline and on the canvas. You can also select multiple clips by clicking on an empty portion of the timeline and click and hold the mouse button down over the clips then release the mouse button when all the clips are highlighted.

In both the single and multiple clip selection, if the playhead moves away from the clip in the timeline, a dotted outline of the selected clip will still show on the canvas (See Figure 7.5). This is useful when you are working on positioning or transforming clips that are located on different sections of the timeline.

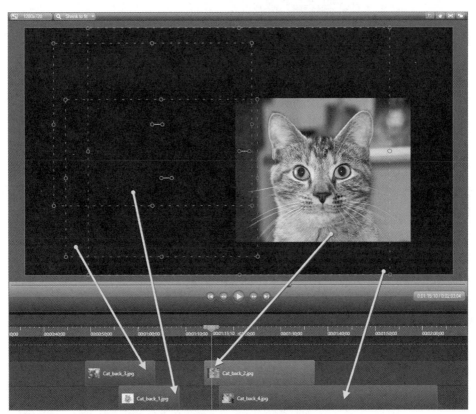

FIGURE 7.5 — Multiple clip selections shown as dotted lines away from playhead

Grouping Media Selections

After selecting multiple clips, right click over one of the selections and click on the **Group** listing in the context menu (See Figure 7.6).

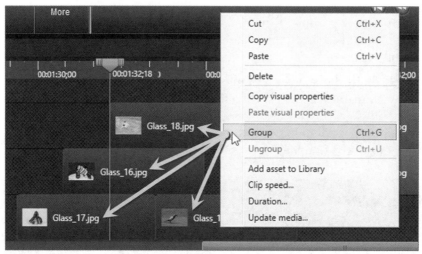

FIGURE 7.6 – Group is highlighted in the context menu.

The files will collapse into a new grouped clip in the timeline. This grouped clip can be expanded to show all the clips enclosed within by clicking the plus sign in the upper left corner of the grouped clip (See Figure 7.7). The clips inside the group can be edited and adjusted the same as clips outside the group.

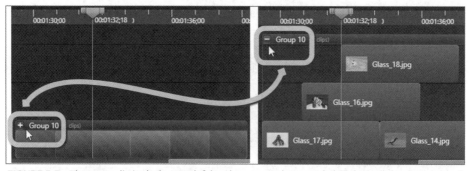

FIGURE 7.7 – The group clip in the bottom left hand corner can be expanded to show all the clips enclosed.

Groups can be selected and combined with new clips to form a new group. Transitions and animations can also be selected to be grouped with the clip files. Group clips can be renamed to identify them on the timeline and then the groups are collapsed.

To ungroup the grouped clips, select the group and right-click. To open the context menu, click on **Ungroup** from the list.

QUICK CLIP Grouping Clips and Arranging the Layer Order

Media Layering

Objects that appear on the canvas represent the layering order of the timeline. If on the timeline, a clip is on an above track over another clip on a lower track, then the clip of the media on the upper track will appear to be overlaid on the lower track media (See Figure 7.8).

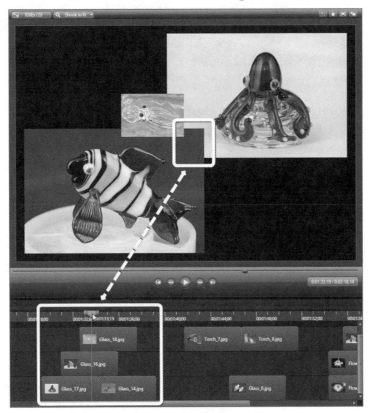

FIGURE 7.8 — The middle yellow outlined box shows overlapping media.

The media on the higher tracks will always overlay the media on the lower tracks. If one clip is on a higher track and fully covers over another clip on a lower track, the clip on the lower track will not be seen in the preview window or your video project. To change the layering of the media, change the hierarchy of the media on the tracks (See Figure 7.9).

FIGURE 7.9 — Shows an example of changing the layer order of media on the timeline.

Resizing, Rotating, and Movie Media

Selected media can be arranged, moved, rotated, and resized in the canvas. Once selected, a clip will have adjustment handles on the sides and corners along with a thin white outline. The white outline and handles will show if the clip is under another clip in the preview. The cursor will change icon shape when you hover over a movable area or handle.

QUICK CLIP | Resizing, Rotating, and Movie Media

 Project: Use the media in the project folder to resize, rotate, and move media on the canvas.

Move a clip

To move a clip, hover the cursor over the clip and it will change to a four-way directional icon. This indicates that the cursor can click on the clip and move it in any direction around the canvas (See Figure 7.10).

If there cursor does not change into the directional icon, the track the clip is on might be locked and unable to be moved.

FIGURE 7.10 — The clip can be moved in any direction around the canvas by hovering over it.

Resize a clip

Click on one of the handles, hold the mouse button down, and drag the handle to a new location. This will resize the clip in the direction you have moved the mouse (See Figure 7.11).

FIGURE 7.11 — Grabbing one of the side handles will stretch the clip to move in the direction of the handle.

If you grab one of the side handles, it will stretch the clip in the direction you are moving the handle. Using the corner handle will resize both of the adjoining sides evenly in the direction you are moving the cursor. Hold the **SHIFT** key down when using the corner to resize, to expand, or to decrease the clip evenly around the center point.

You can flip or distort the clip by selecting one of the sides of the clip and flip, stretch, or condense the clip by moving the handle around the canvas (See Figure 7.12).

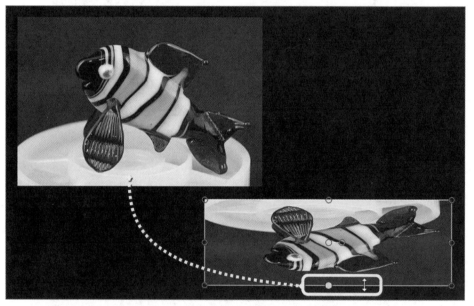

FIGURE 7.12 — The bottom picture shows how you can resize and flip your clip.

The resizing and flipping action can be performed on videos, images, and callout animations.

Rotate a clip

When a clip or multiple clips are selected, there will be two small white circles in the middle of the clip or clips. When the cursor hovers over the circle on the right, the cursor icon turns into an arrow in a circle shape. Click on the circle and move the cursor around the canvas to rotate the clip (See Figure 7.13).

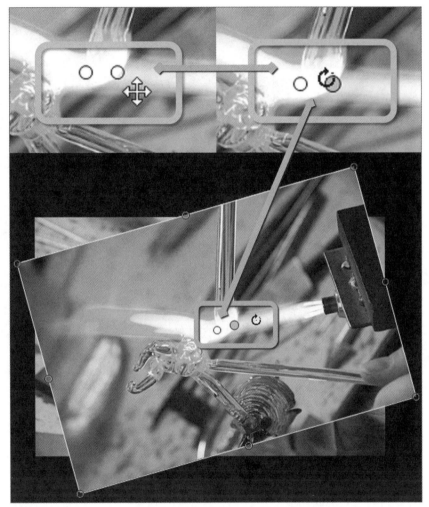

FIGURE 7.13 — You can hover over the small white circle to the right of the clip until it changes into an arrow in a circle shape and then click on it and move it to rotate the clip.

If multiple clips are selected, all of the clips will move in relation to the clip you are rotating.

Aligning Media and Snapping Guides

Any media can be aligned with the background or other clips inside on the canvas. The aligning yellow guidelines are at the edges and center points of the media (See Figure 7.14).

FIGURE 7.14 — The canvas shows the aligning yellow guidelines at the edge and center point.

When moving one clip around the canvas, yellow guidelines will appear when the clip you are moving is aligned by the edge or center points of the background or other viewable clips (See Figure 7.15).

The yellow guidelines show even for clips that are hidden behind other clips or are selected away from the playhead location. This allows for aligning between media that are not seen at the same time.

Snapping guides

When dragging a clip around the canvas and yellow guide lines appear, you might feel a tug or a hesitation for the clip to move over certain points. The clip is snapping to the guide making it easier to find the exact edge of the alignment. If you do not want the clips aligned, ignore the snap and keep moving the clip.

FIGURE 7.15 — The yellow guidelines will appear when you move the clip around and is aligned with other points in the canvas

7.3b — Cropping Media

Media from the clip bin or library are not always cropped to fit your project. To crop the media in your timeline, select the **Crop** button in the **View Options** panel in the upper right hand side of the **preview window** (See Figure 7.16).

FIGURE 7.16 — In the yellow box is the crop button in the view options.

When the **Crop** button is activated, the selected media outline box will turn blue. Video and image clips can be cropped to match or trim the media (See Figure 7.17).

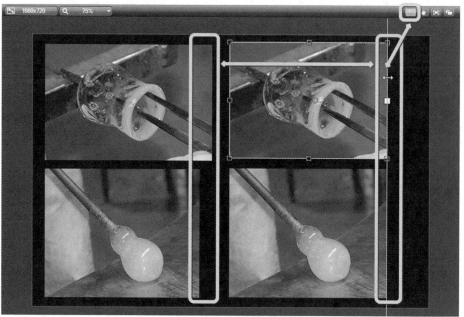

FIGURE 7.17 — The blue media outline box is activated by the crop button. Now they can be cropped.

Hold the **ALT** key and toggle the crop function on and off. Keep holding the key down and click on an adjustment handle to crop or adjust the media. However, once selected, the crop button will stay active until it is selected again.

 Project: Use the media in the project folder to align and crop the media.

7.3c — Editing Dimensions

In the upper-left hand side of the **Preview Window** is the **Editing Dimension** button that launches the Editing Dimension dialog box (See Figure 7.18).

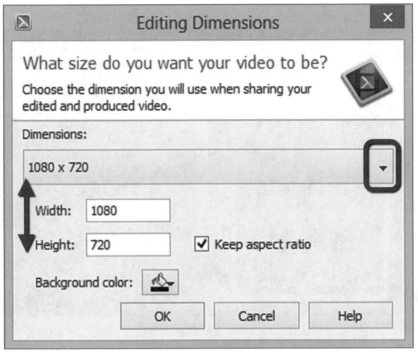

FIGURE 7.18 — What size do you want your video to be? (Shows the dimensions, width, height, aspect ratio, and background color)

The dropdown menu can change the dimensions of the overall video project. There are preset sizes along with the recording video size. You can add custom sizes and types into the **Width** and **Height** fields. It is recommended to keep the aspect ratio box checked. The dimensions can be changed anytime throughout the editing process, however it is recommended to keep the project at the recording dimensions or at the size of the end use of the video project.

Active and Nonactive Areas

The edge of the canvas background is a gray field that surrounds the canvas. This marks the end of the canvas or the video area. Any portion of animation outside of the canvas will not be seen in the final video project. Keep all important information within the canvas area. When a clip is over the edge of the canvas, the portion over the edge will appear in a light gray tone (See Figure 7.19).

This space can be used to see animation and callout effects and placement.

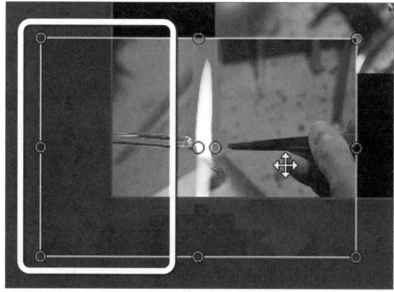

FIGURE 7.19 — Only the canvas area will be seen in the final project. The clip part over the edge of the canvas will appear in a light gray tone.

FIGURE 7.20 — Click on the right corner button of the color palette to choose a new background color.

Changing the Canvas Background Color

Think of the canvas like a painter's canvas; when there are areas without paint, the canvas will show. If the clips do not cover each other or the background fully, the canvas background color will show. To change the color of the background, click the **Editing Dimensions** button in the upper left corner of the preview window. The **Editing Dimensions** dialog box will pop up with a **Background color** button with a **paint bucket** icon. Click on the button to open the **Color palette** and select a new background color (See Figure 7.20). The color will change for the whole video project.

7.3d — View and Playback Options

The last three icons in the **View Options** panel changes the view of the previews but does not change the dimension of the video project (See Figure 7.21).

FIGURE 7.21 — Three icons in the view options panel are the hand, full screen, and video detachment.

1. The **hand** icon is the pan toggle. When activated, it will grab and move the canvas view window but not the media clips within the timeline. This is useful to navigate around the view area when zoomed into the canvas.

2. The **Full Screen** button will launch the preview window to **Full Screen** mode. Hit the **ESC** button to exit the mode.

3. The **Video Detachment** button will release the **View Preview** from the interface to float in a movable and adjustable window over the interface. Select the button again to attach the window back into the interface.

Playback

Select the **Play** button in the Preview Window to start the playback of your project. The **spacebar** toggles the playback between start and stop. From the **Menu Options > Play** are more controls for the project playback including **Play from the Beginning** selection.

7.4 — Working with the Timeline

Most of the work during the editing process will be done on the timeline. Media will be imported into the timeline tracks. Once on the timeline, these clips can be edited, moved, enhanced with special effects, and selected for production. During video playback, the playhead will follow along keeping the current frame and moving the timeline accordingly (See Figure 7.22).

Overview Review — The Timeline

1. **Timeline toolbar** — holds the magnifying slider, redo and undo, cut, split, copy, and paste

2. **Tracks** — area lines to add media, animation, and special effects

3. **Add Tracks** — a button to add tracks

4. **Toggle Marker and Quiz Track View** — opens and closes the marker and quiz track

5. **Marker or Quiz track** — a collapsible track holding the markers and quizzes

6. **Time Duration tracker** — indicates where in the duration of the timeline, the media and playhead are located

7. **Playhead** — a slider that can select and move throughout the duration of the timeline that is linked to the preview area

8. **Markers** — pin points spots within the timeline and production

9. **Clips** — the media pulled or imported from the Recorder, Clip Bin, and Library

10. **Snap guides** — yellow guidelines that pull or snap clips to markers, media, or other clips

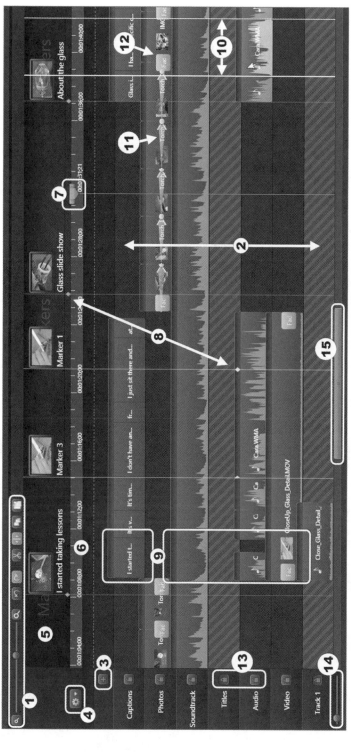

FIGURE 7.22 — The timeline has 15 areas (timeline toolbar, tracks, added tracks, toggle marker and quiz track view, marker or quiz track, time duration tracker, playhead, markers, clips, snap guides, animation indicator, transition indicator, and lock tracks toggle).

11. **Animation indicator** — an icon of a blue arrow that indicates an animation applied to the clip

12. **Transition indicator** — an icon in-between or at the end of a clip to indicate a transition

13. **Lock Tracks toggle** — locks and unlocks tracks

14. **Track height adjustment** — adjusts the height of the tracks

15. **Navigation slider** — a slider bar that will navigate through the duration of the timeline

NOTE   *To increase workflow, use the right-click context menu over different parts of the Editor interface for additional selections and tools.*

A Closer Look — The Timeline

7.4a — Tracks

The tracks area in the timeline is the work area. In the tracks area, the media can be arranged both vertically and horizontally. The media placed vertically on the timeline will take place at the same point of time during the video project. Media placed horizontally will be viewed in time duration progression (See Figure 7.23).

FIGURE 7.23 — The timeline tracks full of media clips both vertically and horizontally.

Media, animations, and effects can be moved in any direction on the timeline as long as the area is not locked or occupied by other media. The timeline tracks layer over each other with media on the higher tracks being seen in the video project over the media on tracks below. Only viewable media on the tracks will be seen in the final video.

Add and Remove Tracks

There are a number of ways to add a track to the timeline. Drag and drop media from the **Clip Bin** or **Library** into the timeline will automatically create a new track. The **plus** button above the track names and **right click** on the context menu will also add new track to the timeline (See Figure 7.24). There is no limit to how many tracks you can add to the project.

FIGURE 7.24 — The plus icon or right clicking on the timeline will insert a track above.

Double-click on the track name to rename a track for organization. The right-click context menu has options to rename, lock, or remove a track from the timeline.

Lock/Unlock Tracks

Tracks can be locked to make the media on the track unable to be edited or moved. Locking a track will prevent accidental editing on clips you did not want to edit. It is recommended to lock tracks that you are not working on to prevent any unwanted changes. On larger projects with a large number of tracks, you might not see all the tracks in the timeline view. For example, the cut tool will cut all media at that point or selection on all tracks even out of view, unless that track is locked.

To toggle locking and unlocking tracks, click the lock icon next to the track names. Diagonal gray lines will appear over the track and all media will not be able to be selected (See Figure 7.25).

FIGURE 7.25 – The diagonal gray lines will appear over the track so other media will not be selected.

QUICK CLIP Add and lock tracks.

7.4b — Playhead

The playhead is a movable slider that runs through the duration of the timeline. Use the playhead to navigate through your project and make duration selections to the media. The position of the playhead will show the current frame in the preview window. Any added effect will be added to the location of the playhead. The playhead has **In** and **End** markers and a current frame point and line (See Figure 7.25).

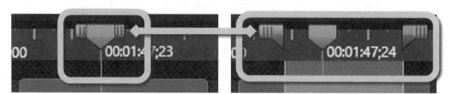

FIGURE 7.26 – The playhead has three main parts (green in point, grey in middle, and red end point).

The playhead consists of a three main parts:

1. **Green in point** — an indent movable slider that can mark the start of a selection

2. **Grey middle** — the downward point and line represents the current frame and duration location of the playhead and preview window

3. **Red end point** — an indent movable slider that can mark the end of a selection

When previewing the project in a video playback, the playhead will move through the timeline always keeping on the current frame. Slide the playhead back and forth to change where in the duration of the project the current frame is.

Making a Selection with the Playhead

To make a selection with the playhead, click and drag the Green In point and Red End point to the start and end of the selection. The selected area is highlighted in the blue area running from the In and End points (See Figure 7.27).

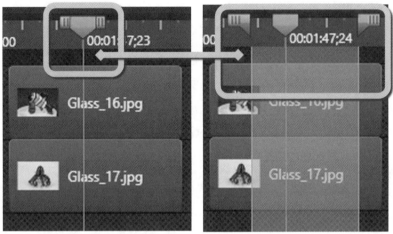

FIGURE 7.27 — Playhead selection shows how to click and drag the green in point and red end point to start and end the selection. The blue highlighted area runs from in to end points.

During a video playback with a playhead selection, the playhead middle part will move as before, only stopping at the end point. If **play** or the **spacebar** are selected again, the playhead will start at the **In** point marker and stop at the **End** point. This is helpful when examining a portion of the project for editing. Double click the gray area of the playhead to collapse the green point in and red point out markers.

QUICK CLIP | Making a Selection with the Playhead

A playhead selection can be individually produced by selecting **File > Produce special > Produce Selection as**. This action will launch the Production Wizard to produce the selection.

Saving Frame as an Image

An image file can be created from the current frame where the playhead is located. **Navigate to File > Produce special > Export** frame to open the Export Frame as dialog box to select file format and save location. Available formats are **.bmp**, **.gif**, **.jpg,** and **.png**.

7.5 — The Clips

The media clips imported from the **Recorder**, **Clip Bin**, and **Library** are the main substance of your video project. They can be cut, split, trimmed, arranged, moved, and deleted within the timeline. Editing the clips together will form your project.

NOTE

*To split the audio from a video clip, select a clip and right-click to bring up the context menu. Then select the option to **Separate audio and video** to create to individual clips.*

QUICK CLIP

Cutting, Splitting, and Trimming Clips

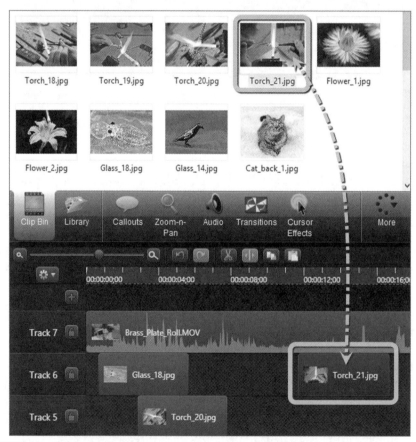

FIGURE 7.28 — Click on media and drag onto the timeline to get clips from the clip bin or library.

7.5a — Adding Clips

When using the **Camtasia Recorder**, the **Save and Edit** selection will open the editor and place the recording clip into the timeline. To add clips from the clip bin or library, click on the media and drag the clip onto the timeline (See Figure 7.28).

Media Clips on the Timeline Tracks

There are a number of different types of media that can be imported or created in the timeline (See Figure 7.29). Each type of media will look slightly different to differentiate or show important information about the media.

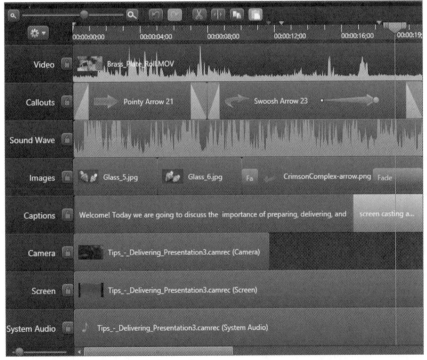

FIGURE 7.29 — Types of media on timeline tracks.

- **Video clip** — shows a small thumbnail of the video and sound wave (if sound is present)

- **Callout and Animations clip** — includes a symbol of the callout with animation arrows and fade in and out (if fades are present)

- **Sound Wave clip** — audio clips are represented with the sound wave

- **Image clip** — with no audio the image clips only have a thumbnail of the image
- **Caption clip** — the text of the caption is represented on the track
- **Camera clip** — has a thumbnail of the camera recording
- **Screen Capture clip** — has a thumbnail of the screen recording
- **System Audio sound clip** — when activated during the recording, the clip will have a sound symbol and description

7.5b — Moving and Arranging

Moving clips within the timeline is easy. Click on the selection and drag the clip in any direction through different tracks in the timeline (See Figure 7.30).

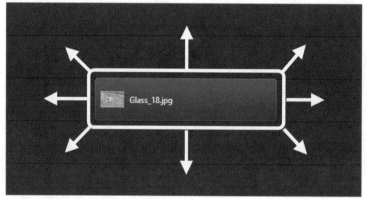

FIGURE 7.30 — Click on a section of the clip and drag in any direction to move the clip on the timeline.

A clip cannot be moved onto a locked track or on the same position as another clip. Multiple clips of the same media work independently from each other and can be moved independently.

Multiple clips can be moved at the same time a few different ways. Select each clip you want to move while holding down the **Shift** key or click on an empty area of the timeline while holding down the Shift key and drag the cursor over the clips to be selected.

To quickly move multiple clips on the same track, click on a clip and hold the **Shift** key down to temporarily included all the clips farther down the timeline with the movement of the selected clip. This group movement also works on multiple tracks and clip selections.

The playhead can also be used to move multiple clips on the tracks. Move the playhead to the point where you want to move all clips on all unlocked tracks, click on the gray area of the playhead while holding down the **Shift** key. This will select everything that is eligible to the right of the playhead in the timeline.

7.5c — Cutting a Selection

The **cut tool** in the timeline will remove a clip or playhead selection. This can be performed on a single clip or multiple clips. The playhead selection that is **cut** can span multiple clips and tracks (See Figure 7.31).

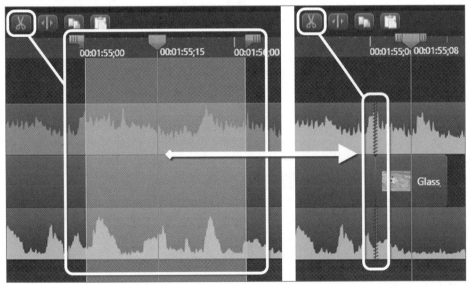

FIGURE 7.31 — With the cut tool in the timeline, you can remove a clip or playhead selection.

Cutting multiple tracks at one time does not include locked tracks. The section that was removed can be pasted on another part of the timeline. Any cut made with the cut tool does not affect the original media, or other clips of the same media in the timeline.

NOTE

Look for Jump Cuts when cutting a selection from the clips. A Jump Cut is an edit that removes the middle section of a continuous shot and joins together the beginning and end of the shot; any moving objects in the shot will appear to jump to a new position.

Stitching

Audio and video files will be stitched together making a clean edit and attached to the two sides of the cut. Animations can move over stitched clips but not unstitched clips. Clips can be stitched or unstitched together by cutting them or selecting the clips and using the right-click context menu and selecting **Stich selected media** or **Unstitch** (See Figure 7.32).

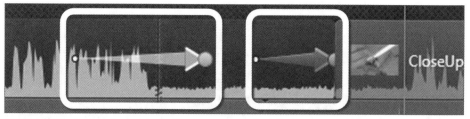

FIGURE 7.32 — Image of an animation flowing over a stitched clip but not unstitched clips.

7.5d — Splitting Clips

A split in a clip will make two clips out of one at the point of the playhead. This split can be used to insert transitions, clips, graphics, or edit points. Any kind of media can be split. To split a selected clip or multiple clips, move the playhead to the frame location. Select the clip or multiple clips and click on the split icon button (See Figure 7.33).

Only selected media at the location point of the playhead will be split. If no clip is selected, the split tool will not be activated. After splitting a clip, you will have two clips with the same name that can work independently of each other. Add splits to extract or delete portions of a clip.

7.5e — Trimming Clips

Trim the time from the beginning or from the end of a clip. The trim hides a portion of the clip instead of cutting it. Select a clip on the timeline and hover the cursor over the beginning or end until the cursor changes icons. When you see the double arrow, pull the clip back or forth through the timeline duration to trim off time from the clip (See Figure 7.34).

The cursor will snap to the edge of the clip making it easier to hover over the edge of the clip. Reverse the process to reveal the hidden portion of the track. With images, the trim can extend the clip for however long it needs to be. On audio or video, the trim can only hide existing portions of the clip.

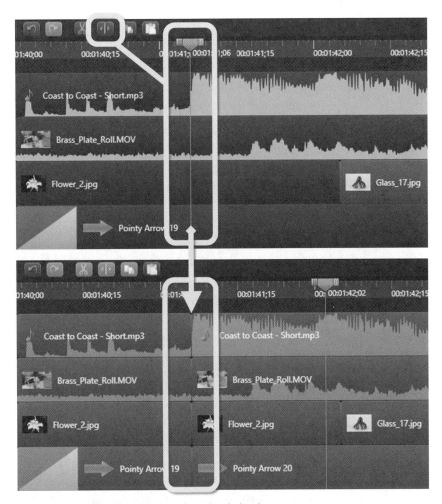

FIGURE 7.33 — The before and after clip split in the playhead.

FIGURE 7.34 — Use the double arrow to pull the clip back or forth through the timeline to trim off time from the clip.

When editing clips and animations, use the playhead selection and the playback options to quickly review edits by isolating the section of the timeline you are working on. This is especially useful when the clip is highly magnified and the playhead moves quickly over the magnified timeline.

7.5f — Clip Speed and Duration

The **Clip Speed** option will speed up or slow down audio or video playback of a selected clip. The change in playback speed is only for the selected clip and not the entire timeline. The higher the speed, the faster the playback and the lower the speed, the slower the playback of the clip.

QUICK CLIP | Changing the speed and duration of a clip.

To adjust the time speed, select a clip and right-click to open the context menu. From the list, select the option for **Clip Speed** to open the **Clip Seed** dialog box (See Figure 7.35).

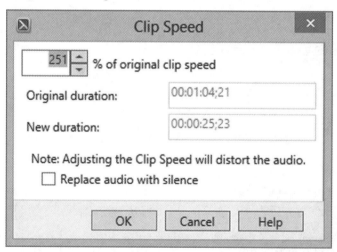

FIGURE 7.35 — Clip speed (original clip speed, original duration, new duration, and replace audio with silence).

When adjusting a video clip, you can silence the audio if you do not want the sound distortion. Use the percentage input field to increase or decrease the duration and speed of the clip. If you need the clip to fit in a certain timeframe, you can make adjustments to the speed to of the clip.

On the timeline of the clip, you will have a new **Clip Speed** adjustment bar. Hover over the end of the clip in the green Clip Speed bar for the cursor icon to change shape (See Figure 7.36).

FIGURE 7.36 — Hover over the end of the clip speed in the green to change the cursor icon's shape.

Click and drag the bar to speed up or slow down the clip speed. The clip speed will only change if the Clip Speed bar is open. Click the down arrow at the bottom of the clip to expand and close the Clip Speed adjustment bar. The Clip Speed adjustments only work for audio and video clips.

Image Clip Duration

To adjust the duration of an image clip, you can use the trim edit. Another way is to right-click on a selected clip to bring up the context menu and select Duration from the list. This will launch a **Duration** (seconds) dialog field over the clip (See Figure 7.37).

FIGURE 7.37 — The duration in seconds over the clip.

Type in the new duration and the clip will adjust on the timeline. If the duration is longer than the position of the next clip on that track, the later clip will be pushed down the timeline on the track.

Extend a Video Clip Frame

The **Extend Frame** option extends the duration of an individual frame in a video clip by creating an image of a frame in the clip. The image frame is stitched into the video clip at the point of the playhead (See Figure 7.38).

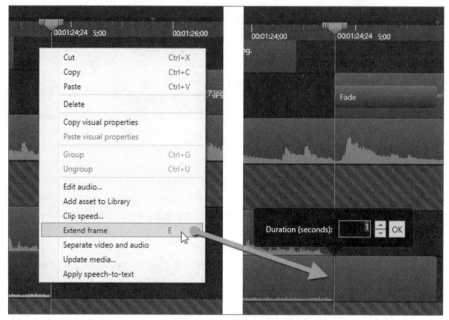

FIGURE 7.38 — Extend Frame option extends the length of the individual frame.

The duration of the image clip can be adjusted to match the selected clip to other media clips in the project like narration or music tracks.

 Project: Use the practice files to cut, split, trim, and change the duration of the clips.

7.6 — Markers

Markers are very useful in a video project. They can be used for creating a table of contents list, or navigation points, identifying places for edits and creating points to split the video into multiple videos. In the timeline, markers can be pinned to the overall timeline, individual clips, or a group. Once placed, the markers can be moved and renamed to best fit the project when the marker track is open (See Figure 7.39).

FIGURE 7.39 — Markers can be used in a variety of ways in a project and is shown at the top of this canvas.

Markers are represented as a small diamond at selected points on the timeline above the playhead slider when the markers view is closed. When expanded, the points in the timeline or on a clip will be highlighted with a vertical line running through all the tracks, as a diamond icon, and thumbnail of the video frame at the point of the marker.

QUICK
CLIP | Adding Markers to the Timeline

Marker view

Open the marker view by clicking on the **Marker/Quiz** button that is located just above the track names in the timeline. This opens an additional track above the media tracks where all the timeline markers will be located. The markers can be moved, renamed, or deleted when the marker view is open, but not when it is collapsed. The marker view will automatically open if the **M** hotkey is used to add a marker at the point of the playhead (See Figure 7.40).

Markers on the timeline

When markers are added while editing, they are pinned to the overall timeline by default. The markers pinned to the timeline will stay at that timeline duration point until moved no matter how the tracks or media are edited below that pin. The color for a clip marker is green.

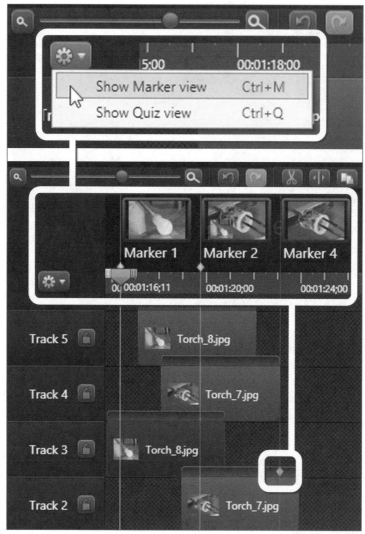

FIGURE 7.40 — An additional area is opened above the media track where markers can be moved, renamed, or deleted.

Markers on media clips

Markers can be pinned onto an individual clip or a group within the timeline. These markers will move with the clip or group within the timeline or added to the library. The diamond marker is located on a small track above the clip. The color for a clip marker is blue. If the clip and group markers are on a locked track, the marker cannot be edited.

7.7 — Hotkeys Within the Editor

Not all of the Editor Tasks or hotkeys are eligible to be assigned. To change the hotkeys for the eligible functions, navigate to **Tools > Options > Hotkeys tab** to open the **Options** dialog box (See Figure 7.41).

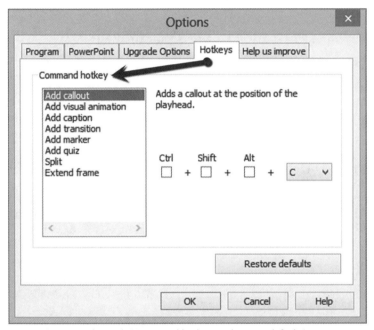

FIGURE 7.41 — Options > Hotkeys tab (Command hotkeys and restore defaults).

Editor: Canvas Hotkeys

ALT Key	toggles the crop function
CTRL Key + Mouse Scroll Wheel	scale a zoom animation for the selected media
CTRL Key	while resizing media, overrides maintaining the aspect ratio
Keyboard Arrow Keys	moves selected media in the direction of the arrows

Mouse Scroll Wheel increase or decrease the magnification view

Shift Key holding down the shift key will resize media from the middle point, while when in pan mode it moves the canvas view

Editor: Timeline Navigation Hotkeys (not customizable)

Beginning of the timeline CTRL + SHIFT + Home

End of the timeline CTRL + SHIFT + End

Jump to beginning of timeline CTRL + Home

Jump to end of timeline CTRL + End

Make a selection step-by-step CTRL + SHIFT + Right Arrow or CTRL + SHIFT + Left Arrow

Next clip CTRL + ALT + Right Arrow

Next marker CTRL +]

Play/Pause Spacebar

Previous clip CTRL + ALT + Left Arrow

Previous marker CTRL + [

Select between markers CTRL + SHIFT [or CTRL + SHIFT]

Select next clip CTRL + SHIFT + ALT + Right Arrow

Select previous clip CTRL + SHIFT + ALT + Left Arrow

Step backward CTRL + Left Arrow - Hold the keys down to rewind

Step forward CTRL + Right Arrow - Hold the keys down to fast forward

Stop	CTRL + ALT + Space
Zoom in	CTRL + Plus or CTRL + Mouse scroll wheel up
Zoom out	CTRL + Minus or CTRL + Mouse scroll wheel down
Zoom to fit	CTRL + F9 or CTRL + SHIFT + Mouse scroll wheel down
Zoom to maximum	CTRL + F11 or CTRL + SHIFT + Mouse scroll wheel up
CTRL + F10	Zoom to Selection
Move the playhead	Double-click

CHAPTER SUMMARY

We have shown how the Timeline and Preview Window are linked and why it is important. The use of the Preview Window in editing your clips has been illustrated. We have taken an in depth look at using the Timeline tracks and playhead and have explained how to add, move, arrange, cut, split, trim, add clip speed, and duration of clips. We have also illustrated how to use markers and have shown and explained the hotkeys in Editor.

CHAPTER PROJECTS

1. Why are the playback controls important and give an example?

2. What are the three main areas on the Camtasia Studio Editor Interface? In detail, explain why they are important and what you can do with them.

3. How are the Timeline and Preview Window linked and why is the linking important?

4. Name the four parts of the preview window and why they are important.

5. Why do you have to be careful of when you layer your media and what can you do if it happens?

6. How can you move, resize, and rotate a clip?

7. Explain how to align media using snapping guides.

8. How do you crop media?

9. How do you change the background color?

10. Name the twelve areas on the Timeline and what they do? Try three of them and share the information.

11. Why are markers useful and give an example of how you would use them?

12. Name two hotkeys you feel are the most helpful to you and explain why you think so.

CHAPTER **8**

EDITING:
TASK TAB ENHANCING

IN THIS CHAPTER

In this chapter, we will learn how to use the task tab with callouts (text, special and animated, hotspots, and keyboard). We will also work with Zooms-n-Pans. Audio editing provides a range of capabilities such as fading in and out, adding points, leveling audio clips, removing background noise, and adding music in the background. We will learn different cursor effects, visual properties, voice narration, and quizzes. Adding captions, being ADA compliant, using speech-to-text, and exporting and importing captions will also be shown.

NOTE

The same technical writing method that was used in Chapter 3 will be used throughout this chapter. Menu items, programs, and file extensions will be in bold lettering while the mouse navigation and keystrokes action will be displayed with a ">" symbol.

Once you've completed this chapter, you will be able to:

- Use a variety of Callouts and Zoom-n-pans
- Edit Audio files, add points, level clips, remove background noise, and add music
- Include transitions, Cursor effects, visual properties, voice narration, and quizzes
- Add captions that are ADA compliant, are speech-to-text, exported, imported, and saved

Files: All figures in this chapter are in color located in the chapter folder on the DVD.

8.1 — The Task Tab

The task tab holds all of the special effects and graphics such as callouts, zooms and pans, cursor effects, quizzes, captions, and transitions. These effects, graphics, and animations can be added to the timeline tracks or media clips to enhance your project.

To select each tab, click the icon image button for each task. The **Tool and Media Preview** will change to show the settings for each tool (See Figure 8.1).

Overview Review — The Task Tab

FIGURE 8.1 — Task bar with ten task tabs that can be used for your projects.

1. **Callouts** — graphics that appear in the video project that highlight important objects or processes

2. **Zoom-n-Pan** — gradual change in the focal area will magnify or move the view area

3. **Audio** — tools to adjust the audio volume, quality, and background noise

4. **Transitions** — a fade or wipe animation combining two clips

5. **Cursor effects** — highlights the cursor and mouse clicks

6. **Visual properties** — enhancements and added effects to media clips

7. **Voice narration** — sound and voice recorder to add as a clip

8. **Record camera** — video and screen recording

9. **Captions** — places text or script as a track

10. **Quizzing** — interactive questions and answers

NOTE

All of the Tasks can be selected by using the Menu Options bar.
Menu Options >Tools

*The **More** icon button will show if the width of the task tab is too narrow to show all the tasks. To see the tasks that are hidden, click the **More** icon button for a dropdown menu. Or, adjust the width of the interface panels by using the cursor to click-and-drag the separation line to show tasks (See Figure 8.2).*

NOTE

FIGURE 8.2 — A screenshot of the Movie icon button and the interface adjustment line.

8.2 — Working with Callouts

Callouts are graphical elements that are added to the project to highlight important information or objects. Text and animations can be added to graphic elements. Adding a hotspot callout will add interaction between the viewer and the project.

QUICK CLIP | Using the Callout tab.

To add or remove a callout, place the playhead where you want to add the graphic in the timeline. Then click the **Add callout** button to add the graphic to the timeline (See Figure 8.3).

FIGURE 8.3 — The timeline on the bottom is highlighted and the top left Add Callout button is clicked to add a callout.

The added graphic can be resized, rotated, and moved the same as clips can in the **Preview Window**. Hover over and **click and drag** the **handles** to make adjustments. In the timeline, the callout clips can be moved in any direction and between tracks the same way as the media clips (See Figure 8.4).

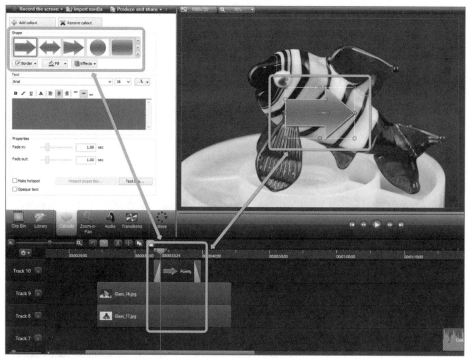

FIGURE 8.4 — The callout clips can be moved between the tracks on the timeline or adjusted in the Preview Window.

The dropdown list shows a variety of selectable graphic elements that can be used as a callout. Click on the downward arrow to open the dropdown selection menu (See Figure 8.5). More elements can be downloaded and added from the TechSmith Website.

The callout graphic can be changed at any time. The change will show in the timeline, preview window, and callout tab. A callout can be selected by double-clicking on the object in the preview window or clicking on the clip in the timeline. A callout needs to be selected before any settings can be changed.

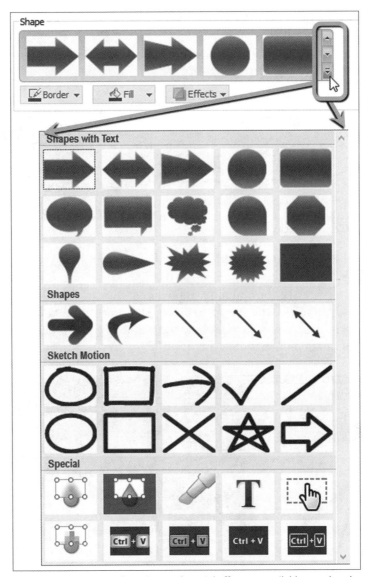

FIGURE 8.5 — Shapes with text, stretch motion, and special effects are available on a dropdown list.

The **Border** button will change the color and width of the border, while the **Fill** button changes the color of the callout. Under the **Effects** dropdown, a style of embossing effect can be selected. These settings can be changed at any time (See Figure 8.6).

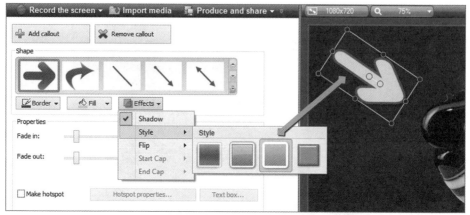

FIGURE 8.6 — The Effects dropdown shows many different effects that can be used.

Under the **Property** field are two sliders controlling the **Fade in** and **Fade out**. These sliders can change the rate of the callout dissolving into and out of view. In the timeline, the callout clip will have a **Fade in** and **Fade out** bar. Move the sliders to change the rate of the fade in and out of the callout. A zero will have no fade in or out. The callout clip will change to match the rate change (See Figure 8.7).

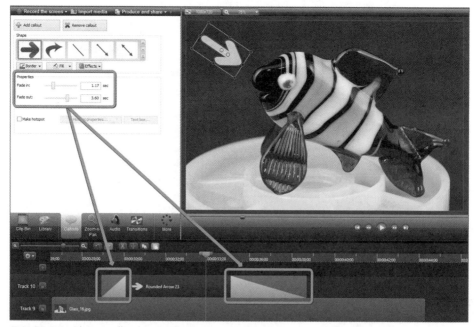

FIGURE 8.7 — The top yellow box shows how to control the fade in and fade out duration.

Callouts can be copied and pasted in the timeline. This saves time and keeps the callouts consistent. The duration of the callout can be lengthen or shortened by **trimming** the clip. Click on the **Spacebar** or hit the **Play** button to preview the callout in the video. Callout clips can be stacked in the timeline with all of the layering properties applying.

8.2a — Text Callouts

To add text to the callout, click the cursor into the text field and begin typing. Use the dropdown menus and style buttons to adjust the text font, style, color, alignment, and size. These changes will show real time on the canvas to preview how the callout will look (See Figure 8.8).

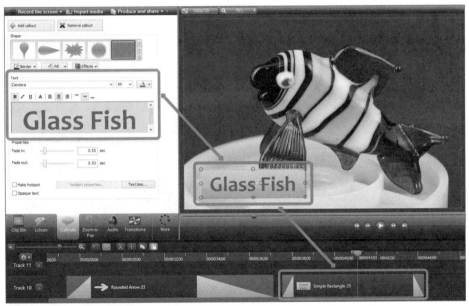

FIGURE 8.8 — The text in the text field is shown in three places (text field, on the canvas, and in the timeline).

The text in the callout can be changed at any time during the editing. The callout settings including the text will not be cleared after adding a new callout to the timeline. You can use this to create multiple callouts with consistent settings at different points on the timeline.

8.2b — Special and Animated Callouts

The special and animated callouts have added features that the plain graphic and text elements do not have. There are a variety of Special callouts to highlight or hide objects and information within your video project (See Figure 8.9).

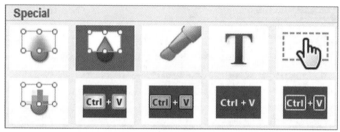

FIGURE 8.9 — Types of Special callouts.

These callouts can highlight, pixelate, blur, or spotlight an area of the project (See Figure 8.10).

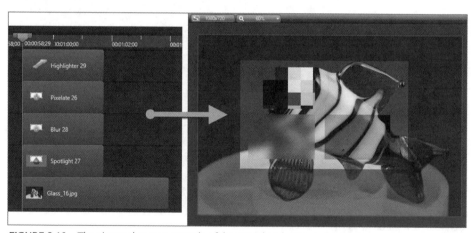

FIGURE 8.10 — The picture shows an example of the special and animated callouts.

Sensitive information, like names and numbers, can be blurred out or pixilated, rendering them unreadable in your project.

The **Sketch Motion** callouts have an animation included in the graphic that represents a drawing motion. The Sketch draw time can be adjusted to fit the project. This movement will draw the viewers' attention to the graphic (See Figure 8.11).

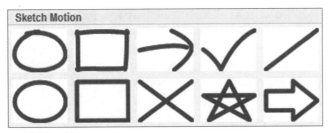

FIGURE 8.11 — Sample Sketch Motion callouts.

Additional callouts can be added to the library by creating your own graphics or downloading new callouts from the TechSmith Website.

8.2c — Hotspot Callouts

A **Hotspot** can be created to add an interactive action element to the video project. The **Hotspot Properties** dialog box holds the setting for the action of the **Hotspot**. Toggle the **Pause at end of callout** and select **Click to continue**, **Go to frame at time**, **Go to marker**, or **Jump to URL** (See Figure 8.12). If selecting **Go to marker**, select the marker from the dropdown menu.

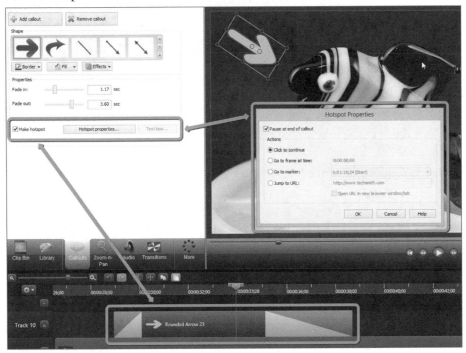

FIGURE 8.12 — The Hotspot Properties window is shown where it would be on the timeline.

Once activated, the color of the callout will change to a purple color when selected and red when not selected. If text is included in the **Hotspot**, an **Opaque text** box will appear. The **Text Box** button will launch the **Callout Text** dialog box to adjust the text box within the callout. This will allow you more control over where the text resides within the callout graphic.

8.2d — Keyboard Callouts

Keyboard callouts can be used to emphasize a key command or hotkey combinations. These callouts work the same as the other types of callouts. They also have a text field to enter in a key stroke that will automatically change the graphic accordingly (See Figure 8.13).

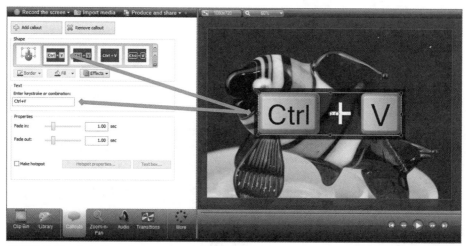

FIGURE 8.13 — Ctrl-V is used as a Keyboard Callout on the left side.

Automatically generate keystrokes

To convert keystrokes recorded in the **.camrec** file into callouts, right-click on the recording clip to bring up the context menu and select **Generate keystroke callout** from the list. This will bring up the **Generate keystroke callout** dialog box with a list of possible callouts to be added. Select the style, keystrokes, and placement on the screen (See Figure 8.14).

The keystroke callouts will then be automatically generated and placed on the timeline over the location of the keystroke during the recording.

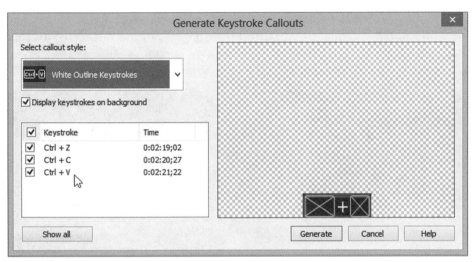

FIGURE 8.14 — Generate Keystroke Callouts with Select Callout Style Shown

---

NOTE

Manually added Keystroke callouts can be added within the Editor. To use the function to automatically generate the keystrokes, a .camrec recording clip will active keystrokes will need to be used.

8.3 — Working with Zooms-n-Pans

The Zoom-n-Pan tab can include zoom in, zoom out, and pan animations to the project. These features can be used to highlight actions, or add motion to the project.

 ZOOM — a gradual change in the focal length of the view that magnify in and out parts of the screen.

Key Term **PAN** — panorama — to move across an area or view with a camera or preview window.

QUICK CLIP   Using the Zooms-N-Pan tab

To add **Zoom-n-Pan** animations, move the playhead to the area where you want the animation to start on the timeline. In the **Zoom-n-Pan tab**, grab the anchor point in the smaller window and move point and object box around to a new position (See Figure 8.15).

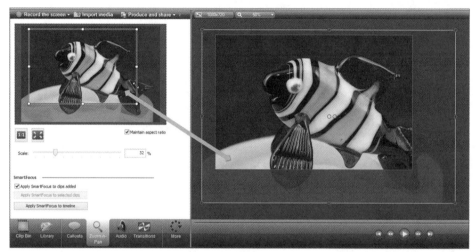

FIGURE 8.15 — The project can be grabbed at an anchor point in the smaller window and moved around.

The image in the **Preview Window** will move in connection to the **Zoom-n-Pan tab**. The movement of any adjustment handles or the whole image frame will affect the animation. In the timeline, the animation is represented as an arrow pointing forward on the selected clip. This animation arrow is light blue when not selected and yellow when selected.

Grab one of the **anchor points** at the tail or tip of the arrow and pull the point back or forth to extend the duration of the animation (See Figure 8.16). Play the clip to view the overall effect of the animation in the preview area. Adjustments to the animation can be made in the **Zoom-n-Pan tab** or on the timeline clip as many times as needed.

FIGURE 8.16 — The Zoom-n-Pan animation can be moved back and forth by grabbing one of the anchor points.

Double click on the animation arrow to swing the playhead to that location, open the task tab, and select the animation. Move the playhead to a new location on a clip or the timeline to add another Zoom-n-Pan animation. Multiple Zoom-n-Pan animations can be added on the same clip and multiple animations can be applied to multiple tracks at the same point in the timeline (See Figure 8.17).

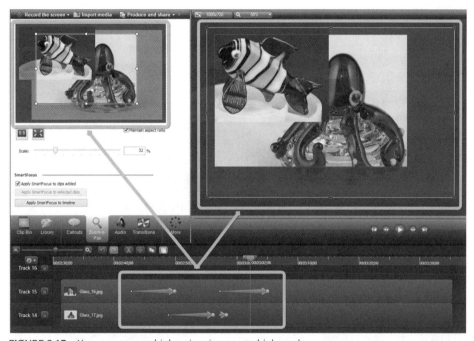

FIGURE 8.17 — You can move multiple animations on multiple tracks.

Multiple clips can be selected while applying the same animation at the point of the playhead. If no clips are selected, then all the eligible clips at the spot of the playhead will receive an animation. The combination of using multiple animations in the same clips, groups, layers, and tracks can produce some very creative and detailed movement in the video project.

 Project: Use the illustrations in the project folder and add zooms and pans to create a moving storyboard.

Using SmartFocus

The **SmartFocus** will automatically generate zoom and pan animations from **.camrec** recordings on the timeline. You can apply the options to one clip or the full timeline. Once selected, the zoom-n-pans animations will be automatically added (See Figure 8.18).

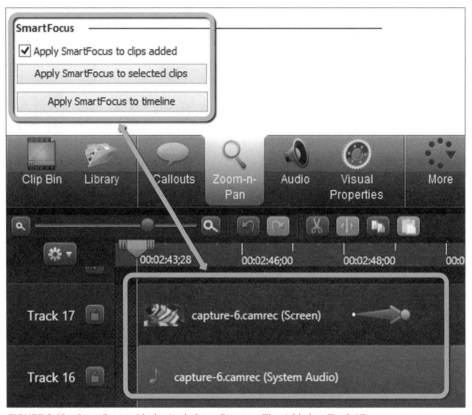

FIGURE 8.18 — SmartFocus with the Apply SmartFocus to Clips Added on Track 17.

Automatically generated animations will most likely need adjustments; however, it's easier to adjust animations than to make them all from scratch.

The automated Zooms and Pans will keep the center of the video focused on the action being shown. SmartFocus works best if you record at a larger size setting, and then produce the video at a smaller setting. A **warning** dialog box might appear if you are editing the project at the same dimension or higher than the recording dimensions.

8.4 — Audio Editing

To edit audio tracks in your project, click on a clip containing audio, and then click on the **Audio tab** (See Figure 8.19). Tools for removing noise, fading audio in or out, adding or deleting audio points, removing clicks, or silencing the audio are all available.

FIGURE 8.19 — Sound tab used to edit your audio.

Once the Audio tab is opened, all of the audio tracks in the timeline will turn green. This color change indicates that the audio can now be edited (See Figure 8.20).

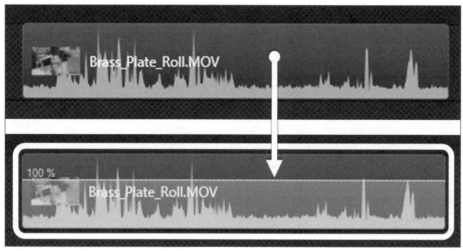

FIGURE 8.20 — The green audio track shows it can now be edited.

On the track, the green area overlays the audio waves with the white dotted line in the middle of the track representing the volume level. Click on the line and move the line up and down to change the volume higher and lower (See Figure 8.21). The cursor will change to the double arrow when you can click on the volume line to move.

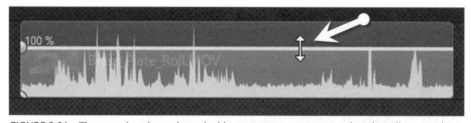

FIGURE 8.21 — The cursor has changed to a double arrow so you cannot move the volume line up or down.

Audio clips recorded at different times could have different volume levels. Adjust the clip's volume levels to even-out the overall sound levels. On average, the top and bottom of the wave should be in the middle of the track. The volume can be adjusted using the **Volume Up** and **Volume Down** buttons in the **Audio tab**.

NOTE

A .camrec recording will have the system audio added to the timeline as a separate audio track.

QUICK
CLIP

Using the Audio Tab

8.4a — Audio Fade In and Out

Audio clips can sometimes have a sudden start from silence before the clip to full sound after the clip starts. It is recommended to **Fade In** and **Out** the audio of a clip to smooth the overall audio sound. Even a brief fade will help the transition between silence and sound.

To create a **Fade In** and **Out** effect, a selected clip or multiple clips and click the **Fade In** or **Fade Out** button in the **Audio tab** (See Figure 8.22).

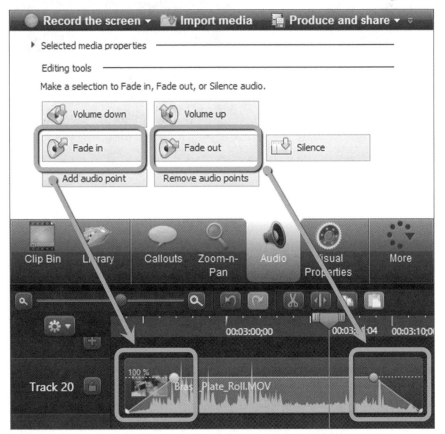

FIGURE 8.22 — The Fade in and Fade out are shown on the bottom of the screen in Track 20.

To adjust the duration and volume of the fade, grab the audio point and drag it to a new location. Moving the point up or down will adjust the volume and to the left or right to change the speed of the fade. The waveform adjusts accordingly when you move the points (See Figure 8.23).

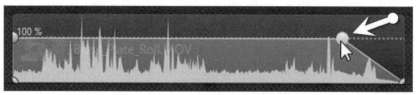

FIGURE 8.23 – Moving the audio point left or right will adjust the speed of the fade.

Click and drag the volume bars and audio points to manipulate the audio waves. Each point can be moved independently and each area between the points volume can be moved (See Figure 8.24).

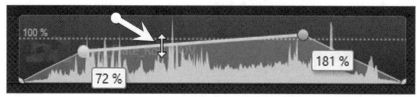

FIGURE 8.24 – Moving the volume bars and audio points will manipulate the audio waves.

The percentages are the volume of the sound at that point in the clip. Playback the clip and keep making adjustments until the sound has the desired effect.

8.4b — Adding Points and Leveling Audio Clips

Adding audio points to the wave clip will add more instances to adjust the sound wave. This gives you more control in editing the audio. To add a point, select a clip with audio, move the playhead to the position you want the point, and click the **Add audio point** button in the **Audio tab**. Move the playhead to a new location on the clip to add a new point (See Figure 8.25).

Use audio points and the **Silence** button to edit the audio track. If there are clicks or unwanted voice sounds, add points before or after to decrease the volume so the unwanted sound is not audible without cutting or trimming the actual media clip.

Another way to edit the wave track is to highlight an area with the playhead and click the **Silence** button in the **Audio tab** to bring the volume of that selection down to zero (See Figure 8.26).

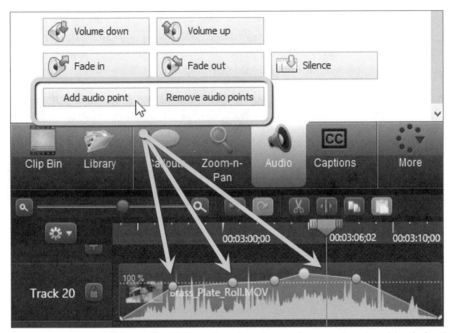

FIGURE 8.25 — You can add an audio point any place along the sound wave at the point of the playhead.

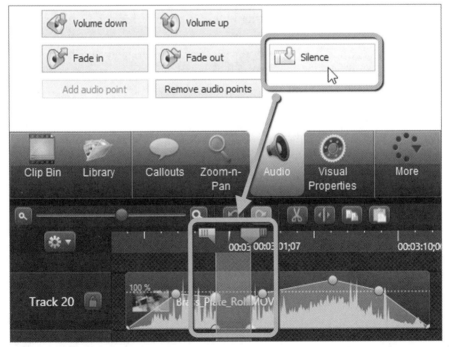

FIGURE 8.26 — After highlighting a track on the playhead, you can click the silence button to have no sound.

This action does not delete the wave and this action can be undone at a later time. The **Silence** button will also add audio points on the wave track to fine tune the fade into and out of the sounds areas (See Figure 8.27). The slight fades will smooth out the transitions.

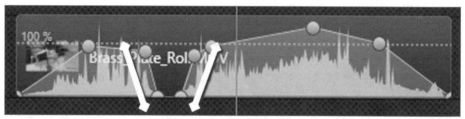

FIGURE 8.27 — Adding fades will smooth out the transitions.

<table>
<tr><td>

NOTE

</td><td>

When working with audio waves, it is helpful to increase the magnification view of the wave clip to better see the high and low points of the wave clearly for precise editing.

</td></tr>
</table>

8.4c — Background Noise Removal

Background sounds such as fans, air conditioning, and hums can be automatically removed using the **noise removal** feature. To activate, click on an audio track and then open the audio tab. Check the Enable noise removal to enable the feature. Then select the **Auto noise training** or **Manual noise training on selection** button to remove noises from the audio track.

For better results, make a selection with the playhead on the clip at a space where only the background noise is audible. Do not include voices in the selection. Then click the **Manual noise training on selection** button for the program to identify the selection as background noise and remove it from the whole clip. Click undo and the **Adjust sensitivity** to fine tune the removal (See Figure 8.28).

<table>
<tr><td>

NOTE

</td><td>

Leave space before and after your recording without music or voice playing to capture just the background noise. This will make the selection of just the background noise easier.

</td></tr>
</table>

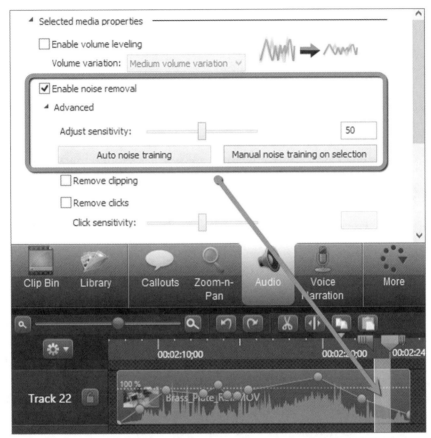

FIGURE 8.28 — Check the box Enable noise removal to remove the noises from the audio track.

The noise removal feature is applied to an entire audio clip. One or more clips can be selected at a time for noise removal. However, it is recommended that if the audio clip were recorded at different times or with different equipment to use the noise removal feature individually. This will give you more control over the settings for even sound. Once the noise removal feature is applied, the wave will turn from gray to orange (See Figure 8.29).

FIGURE 8.29 — The orange shows the noise removal feature has been applied.

Removing Background Noise

8.4d — Adding Background Music

One of the biggest mistakes in a video project is the background music being too loud in volume and drowning out the voice narration. Many times the music track is placed into the timeline as a whole without fades or volume adjustments. Treat the music track as any other audio track and use the fades and volume settings to keep the music in the background.

8.5 — Transitions

Transitions are effect elements that are places between clips as they move one clip to another. To add a transition, click on the **Transition tab**. In the tab field, there will be a thumbnail view of the different transition effects available (See Figure 8.30). To preview the transition animation sample, double click on the transition and a preview will show in the canvas.

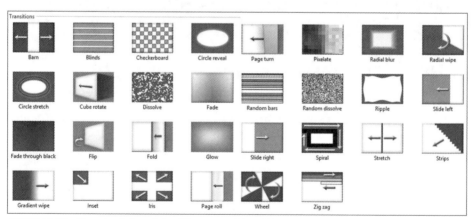

FIGURE 8.30 — Thumbnail view of the different transition effects.

Click on the transition you want to insert. The locations eligible for transition will be highlighted with yellow. Drag and drop the transition from the tab to a highlighted yellow area (See Figure 8.31).

FIGURE 8.31 — The highlighted yellow area can have a transition.

To make adjustments to the duration of the transition, select the bar indicating the transition. Then pull or push the edge to lengthen or shorten the speed of the transition change (See Figure 8.32).

FIGURE 8.32 — Pull or push the transition bar to lengthen or shorten the speed of transition

If the clips are moved, the transition will move with the clip. Multiple types of transitions can be used on the timeline.

QUICK CLIP | Using the Transition Tab

8.5a — Using Trimmed Content

If a clip is trimmed during editing, that trimmed area can be used in the transition. Using this feature can make a smoother transition by not using the part of the clip that was not trimmed. To toggle on and off the feature, right-click on the placed transition on a clip that was trimmed and select **Use trimmed content in transition** (See Figure 8.33).

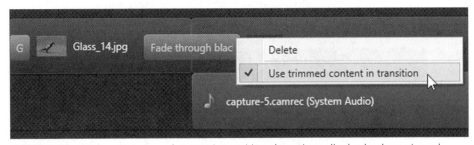

FIGURE 8.33 — Click on Use trimmed content in transition when using a clip that has been trimmed.

8.5b — Title Clips

Transition can be used at the beginning and end of the whole video project and not just between clips. Title clips can be used to ease the view into the project at the start with a **Fade In** and title of the project. At the end of the project, it will ease the view out of the project with a **Fade Out** and credits. Music and graphic elements are commonly used in title clips. The library has a list of premade title clips for use and to edit to fit your needs.

If you are going to use a title clip more than once, you can copy or save the clip. After you add all the elements of the title clip, you can group the clip to form one group (See Figure 8.34).

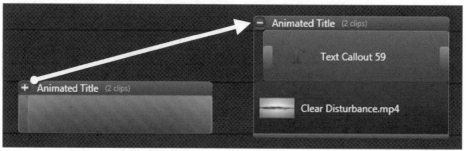

FIGURE 8.34 — Title clips can be group together to form one group.

This group can be cut and pasted in the project or into the library for use in other projects. This will keep the title clip consistent between projects.

8.6 — Cursor Effects

When recording with the editor, you have the option to burn the cursor effect into the recording or add the effects using the **Editor**. Generally, it is more effective to add the cursor effects from your recording using the **Editor**.

QUICK
CLIP
Using the Cursor Effects Tab

NOTE   *To add cursor effects within the Editor, a .camrec file with cursor action needs to be used.*

NOTE

The cursor effect animations work independently from the embedded cursor action that was recorded within the .camrec file. You can add, move and delete multiple cursor effect animations to a clip while the recorded cursor action remains unchanged.

To add the cursor effects within the **Editor**, place a **.camrec** file into your timeline. Click the **Add Animation** button in the **Cursor effects tab**. This will automatically activate the cursor effects from the recording. Once the cursor effects are activated, the rest of the **Cursor Effects tab** will be eligible for selection (See Figure 8.35).

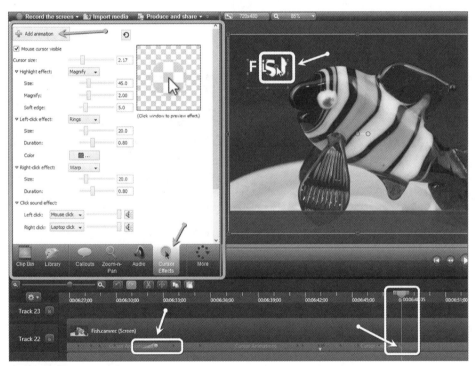

FIGURE 8.35 — The Cursor Effects tab and clip showing the activated effects.

The clip will have a small animation bar on the bottom of the clip with a little cursor arrow representing the points of the cursor clicks and action (See Figure 8.36). To open or close the animation panel, click the small downward arrow in the middle of the clip.

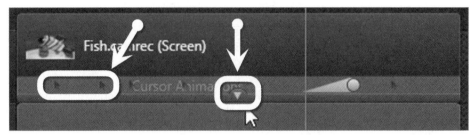

FIGURE 8.36— The small animation bar has a little cursor arrow showing the point of the cursor clicks and action.

The yellow animation sliders adjust the position and length of the effects (See Figure 8.37). Delete the yellow slider to delete the cursor animation effect. This does not delete the cursor action embedded within the clip and you can always add effects later.

FIGURE 8.37— The small animation slider that can be moved and lengthened on the clip.

There are settings to change the cursor size and visibility along with highlighting, left and right mouse clicks animations, and sound effects. The large number of customization tools allows the cursor effect to enhance the project and not distract from it.

8.7 — Visual Properties

The settings in the **Visual Properties tab** allow you to manipulate clips in the timeline. These settings include adding color, adding a drop shadow or border, changing the opacity, and subtracting color to most visual media on the timeline like video, callouts, and images.

QUICK
CLIP   Using the Visual Properties Tab

NOTE *Animations can be copied and pasted to new locations and clips. This saves creation time and enforces consistency.*

To add a visual effect, click the playhead on the selected clip or clips and select the **Visual Properties tab**. Then click the **Add Animation** button at the point you would like the visual effect to start (See Figure 8.38).

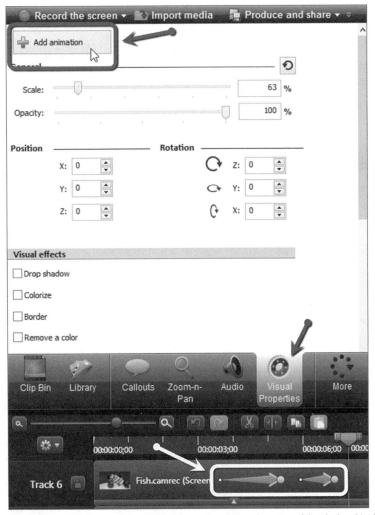

FIGURE 8.38 — The Add Animation button will add an animation at the point of the playhead in the timeline.

Multiple animations can be added to a clip or clips. Use the adjustment handles on the animation arrow to adjust the duration of the animation.

Position and Rotation

Video and image media clips can be manipulated through various planes and axis. Multiple position and rotation effects can be used at the same time in an animation (See Figure 8.39).

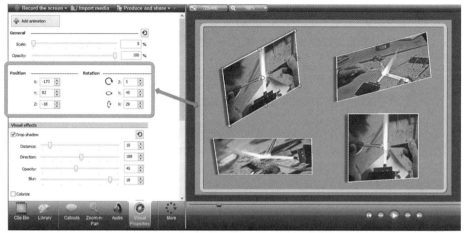

FIGURE 8.39 — Four different positions and rotations of a visual clip are shown.

These animations can move outside of the canvas area and will give the appearance of moving into and out of the video project.

Colorize

A clip can be altered by adding a color stylization to the animation (See Figure 8.40). Select the paint bucket tool to select a color to add wash over the image. The Amount slider will change the intensity of the color amount.

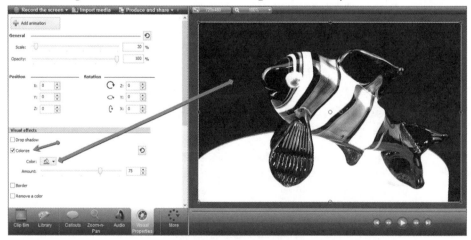

FIGURE 8.40 — The intensity of the color amount can be changed by the Amount slider.

Drop Shadow or Border

The edge of the clip can be highlighted by adding a border or drop shadow. This can make the clip stand out from the background or other clips (See Figure 8.41).

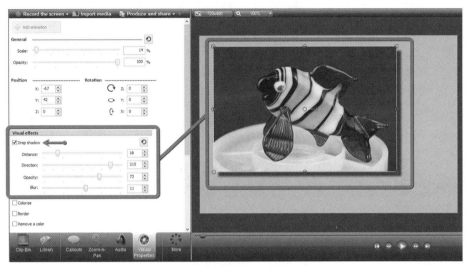

FIGURE 8.41 — The clip is shown with a drop shadow around it.

The color and thickness of the border can be changed while the distance, direction opacity, and blur of the shadow can be changed to fit the style of shadow that works best for your project.

Remove a Color

The ability to remove a color from the clip is very useful. For example, if you have a green or blue screen, the subject can be recorded in front of the screen. Then during editing that color can be removed to have the appearance of the subject being cut out of the background. Any clips below this clip in the timeline will appear to be behind the subject. This process is called **Chroma key Compositing** and is used in television and movie sets.

Chroma Key Compositing — an editing technique for combining two images or frames, making one color of one image or frame transparent to reveal the other image or frame behind it.

To remove a color, select **Remove a color** in the **Visual effects tab**. Then select a color to remove (See Figure 8.42).

FIGURE 8.42 – Under Visual Effects, select remove a color.

You can use the eyedropper tool to pick a color from the clip or use the **More colors** button to select from a palette. The effect will take place in real time so you can watch how the settings affect the clip (See Figure 8.43).

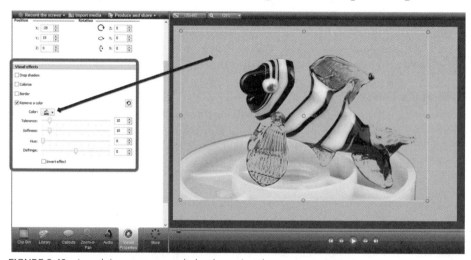

FIGURE 8.43 – In real time you can watch the change in color.

Use the slider bars to change the tolerance, softness, hue, and defringing effects. Select the curved arrow to return the settings to the default state.

Project: Use the media in the project folder and use the Visual Properties tab to adjust the clip settings.

8.8 — Voice Narration

There are times when you might need to add audio to your project that was not captured during the original recording. For natural, background, and other types of sounds, import the audio clip into the clip bin to use. For desk top or narration additions, you can use the **Voice Narration tab** (See Figure 8.44).

QUICK CLIP — Using the Voice Narration Tab

FIGURE 8.44 — Click the Voice Narration tab to add your narration.

The audio device setup is the same as used in the **Recorder**. Try and keep your audio levels in the middle of the volume bar. If you just need to record voice audio without lining up a visual, you can start recording at any time. Once finished, hit stop to save the recording and generate it as a clip in its own track on the timeline.

To lineup a visual portion of the project to the narration, place the playhead at the start of the area. Hit the play button and the record button to start the project playing while recording. Because the project is playing in the background, you can line up the dialog. Use the **Mute speakers during recording** checkbox if you have audio that will playback during the recording. Once saved and generated into the timeline the new narration clip works the same as other media clips and is able to be edited.

8.9 – Record Camera

The record camera feature will record the activity displayed through the Web camera, like it would be when using the **Recorder**. This feature can be used to add missing video recordings or fix errors.

To start recording make sure your Web camera is plugged in and working. Then click the **Record Camera tab** (See Figure 8.45).

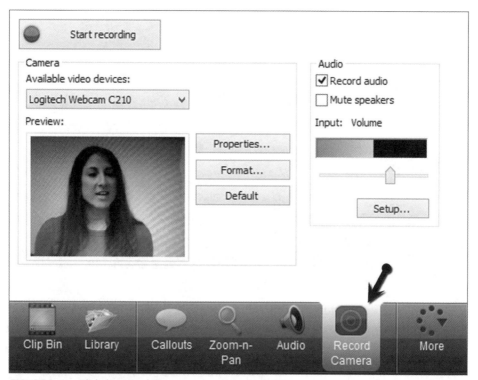

FIGURE 8.45 – Click the Record Camera to start recording.

QUICK
CLIP   Using the Record Camera Tab

A live action preview of the camera will appear in the tab along with the audio input. Click the **Start recording** button to begin.

If you just need to add a recording, you can start the capture at any time. If you want to try and match any part of the project, place the playhead at the location of where you would like to start the recording. During the recording, the playhead will move through the timeline. Once the recording is finished, select **Stop recording** to save the recording to your computer while also generating a clip to the timeline.

8.10 — Captions

If you have an outline or script, it is recommended that you add the text to your project as captions. The captions display text overlaid on the video project can be used to provide additional information, language translations, and the dialog of the narration. Viewers with hearing loss or in a public location can follow along through the video by reading the captions.

There are two types of captions:

Open Captions

These are captions that are burned into the recording and cannot be turned off or removed. During the recording, the style of the caption can be customized by changing the type style, size, color, alignment, and placement. During production these captions can be made searchable using an **.mp4** file format.

Closed Captions

These captions can be turned on and off using the video playback controller **CC** button. The type style, size, color, alignment, and placement can all be adjusted and made **ADA compliant**. During production, the captions can be turned on or off before rendering and can be made searchable using an **.mp4** file format.

8.10a — Adding Captions

Captions can be added by importing, typing, speaking, or cutting and pasting text into the **Captions tab**. Use the best way that fits into your workflow.

To add captions manually by cutting and pasting the text, move the playhead to the point of the timeline you would like to start the captions. Then copy your text, script, or outline (See Figure 8.46).

I started torch work about four years ago, when I was a kid I watched 3-2,-1 Contact and they had a segment on glass blowing and I loved it from that minute on.

I started taking lessons

It's very relaxing

It's time to myself, I don't have anything intruding in on me from the world; I just sit there and burn glass and even if I don't make anything at least I'm practicing.

Glass is all about chemistry. I have to purchase specific colors of glass. Silver will make a kind of interesting haze on it, that will change color and you never quite know what you get. Gold makes these beautiful purples and pinks. A lot of the experimentation is how the different chemicals in the different glasses react to each other once they are burned together.

You have to use a lot of tools like tweezers and graphite paddles, and some brass implements to shape the glass; and presses and all sorts of specialized tools out there to squash it, to pull it, to mold it into shape.

I started making beads with like patterns on them. I have made little sculptural pieces like cats and rabbits and just free form kind of stuff; whatever floats my fancy that day

This is actually the hardest craft I have ever done. Bar none, it's dangerous in that you can burn yourself, but the result is beautiful.

I don't know, I love it

FIGURE 8.46 — A sample of text that can be added.

Then open the **Captions tab** and **paste** the text into the open captions field within the tab (See Figure 8.47).

The copy will be added in a long box with mostly red text if you copy is over three lines (See Figure 8.48).

Use the **split** button to cut the text at natural brakes, during points in video action (See Figure 8.49).

Keeping the segments to three lines will keep the captions ADA compliant and keep the text in manageable chunks for the reader to read on screen (See Figure 8.50).

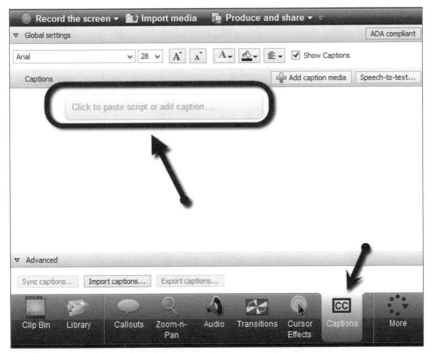

FIGURE 8.47 — Use the Click to Paste Script or Add Caption to insert the text.

FIGURE 8.48 — The copy is on the right hand side in red because it is over three lines long.

FIGURE 8.49 — The text is split to add to different points in the video action.

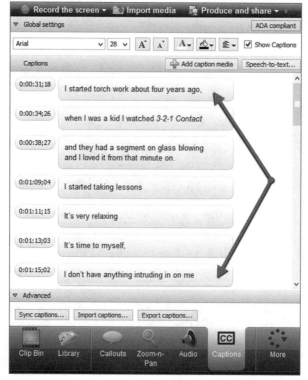

FIGURE 8.50 — The text had been divided into seven sections to go with the visual actions.

The captions are added on an individual track on the timeline. This track can be moved in the timeline and split or trimmed like other types of media clips. The captions will show in the tab, timeline, and preview window at the frame of the playhead (See Figure 8.51).

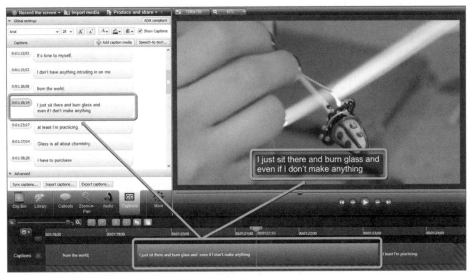

FIGURE 8.51 — The captions on the left are be added to the timeline.

The time next to the text indicates the time within the timeline of the caption. The captions can be changed and moved at any point during the editing process.

QUICK CLIP | Using the Captions Tab

Project: Add Cat Thoughts captions to add captions and arrange clips to create a video project.

8.10b — ADA Compliant Captions

When creating captions, try and keep them **ADA compliant** even if the project will have a controlled viewing audience. It is a good habit to always add captions and make them compliant. This practice will increase possible viewers and save time reediting to make them compliant at a later time.

ADA compliant captions include:

- one to three lines of text that appear on-screen at a time
- 32 characters or less a line
- Helvetica medium or similar style of font
- upper- and lowercase letters
- text should not cover up graphics or other essential elements
- captions stay there for a few seconds
- text is timed to the audio

8.10c — Speech-to-Text

With the Speech-to-Text feature you can automatically create captions from voice narration or audio clips in the timeline. This feature provides voice during video playback and trains and adapts to recognize your voice and style of speaking the more you use it.

To start the feature, select the **Speech-to-text** button in the **Captions tab** (See Figure 8.52).

FIGURE 8.52 — Select the Speech-to-text tab in the captions section to automatically create captions from voice narration or audio clips in the timeline.

The **Tips for Generating Accurate Speech-to-text Caption** dialing box will pop up (See Figure 8.53).

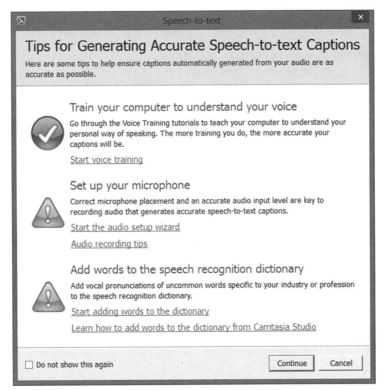

FIGURE 8.53 — List of Tips for Generating Accurate Speech-to-text Captions.

It is strongly recommended that the voice that runs through the training also is the voice of the narration. The program learns from hearing the voice and using the same voice will help generate more accurate captions. It is also recommended to run through the fill tip and training before generating the captions.

After the training, click the **Continue** button to generate the text. There is a high possibility that you will have to make frequent adjustments to the captions after generation. However, it might be faster than starting from scratch. The effectiveness will depend on your workflow.

NOTE   *During the Speech-to-text process, capitalization and punctuation data is not collected.*

There is an option to **Sync captions** that will automatically split captions from video playback (See Figure 8.54).

FIGURE 8.54 — Shows How to Sync your captions.

This feature will run through the video while splitting the caption block at the appropriate time. There is a bit of a learning curve when using this feature. It is recommended that you practice or work with manual input to train and get more familiar on how the caption editing works.

8.10d — Exporting, Importing, and Saving

If your project contains captions, they can be exported into a **.srt** file (See Figure 8.55). These files can be imported into other projects and used for language translations.

FIGURE 8.55 — This is a sample of a .srt file that can be imported into your project.

The exported **.srt** file includes the text of the caption along with timing information and the caption number (See Figure 8.56).

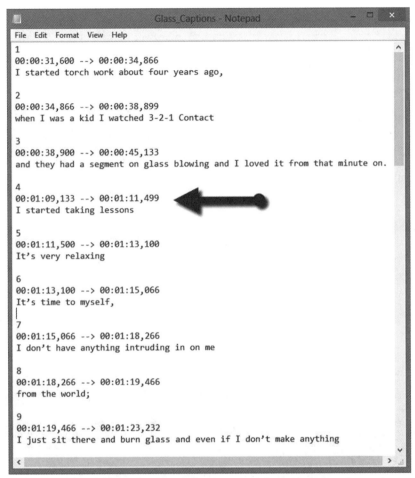

FIGURE 8.56 — The text of the caption also includes the timing information and caption number.

Use the **Import captions** or **Export captions** in the **Captions tab** to start the selected process.

Saving

For **Closed** or **Open** caption function needs to be selected in the **Production Wizard** during the production process in order for the captions to display in the final video.

8.11 — Quizzes

You can easily add a quiz or multiple quizzes to your presentation. These quizzes can be added at any time during the project.

Using the Quizzes Tab

To add a quiz, move the playhead to the area of the timeline where you want to start the quiz, and then open the **Quizzing** tab. Click the **Add quiz** button to add the quiz onto the timeline (See Figure 8.57).

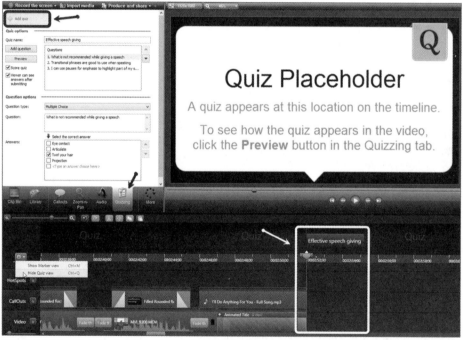

FIGURE 8.57 — Click the Quizzing tab and the Add Quiz button to add a quiz to the timeline.

Quiz placement works like the **Markers** and have their own track in the timeline. Click the **Show Quiz view** button located above the track names to open the track to edit the quiz. Then fill in the quiz questions and names in the text fields in the **Quizzing tab** (See Figure 8.58).

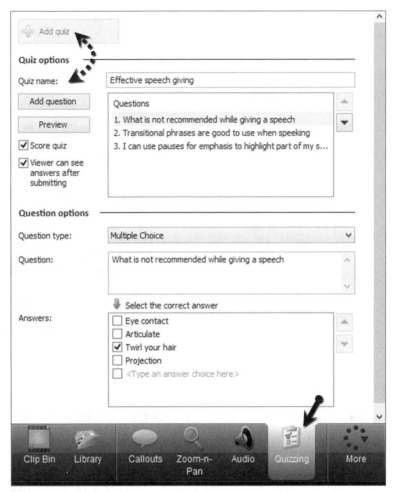

FIGURE 8.58 — Add Quiz includes Quiz Options, Question Options, and Answers.

The fill out the quiz fields and dropdown menus to create the quiz that fits your viewers and your style of project.

Types of Quizzes

- Multiple Choice
- Fill in the Blank
- Short Answer
- True/False

There are also options to score the quiz and have the viewers see the results.

To preview the quiz at any time, click the Preview button in the Quiz options within the Quiz tab. The full quiz will not be able to be used until it is rendered. For an active quiz the .mp4 format setting will need to be use in the render (See Chapter 9 for more details on how to render a video file with an active quiz).

After the production process, the quiz will appear in the video depending on the setting chosen in the Production Wizard. At the point of the video where the quiz is located a **Take Quiz now** button will overlay on the video playback (See Figure 8.59).

Once the quiz starts, the viewer can interact by selecting or filling in the answers to the quiz (See Figure 8.60).

After the quiz ends, the viewer will have the option to repeat the quiz or review the results depending on the setting you selected.

FIGURE 8.59 — The Take Quiz Now button will be in your video playback.

FIGURE 8.60 — A sample of a quiz you can generate.

NOTE

*During the production process, the video project needs to be saved in a format that is compatible for the use of quizzes. Use the **MP4 video file with a player** preset, or equivalent, to include a quiz or survey.*

CHAPTER SUMMARY

In Chapter 8, we learned how to use callouts, zooms-in-pans, plus additional task tab tools. Editing audio can do done in many different ways as shown in this chapter. It depends on what your end goal is. We also learned about many different ways to enhance your project using cursor effects, visual properties, voice narration, captions, and quizzes. In the next chapter, you will learn about producing and sharing your project.

CHAPTER PROJECTS

1. Discuss four special effects you can add to the timeline and why you would use them.

2. What is one way of creating pans and zooms in your project?

3. When you add additional sound tracks such as background music and voiceover to your presentation, what is the best way of doing it?

4. When you are editing captions, how would you: change text, change font, move and size it, change duration, and delete captions?

5. Why is Sketch motion callout important and how would you use it?

6. Give an example of how you would use each of the ten tasks on the task tab.

7. What are the similarities and differences of using a text, special and animated, hotspot and keyboard callouts?

8. Use eight shapes, sketch motion, or special callouts. Which do you like the best and why?

9. Why are Fade In and Fade Out for both visual and audio important? Show an example you have made of each.

10. How would you render sensitive information unreadable? Show an example you have made.

11. What is a hotspot and why whould you use it?

12. Describe how to remove background noise and why it is important?

13. Make project with three different transitions in it.

14. Show a clip with two multipositions and two rotation effects.

15. Make a project with ten lines that are split using ADA compliant captions.

16. Make up a quiz on this book using Camtasia Studio. It needs to have ten or more questions and you need to give it to someone as a test.

CHAPTER 9

PRODUCING AND SHARING

IN THIS CHAPTER

In this chapter, we will learn how to produce and share videos. We will study how to use the Production Wizard and all of its processes. In addition, we will study a variety of production presets and custom settings. Another important process is learning how to add and edit presets and knowing how batch and advance settings are processed. In Chapter 10, we will learn how to edit and produce high quality screen captures using Snagit by TechSmith.

NOTE

The same technical writing method that was used in Chapter 3 will be used throughout this chapter. Menu items, programs, and file extensions will be in bold lettering while the mouse navigation and keystrokes action will be displayed with a ">" symbol.

Once you've completed this chapter, you will be able to:

- Produce and share videos
- Operate Production Wizard
- Use Production presets
- Apply Custom settings
- Utilize batch and advance settings

Files: All figures in this chapter are in color located in the chapter folder on the DVD.

9.1 — Producing and Sharing the Videos

Once the recording and editing processes are done, the project is ready to be produced. The **Production Wizard** is the main tool to render the project into the final sharable video.

Key Term — **Render** — video rendering is the process the computer takes to generate images.

To start, it is best to stay with the default setting before using the customization tools. The presets are premade for optimal rendering to fit most popular end uses. These include YouTube and Web or mobile device output.

Overview — Producing and Sharing the Videos

Step-by-Step to Producing

Before we take a closer look at the different ways to produce and share the videos, let us take a quick overview of the production process. This list will vary depending on what type of end use you will want.

Quick List: Producing the Video Project

1. Open the **Production Wizard**

2. From the dropdown menu, select a **Preset** or **Custom** production setting, then click **Next**

3. If a **Preset** is selected, skip to Step 8

4. Select file format if a custom setting is selected, then click **Next**

5. *Optional:* Select player style and size, audio and video options, **Captions**, then click **Next**

6. *Optional:* Add meta data and **Watermark**, then click **Next**

7. *Optional:* Select **Marker** information, then click **Next**

8. *Optional:* **Quiz** options, then click **Next**

9. Select output file destination and name in the Output file field

10. Click **Finish** to render the video

11. Click **Finish** after verifying production results

A Closer Look — Producing and Sharing the Videos

9.2 — The Production Wizard

The Production Wizard is an extremely useful tool for the production of all your video projects. It walks the user step-by-step through the production process in a clear and organized way. The wizard will change its selections and walkthrough based on what production type is selected (See Figure 9.1).

Overview Review — The Production Wizard

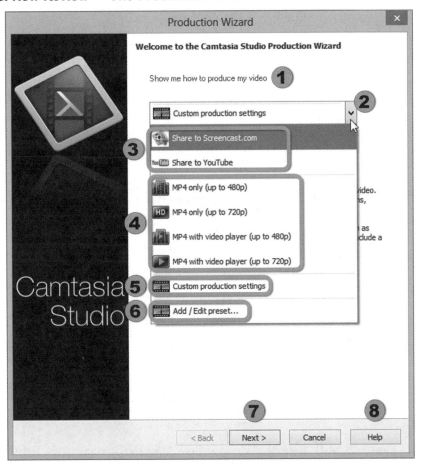

FIGURE 9.1 — Production Wizard used to render video projects for final use

1. **Help link** — a link to the TechSmith Website opened to a tutorial page

2. **Option dropdown** — a dropdown menu that holds the type of production

3. **Preset site production** — presets to produce and upload to Screencast.com and YouTube

4. **Preset video production** — preset to produce videos with additional sharing files

5. **Custom production** — a selection to produce with custom settings

6. **Add/Edit preset** — an option to add or edit a preset or create a new one

7. **Next** —will navigate through the Production Wizard windows

8. **Help** —launches the help documents

A Closer Look — The Production Wizard

9.2a — Opening the Production Wizard

There are a number of different ways to launch the **Production Wizard**. From the **Recorder**, click the **Produce** button. Within the **Editor**, click the **Produce and Share** button from the **Application Menu** or right click on a **playhead selection** in the **Timeline** (See Figure 9.2).

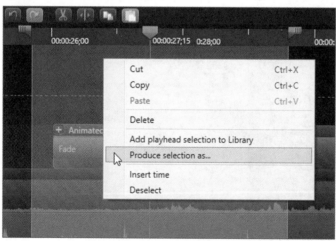

FIGURE 9.2 — A right-click context menu with a playhead timeline selection — (Produce selection as).

You can also open the **Production Wizard** through the **Editor** by using the hotkey command or **Menu Options > File Produce and Share**.

9.3 — Using Production Presets

A preset is a saved group of settings for a production. When using a preset, all the video production settings are already selected for that type of render. This reduces the steps in your workflow saving you time. Custom settings can be saved into a preset to be shared between multiple projects. If you have a number of projects using the same video production settings, a saved preset will keep the renders consistent.

The dropdown menu, in the Production Wizard's opening window, holds six common preset settings (See Figure 9.3). These base presets will cover most of your production needs. When in doubt of the type of render you need for your project, use one of the presets to start with.

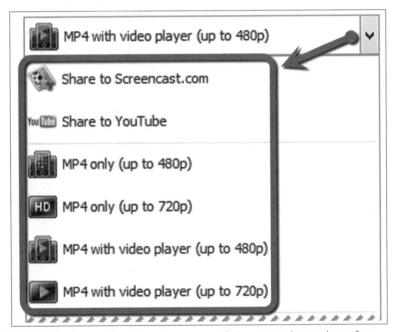

FIGURE 9.3 — The Production Wizard dropdown menu with six preset settings to choose from.

Preset Options

1. **Share to Screencast.com** — ideal settings for Screencast.com including upload walkthrough

2. **Share to YouTube** — ideal settings for YouTube including upload walkthrough

3. **MP4 only (up to 480p)** — 480 pixels of vertical resolution, progressive scan, video file only

4. **MP4 only (up to 720p)** — 720 pixels of vertical resolution, progressive scan, video file only

5. **MP4 with video player (up to 480p)** — 480 pixels of vertical resolution, progressive scan, video file with accompanying support files

6. **MP4 with video player (up to 720p)** — 720 pixels of vertical resolution, progressive scan, video file with accompanying support files

 480p/720p — Perform a search about video resolution and the differences between 480p and 720p and how they interact with the aspect ratio.

9.3a — Step-by-Step: Share to Screencast.com

Screencast.com is a Website developed by TechSmith to host and share screencast recordings. You can upload video projects directly through the Production Wizard using the Screencast.com preset. Once uploaded, the Production Wizard will display an URL address and an embedding code to add to Websites to share your video with your audience. You can log into your Screencast.com account at any time to view your videos and retrieve video and embedding information.

Quick List: Producing the Video Project

1. Open the **Production Wizard**.

2. From the dropdown menu, select a **Share to Screencast.com**, then click **Next**.

3. Enter your account information in the **Sign In to Screencast.com** screen dialog box, then click **Next**.

4. Name your video project and select a sorting folder.

5. *Optional:* Select **Option**s to set playback controller settings, toggle features including quizzes, video and audio quality, table of contents, and captions.

6. *Optional:* Select **Preview** to temporarily render your video to preview at current settings.

7. Click **Next**.

8. *Optional:* If a quiz is activated, fill in the results information in the dialog box. Click **Quiz appearance** to adjust the quiz settings.

9. Click **Finished**.

10. The video will start to render then upload to **Screencast.com**.

11. After upload, Screencast.com will launch with the video ready for playback along with a **Production Results** dialog box with URL and embedding code information.

12. Click **Finished** when done reviewing results to close the **Production Wizard**.

Project: Use project files and create a video project and Screencast.com account, and then use the Production Wizard Screencast.com preset to upload the practice file.

A Closer Look — Share to Screencast.com

When you are ready to render your video project, click on the **Produce and share** button to launch the **Production Wizard**. Click the **dropdown menu** and select the **Sreencast.com** option from the list (See Figure 9.4).

FIGURE 9.4 — A video project opened in the Editor with the Production Wizard opened in the top left.

Next, a dialog box will pop up asking for sign in information (See Figure 9.5). If you do not already have a Screencast.com account, click on the hyperlink below the **Remember me** checkbox. This will launch the Screencast.com Website to create a new account.

FIGURE 9.5 — Sign In To Screencast.com asking for your e-mail address and password.

After signing in, type in the video project's title and select a navigation folder (See Figure 9.6). Select **Preview** to temporarily render and view the video project.

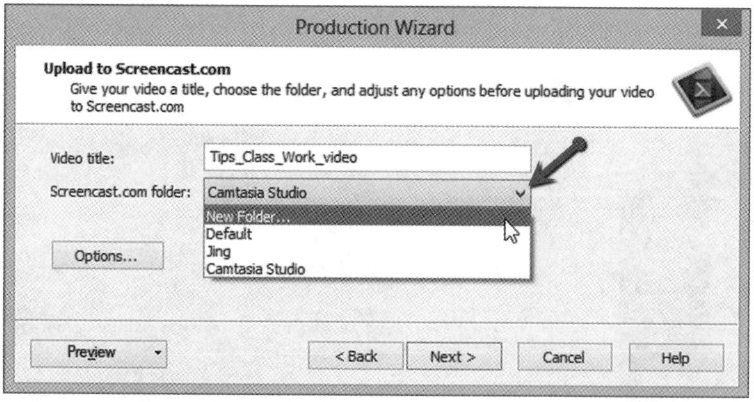

FIGURE 9.6 — Upload to Screencast.com (video title, Screencast.com folder, options, and then preview).

To change the project settings, select the **Option** button from the dialog box. The **Screencast Options** has tabs to adjust the controller, size, video, and audio of the project. The **Options tab** holds toggles and placement settings for features like adding a table of contents, captions, and quizzes (See Figure 9.7).

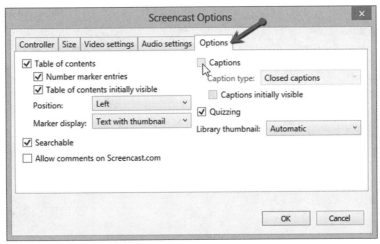

FIGURE 9.7 — Screencast.com dialog box opened to the Options tab (table of contents, captions, quizzing, library thumbnail, searchable, and allow comments).

If a quiz is activated, a dialog box will pop up with **Quiz Reporting Options** (See Figure 9.8). Enter the e-mail address along with selecting the view identity requirements. Using the quiz for a classroom setting or for a grading tool might require the viewer's name and e-mail address. Other uses like surveys or general information would not require the viewer to write down personal information.

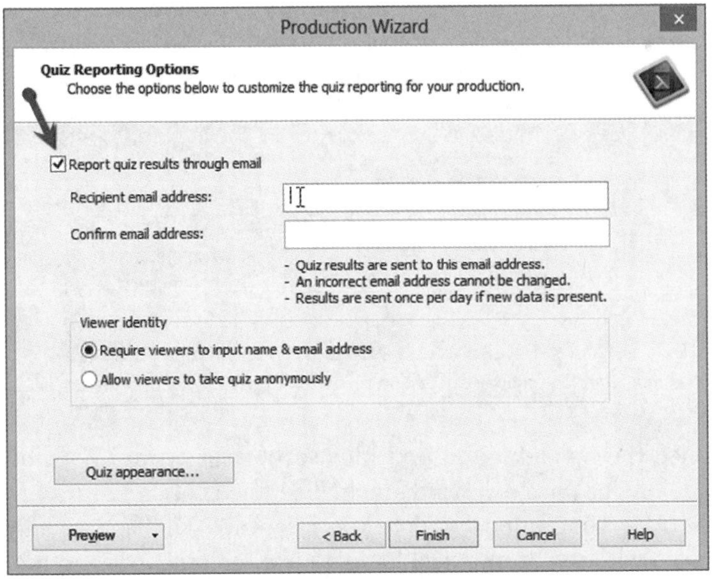

FIGURE 9.8 — Quiz Reporting Options (report quiz through e-mail, e-mail address, viewer identity, quiz appearance, and preview) and you can receive the results of the viewer's quiz.

To change the quiz control name labels, select the **Quiz appearance** button in the dialog box (See Figure 9.9). Changing the name labels allows you to customize your quiz to fit the style of your project.

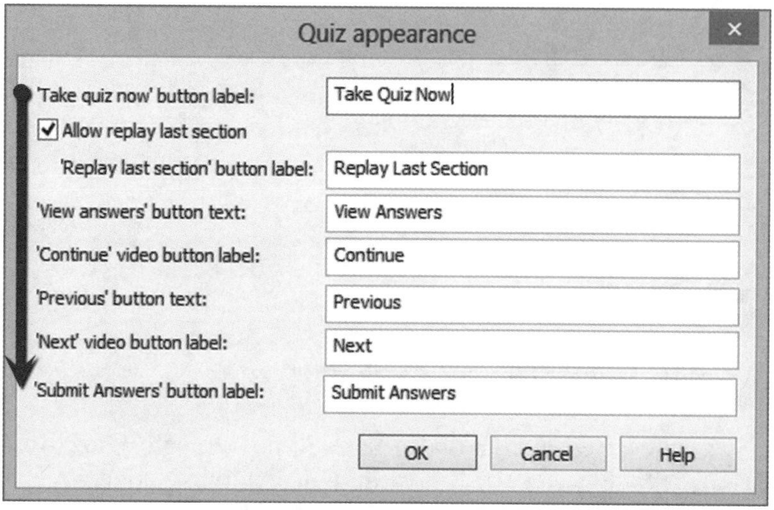

FIGURE 9.9 — The quiz generic format is unchangeable, however you can customize the label names.

Click **Finished** when you are done making adjustments to start the rendering process. The duration of the render will depend on how long and detailed your video is and how fast your computer can process. After the rendering is completed, uploading to the **Screencast.com** Website will automatically start (See Figure 9.10).

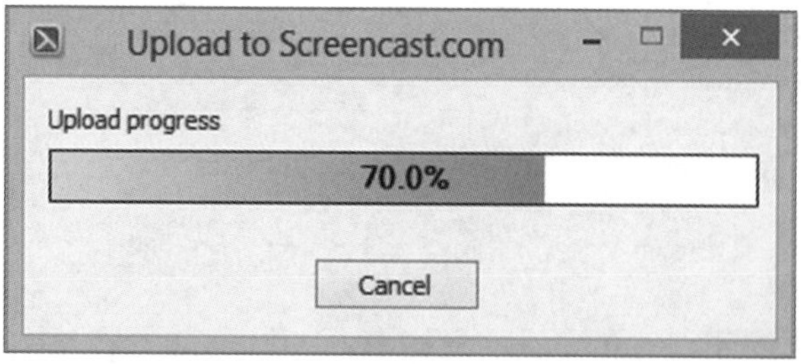

FIGURE 9.10 — Rendering and upload speed and progress will depend on the connection and equipment you are using.

Once the upload is finished, the **Screencast.com** Website with your video ready for playback will launch. The top **URL** is the new location on the Web for your video project (See Figure 9.11). The playback window and video will have the special features like the table of contents, captions, and quizzes working and ready to be used and viewed.

FIGURE 9.11 — A Web browser view of a video that was uploaded to Screencast.com.

The **Production Results** dialog box will pop up to display the video **URL** and **Embed code**. The **Copy** button will copy the text to your pasteboard for pasting into a Web browser or other locations (See Figure 9.12).

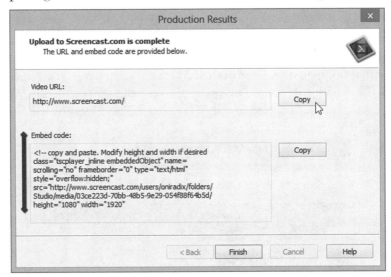

FIGURE 9.12 — Upload to Screencast is complete. (The video URL and Website embedding information after it was uploaded.)

The embedding and URL information can also be located in the **Show Details** button under the video playback on the Screencast.com site.

9.3b — Step-by-Step: Share to YouTube

In only a few steps, the **Production Wizard YouTube** setup will upload the video directly onto the site. Select the **YouTube** preset for the wizard to use and upload the video onto the site. If you do not have a YouTube account, you must make one before uploading. If you have an account, sign in through the **Production Wizard** to upload the video to your account.

NOTE	*Some extra features may not be able to be included in the production.*

Quick List: Share to YouTube

1. Open the **Production Wizard**

2. From the dropdown menu, select **YouTube**, then click **Next**

3. Enter your login name to sign into YouTube within the dialog box, then click **Next**

4. Enter your project name, meta data, captions, and select a category

5. Click **Finish** to render the video

6. Video is uploaded onto YouTube and is ready for viewing

A Closer Look — Share to YouTube

After opening the **Production Wizard**, select the **YouTube** preset from the dropdown menu. This preset uses the optimal settings for YouTube and condenses the process to only a few steps (See Figure 9.13).

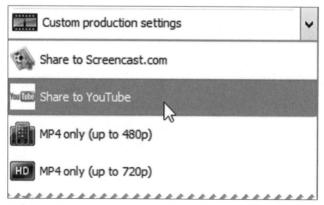

FIGURE 9.13 — Production Wizard dropdown menu with the Share to YouTube highlighted.

Quizzes, hotspots, table of contents, and other features might not be available in all uploads. Knowing how you are going to use and share your video during production will avoid any issues during production. If your project has these features, you can still upload to YouTube; however the features will be disabled (See Figure 9.14).

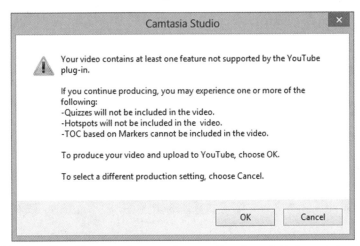

FIGURE 9.14 — You will get this screen when some features will not be available for rendering and to upload to YouTube.

Next, sign into your YouTube account and click **Next** (See Figure 9.15).

FIGURE 9.15 — Sign In To YouTube.com (asking for user name and password).

After you sign-in, enter the title, tags, category, captions, and privacy settings of your video. Click **Finished** to start rendering and uploading your video to **YouTube** (See Figure 9.16).

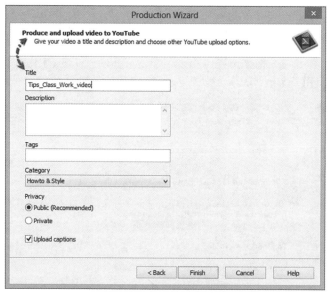

FIGURE 9.16 – Produce and upload video to YouTube (title and description information that will be uploaded to YouTube along with your video).

Select **Finish** when ready for the **Production Wizard** to upload the video to **YouTube**. The **Production Results** dialog box will pop up along with your new YouTube page.

9.3c — Additional Presets

Additional popular settings are created into production presets. Because most of the settings are already programmed in, there are less Production Wizard windows to navigate through. Special features like quizzes will still need some additional information. A description with details on the preset will appear under the dropdown menu for each preset.

Files: All production presets and custom formats are rendered using the same video project as reference examples located in chapter folder on the DVD.

Quizzes, hotspots, table of contents, and captions are not supported in the **Video file only** presets because they need the additional data that is included with the video player support files. If you have any of these features, select the presets with the accompanying video player.

Without Video Player

- **MP4 only (up to 480p)** — 480 pixels of vertical resolution, progressive scan, video file only

- **MP4 only (up to 720p)** — 720 pixels of vertical resolution, progressive scan, video file only

With Video Player

- **MP4 with video player (up to 480p)** — 480 pixels of vertical resolution, progressive scan, video file with accompanying support files

- **MP4 with video player (up to 720p)** — 720 pixels of vertical resolution, progressive scan, video file with accompanying support files

Quick List: Additional .mp4 Presets

Without Video Player

1. Open the **Production Wizard**

2. From the dropdown menu, select **MP4 only (up to 480p)** or **MP4 only (up to 720p)** production setting, then click **Next**

3. Select output file destination and name in the **Output file** field

4. Click **Finish** to render the video

5. Click **Finish** after verifying production results

With Video Player

1. Open the **Production Wizard**

2. From the dropdown menu, select **MP4 with video player (up to 480p)** or **MP4 with video player (up to 720p)** production setting, then click **Next**

3. *Optional:* **Quiz** options, then click **Next**

4. Select output file destination and name in the **Output file** field

5. Click **Finish** to render the video

6. Click **Finish** after verifying production results

A Closer Look — Additional .mp4 Presets

The **.mp4** presets are very similar in the production process, however, the rendering and produced files in the results are very different. There are a number of support files that are incorporated into the preset that includes video player (See Figure 9.17).

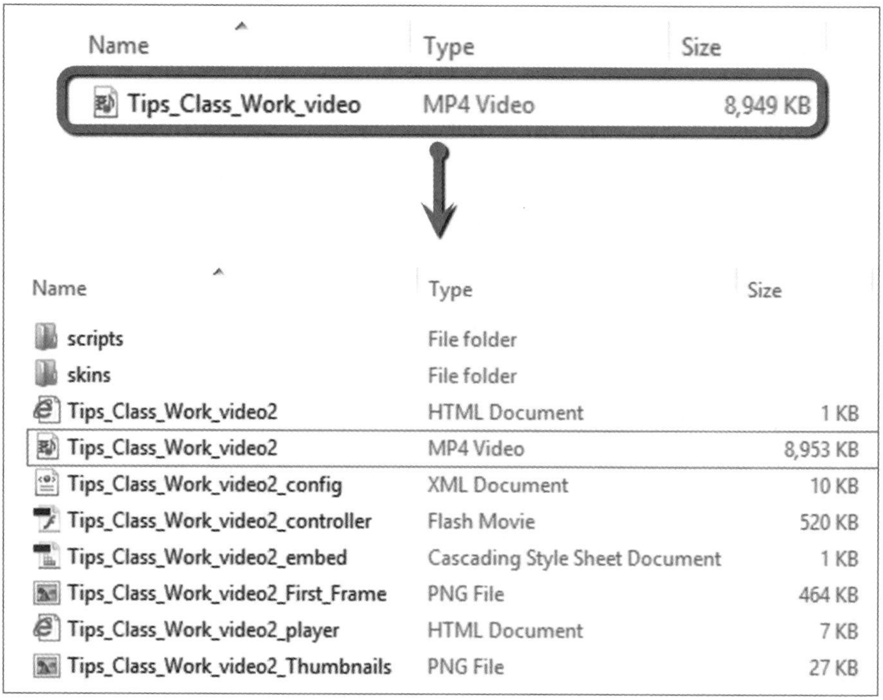

FIGURE 9.17 — Top — video file produced in the video only preset. Bottom — video and support files produced in the video player preset.

The **.html**, **.xml**, **.png**, **.css**, and **.js** files are the support files that run the video playback features, and special features controls. These files are needed for Websites and other sharing methods. The video **.mp4** file can be played and moved to a different location on its own; however the special features will be disabled.

Although the actual production process and included files are quite different, both types of **.mp4 presets** have generally the same steps through the **Production Wizard**. The main thing to notice through the wizard is if a quiz is included in the project. A **warning** dialog box will launch if the video alone preset is selected. The quiz reporting results dialog box will pop up if the includes video player option is selected.

In both cases, the next navigation will be the **save location** and **file name** dialog box (See Figure 9.18). It is recommended for organizational purposes to keep the **Organize produced file into sub folders** checked even if only the video file will be rendered.

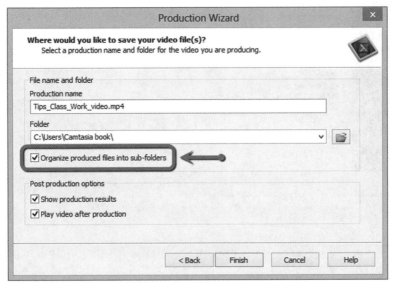

FIGURE 9.18 — Video production name and folder information for the .mp4 preset without the player.

NOTE   *The file save name and location dialog box will slightly vary to include a list of supporting files if the **includes video player preset** is selected.*

Click **Finish** to start the rendering process and have the files saved to the location selected on your computer.

9.4 — Using Custom Settings

The **Custom Production Setting** option in the **Production Wizard** dropdown will allow you more control of the style, size, quality, and video extras that using one of the premade presets dictate (See Figure 9.19). These include a wide range of options including file format, audio and video settings, and watermarks. The Production Wizard will walk you through each step for each file format.

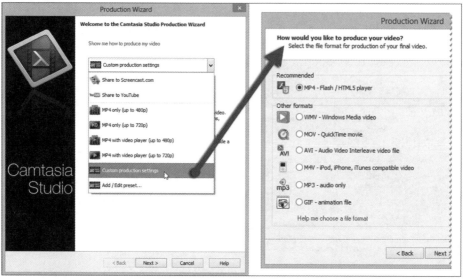

FIGURE 9.19 — Production Wizard with the Custom production setting highlighted and other types of formats available.

1. **MP4 — Flash/HTML5 Player** — .mp4 — Motion Picture expert group 4

2. **WMV — Windows Media Video** — .wmv — Window Media Video

3. **MOV — QuickTime movie** — .mov — Quick Time Movie

4. **AVI — Audio Video Interleave video file** — .avi — audio video interleave video file

5. **M4V — iPod, iPhone, iTunes compatible video** — .m4v — MPEG-4 Video file from iTunes

6. **MP3 — audio only** — .mp3 — MPEG 1 or MPEG 2 audio Layer 3

7. **GIF — animation file** — .gif — Graphics Interchange Format

NOTE *If you are undecided on a file format, select the Help me to choose a file format hyperlink to open the help document for more information on the types of formats.*

Because the .mp4 production format is recommended and will be most commonly used, the step-by-stepswill be more in-depth for the custom .mp4 production and show only the major differences with using the other production formats.

9.4a — Step-by-Step: MP4 — Flash/HTML5 Player (.mp4)

Whether you select a preset or custom option, the .mp4 format serves as the production workhorse and will serve most of your needs. The .mp4 can be produce with all the special features and can be viewed and shared using most methods.

The **.mp4** Flash file format creates a high quality, low file size video for playback. It is extremely versatile being able to be played on multiple Web browsers, local and mobile devices, and programs. This makes it one of the best file formats for sharing video projects and is recommended for use in most situations.

Advantages

- Comparatively small file size

- Excellent overall quality

- Plays on browsers, smartphones, and tablets

Disadvantages

- Not supported by all browsers or devices, if the Flash player is not installed

Quick List: Custom .mp4 Production

1. Open the **Production Wizard**

2. From the dropdown menu, select a **Custom** production setting, then click **Next**

3. Select **MP4 Flash/HTML5 player** output option, then click **Next**

4. Select player style and size, audio and video options from the **player options** dialog box tabs

5. *Optional:* Activate the **captions**, **table of contents**, and **quiz** features under the **Options tab**

6. Click **Next**

7. *Optional:* Add meta data and a **Watermark**, then click **Next**

8. *Optional:* Select **Marker** Information and table of contents, then click **Next**

9. *Optional:* **Quiz** options, then click **Next**

10. Select output file destination and name in the **Output file** field

11. Click **Finish** to render the video

12. Click **Finish** after verifying production results

Custom .mp4 Production

A Closer Look — Custom .mp4 Production

The preset enables most of the available features and uses the default settings. To individually select features or change the style of the player, select the **MP4 Flash/HTML5 player** output option from the **Custom production setting**. The next dialog box will contain control, video, audio, and tool settings within five option tabs. The first **Controller tab** toggles the activation and sets the style and playback controls for the video player that can be produced along with your video (See Figure 9.20). There are options to set the player to auto-hide the controls, be paused on start, and its theme style.

FIGURE 9.20 – Flash/HTML5 Player Options — controller (theme, auto-hide, after video, thumbnail, pause, thumbnail).

The **Size** setting tab controls the **Embedding code** information that will be produced as well as the actual video size. It is recommended to have the **Keep aspect ratio** checkboxes checked unless your project calls specifically for the video to fit a certain width and height (See Figure 9.21).

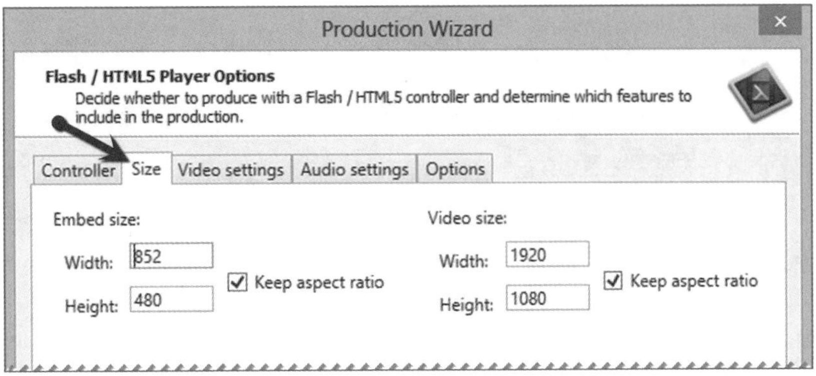

FIGURE 9.21 — Flash/HTML5 Player Options — size (embed size, video size, and keep aspect ratio)

The **Video setting tab** has controls for adjusting the quality of the video project. Generally, the higher the quality of the video settings, the larger the file size will be. If file size is not an issue, then it is recommended to always produce videos at the default or high quality settings. If the size of the project is an issue, try and find the best quality to fit within the size constraints (See Figure 9.22).

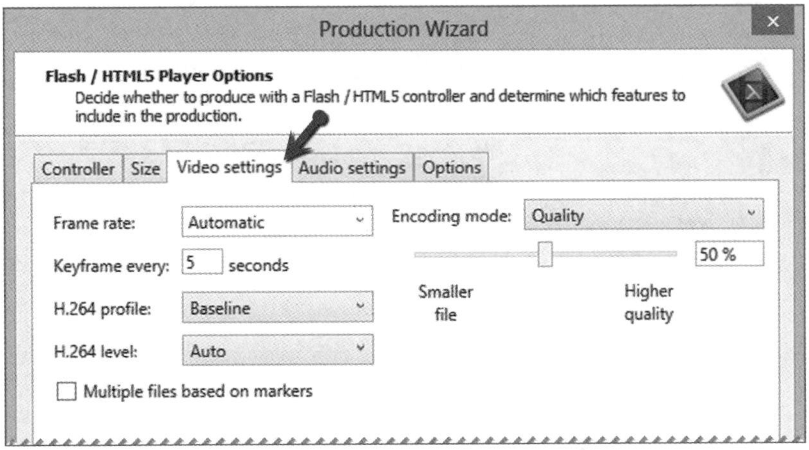

FIGURE 9.22 — Flash/HTML5 Player Options — Video settings (frame, keyframe, profile, level, encoding mode, and quality)

The **Multiple files based on markers** checkbox toggles splitting your video into multiple videos at the marker breaks.

The **Audio settings tab** toggles encoding the audio and its bit rate. Keep the **Encode audio** checked if you want the audio produced with your video (See Figure 9.23).

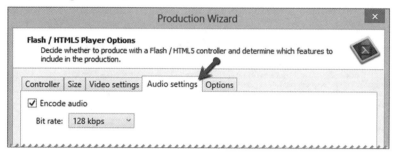

FIGURE 9.23 — Flash/HTML5 Player Options — Audio setting (encode audio – bit rate).

Generally, the higher the bit rate, the higher the quality of sound and file size.

- **56 kbps** — good for voice only recordings, smaller relative file sizes

- **128 kbps** — good overall quality, medium file sizes

- **256 kbps or higher** — almost audio CD quality, largest file sizes

Net Search   **Bit rates** — Perform a search on bit rates in relation to video, audio, and Internet uses. Compare them to file sizes and where the balances are between the quality of a project and the file size.

The **Options tab** toggles the activation of the table of contents, having your project searchable, captions, and quizzes (See Figure 9.24). These

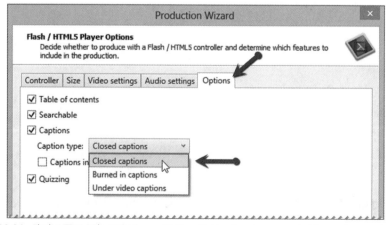

FIGURE 9.24 — Flash/HTML5 Player Options — Options (table of contents, searchable, captions, and quizzing).

checkboxes need to be activated in order for the features to be activated within your project. Additional dialog boxes will hold settings for the table of contents and quizzes.

Click **Next** to continue, when you have set all the options in the tabs. In the **Video Options**, you can add metadata, create HTML, and include a watermark (See Figure 9.25). Select the Option buttons to add information or change the related settings.

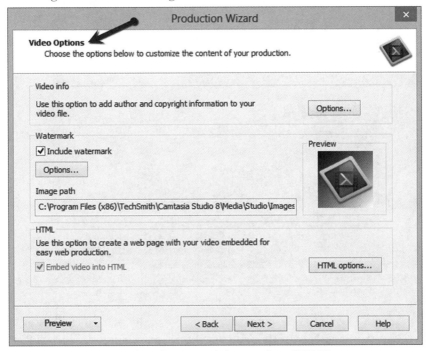

FIGURE 9.25 — Video Options (video info, watermark, image path, and HTML).

The watermark options button opens a pop-up dialog box (See Figure 9.26). The default watermark is a Camtasia icon indicating that the project was created using the program. The icon can be changed to your custom image by browsing through the navigation browse button. The checkboxes and slider bars change the image look, scale, and position when overlaid on your video project.

Click **Next** to continue through the **Production Wizard**. At this point, if there is no table of contents or quizzes, the wizard would skip the new few steps and proceed to the **Produce Video** dialog box. For this sample, both the table of contents and quiz functions are activated.

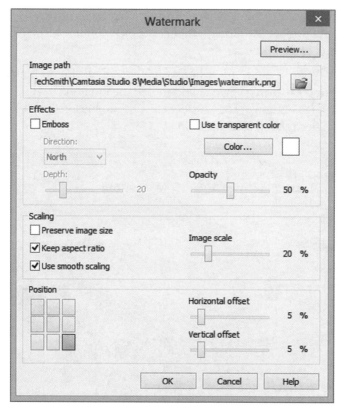

FIGURE 9.26 — Watermark (image path, effects, scaling, position, transparent color, opacity, image scale, plus horizontal and vertical offset).

If your video includes markers, the name of the markers will show in the table of contents list. In the **Marker Options** dialog box, the checkmark next to the list will toggle on and off if that marker will be part of the final production. You can rename, show a thumbnail image, and number the listings. The table of contents display can be moved to the left or right side of the video player (See Figure 9.27).

Click **Next** to continue to the **Quiz Reporting Options** dialog box (See Figure 9.28). The quiz appearance can be adjusted and previewed.

The viewer's quiz results can be sent through e-mail or using **SCORM**.

(Key Term) **SCORM (Shareable Content Object Reference Model)** — standards for Web-based e-learning and shows how to transfer to zip files.

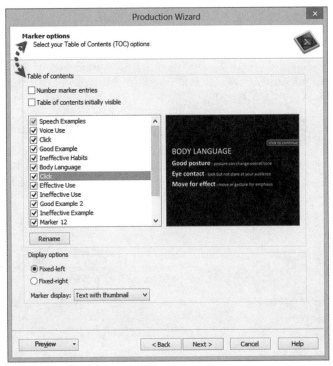

FIGURE 9.27 — Marker options (table of contents, display options, and marker display and number).

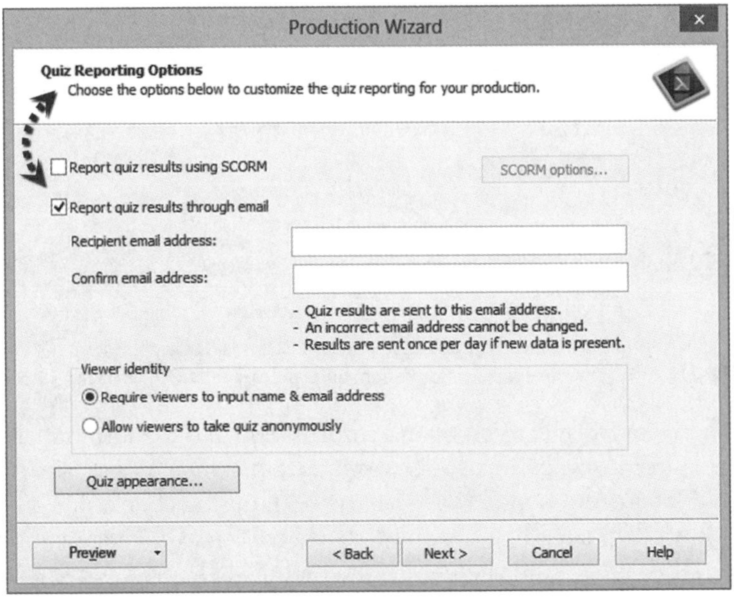

FIGURE 9.28 — Quiz Reporting Options (SCORM, e-mail, recipient's address, viewer identify).

Net Search SCORM — Perform a search on the Internet to see how and when it can be used in your project.

If the using **SCORM** checkbox is activated, the **SCORM options** button will become active and will open the **Manifest Options** in a pop-up dialog box (See Figure 9.29).

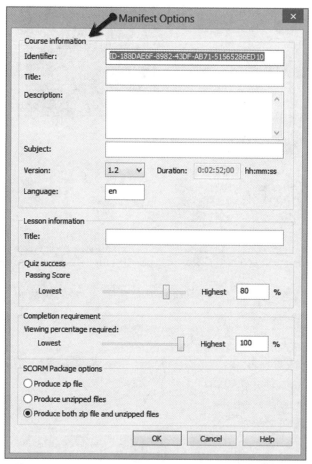

FIGURE 9.29 — Manifest Options (course information, quiz success, and SCORM package options).

These controls focus on course information and organization along with quiz requirements. There are also options to produce files as .zip, unzipped, or both. It is recommended to leave the both option checked. A .zip file can be uploaded to sites like Moodle or other Course Management Systems (CMS), Learning Management Systems (LMS), or a Virtual Learning Environment (VLE) service.

MOODLE (Modular Object-Oriented Dynamic Learning Environment) — open source course management system used by educational institutions to create online courses. It can include participants, course schedule, assignments, quizzes, student comments, forums, glossaries, and links to resources.

Key Term

Net Search **Moodle** — Perform an Internet search to learn how Moodle can be used in the classroom.

Click **Next** to continue to the last step before rendering your video. Enter the name and save the location of your video in the **Produce Video** dialog box (See Figure 9.30). It is recommended to keep the **Organize produced files into sub folders** box checked if producing with most than a video only option.

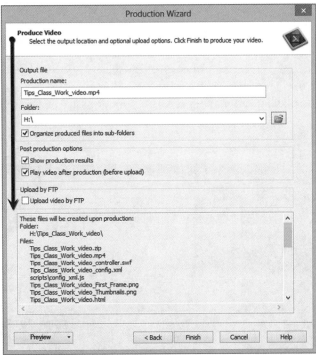

FIGURE 9.30 — Produce Video (output file, folder, post production options, and upload by FTP).

Check or uncheck the post production actions of showing production results and video playback. Check the upload by FTP to activate the FTP Setting dialog box at the start of the rendering process to enter server, path, and port information.

Key Term **File Transfer Protocol (FTP)** — protocol for exchanging files with another computer.

The **Preview button** will produce a short temporary sample of the video with the current settings. If unsatisfied, click the back button to navigate back through the **Production Wizard** to make adjustments.

Click **Finish** to start the video production process. The render time will vary depending on the project length, quality, and computer equipment (See Figure 9.31).

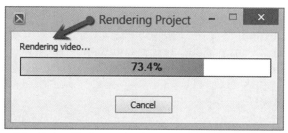

FIGURE 9.31 — Rendering Project 73.4% completed.

Once the rendering process is finished, the video playback will be available to review depending on your production settings (See Figure 9.32). Check the playback to make sure all the functions are working without errors.

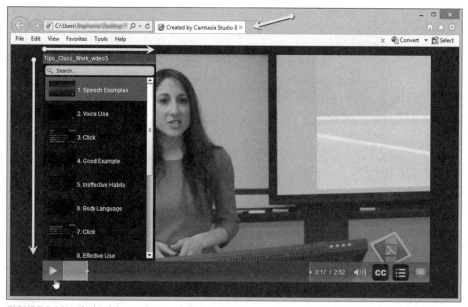

FIGURE 9.32 — Playback key on bottom left corner.

Close the video player and view the **Production Results** dialog box for an overview of the rendered project (See Figure 9.33).

FIGURE 9.33 — Production is complete (results are shown, can create a production preset, and open production folder).

If the custom setting is one that you will use again, you can save the setting as a preset by clicking on the **Create production preset** button. To open the folder with newly created files, click the **Open production folder** button. This will open a window showing the files (See Figure 9.34).

The **.mp4** file is your video file. The other files within the folder and sub-folders are player, feature, and embedding support files. It is recommended to leave the video file within the folder although you can make a copy of the file to use individually. Some features will not work without the player or support files.

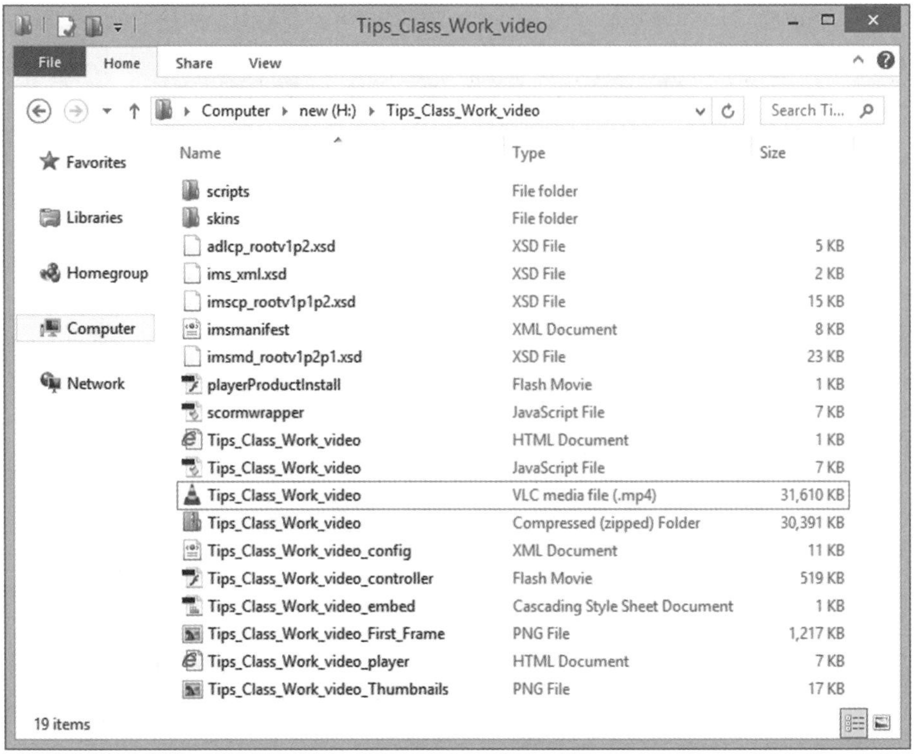

FIGURE 9.34 — The folder Tips_Class_Work_Video shows files produced through the rendering process.

9.4b — WMV — Windows Media Video (.wmv)

The **.wmv** file format is a good balance between quality and file size. The main drawback is the lack of full video feature support, like hotspots, and the availability of support for some video players.

Advantages

- Excellent quality
- Smaller file size

Disadvantages

- Limited mobile device support
- Not all players will be able to play this format, not native to Mac
- Will not support extra video options like quizzes and hotspots

Quick List: Custom .wmv Production

1. Open the **Production Wizard**

2. From the dropdown menu, select a **Custom production setting**, then click **Next**

3. Select **WMV-Windows Media** output option, then click **Next**

4. From the **Windows Media Encoding Options**, select an encoding profile, then click **Next**

5. Set the dimensions of the video in the **Video Size** dialog box, then click **Next**

6. Set the **Video Options** settings

7. *Optional:* Add meta data and the **Watermark**

8. Optional: Use the embed to HTML option for a marker based table of contents

9. *Optional:* Create multiple videos based on the markers in the **Markers Options**

10. Click **Next**

11. In the **Produce Video**, select save file destination and name

12. Click **Finish** to render the video

13. Click **Finish** after verifying production results

A Closer Look — Custom .wmv Production

After selecting the custom dropdown menu from the **Production Wizard**, select the **.wmv** format. If your video contains video features like a quiz, captions, hotspots, or markers, it will have a **warning** pop-up window alerting you that the features will be tuned off or changed. For example, if the captions were closed, they will lose that ability and remain open throughout the playback. After reading the warnings, close the window to continue. If your video project does not have any of these features, you will not see the warning.

The **Production Wizard** will next navigate to the **Windows Media Encoding Options** dialog box to select a profile (See Figure 9.35). The

Camtasia Studio Best Quality and File Size (recommended) profile for the best balance and quality and size. This is the default setting and best to leave as is unless your project needs a different profile specifically.

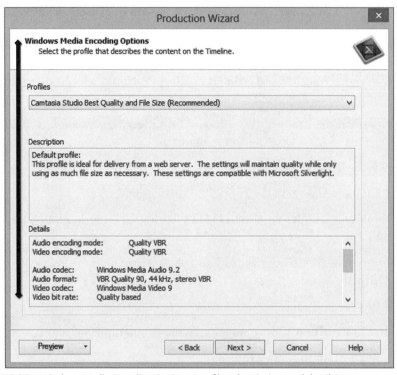

FIGURE 9.35 — Windows Media Encoding Options (profiles, description, and details).

FIGURE 9.36 — Video size (editing dimensions video size or custom size plus a preview).

Next is the **Video Size** options window. Here are controls to keep the recording size or to resize the final video. It is recommended to always keep the **Maintain aspect ratio** box checked. With this checked, if you change the width of the video; the height will change accordingly to keep the ratio (See Figure 9.36).

Next are the **Video Options** window and **Marker Options** window, if your project has markers. These are generally the same as the .mp4 step-by-step with a few changes. One difference is that the **SCROM** settings are under the **Video Options** (See Figure 9.37).

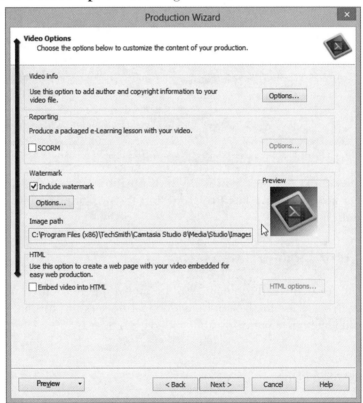

FIGURE 9.37 — Video options (video info, reporting, watermark, image path, and HTML plus preview).

Another difference is that to include a table of contents using the timeline markers, you have to select the **Embed video into HTML** checkbox. This will embed the video into a **HTML code** and player with a selectable table of contents. If your video project is over the size you are using for the HTML setting, you will need to decrease the **Video Size** settings to fit (See Figure 9.38).

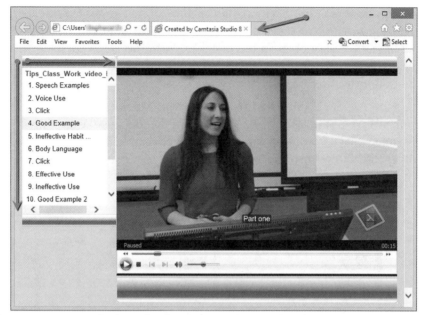

FIGURE 9.38 — An example of a produced .wmv HTML video to a table of contents.

Click **Next** see the **Produce Video options** to name your video and select a save location. Click **Finish** to start the rendering process and view production results.

9.4c — MOV — QuickTime Movie (.mov)

The **.mov** file is flexible and can be embedded into different settings. The drawbacks are the lack of full video feature support, like hotspots, and the availability of support for some video players.

Advantages
- Native video format for Macs
- Plays in iTunes, QuickTime, or other 3rd party players on Windows

Disadvantages
- Limited mobile device support
- Not all video players will be able to play this format
- Not native to Windows
- Will not support extra video options like quizzes and hotspots

Quick List: Custom .mov Production

1. Open the **Production Wizard**

2. From the dropdown menu, select a **Custom production setting**, then click **Next**

3. Select **MOV-QuickTime movie** output option, then click **Next**

4. From the **QuickTime Encoding Options** select **QuickTime options** to adjust settings, then click **Next**

5. Set the dimensions of the video in the **Video Size** dialog box, then click **Next**

6. Set the **Video Options** settings

7. *Optional:* Add meta data and a **Watermark**

8. *Optional:* Use the embed to HTML option for a marker based table of contents

9. *Optional:* Create multiple videos based on the markers in the Markers Options

10. Click **Next**

11. In the **Produce Video**, select save file destination and name

12. Click **Finish** to render the video

13. Click **Finish** after verifying production results

The **.mov** production process is very similar to the **.wmv** production process. The main difference is the **QuickTime Encoding Options** and **Movie Setting** dialog boxes.

To start, select the **.mov** file format in the Production Wizard. A **warning** pop-up window will show alerting you if your video features like quizzes, captions, hotspots, or markers, will be tuned off or changed. Then navigate through the **Production Wizard** to the **QuickTime Encoding Options** dialog box to view format details (See Figure 9.39). The QuickTime options button opens the **Movie Setting** dialog box to change the format settings.

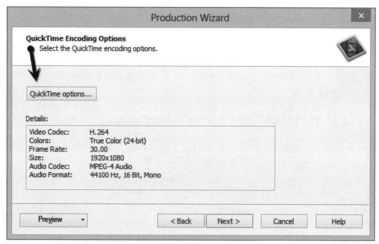

FIGURE 9.39 — QuickTime Encoding Options (options, details, and preview).

Next are the **Video Size**, **Video Options**, **Marker Options**, and **Produce Video Options**. These dialog boxes work the same as in the **.wmv** production setting. Click **Finish** to start the rendering process and view production results.

9.4d — AVI — Audio Video Interleave Video File (.avi)

An **.avi** file format keeps the highest quality during recording and is a good format for editing in Camtasia Studio or other video editing programs. However, the file size of the project will be larger and cannot support video features like hotspots and quizzes.

Advantages

- A standard video format

- Excellent overall quality

- Good to use with additional video editors

- Neutral format that is not bound to Mac or Windows programs

Disadvantages

- Not recommended as a sharable format because it uses specific audio and video codecs that will be required if played on another machine

- Will not support extra video options like quizzes and hotspots

Quick List: Custom .avi Production

1. Open the **Production Wizard**

2. From the dropdown menu, select a **Custom production setting**, then click **Next**

3. Select **AVI-Audio Video Interleave** output option, then click **Next**

4. From the **AVI Encoding Options**, select **Video Compression** and **Audio format options** to adjust settings, then click **Next**

5. Set the dimensions of the video in the **Video Size** dialog box, then click **Next**

6. Set the **Video Options** settings

7. *Optional:* Add meta data and a **Watermark**

8. *Optional:* Use the embed to HTML option for a marker based table of contents

9. *Optional:* Create multiple videos based on the markers in the **Markers Options**

10. Click **Next**

11. In the **Produce Video**, select save file destination and name

12. Click **Finish** to render the video

13. Click **Finish** after verifying production results

The **.avi** production process is very similar to the **.wmv** and **.mov** production processes. The main difference is the **AVI Encoding Options** dialog box.

Select the **.avi** file format in the **Production Wizard**. A warning pop-up window will show alerting you if your video features like quizzes, captions, hotspots, or markers, will be tuned off or changed.

Navigate through the **Production Wizard** to the **AVI Encoding Options** dialog box to view format details (See Figure 9.40). The **Video Compression** and **Audio format options** buttons change the compression audio settings.

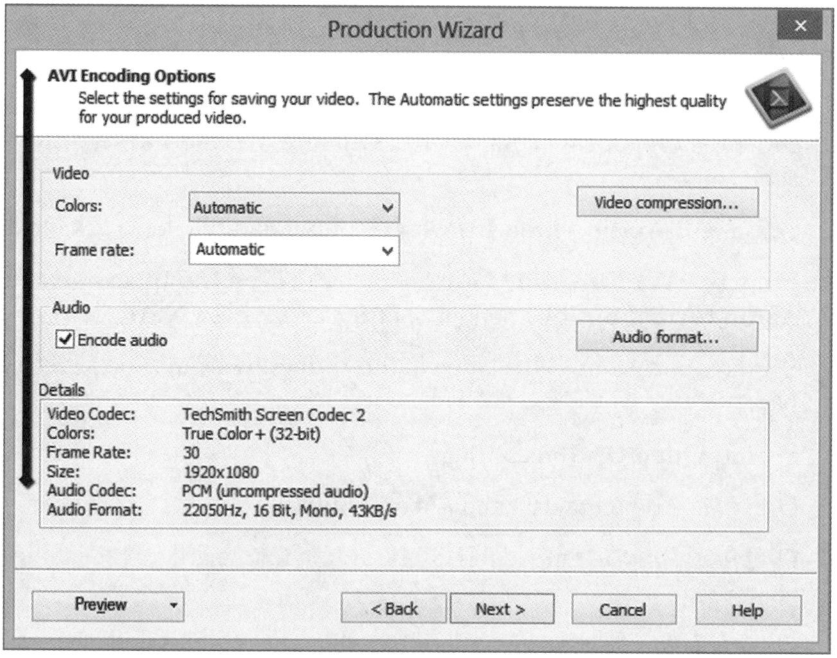

FIGURE 9.40 — AVI Encoding Options (video color and frame rate, audio, details, and preview).

The **Video Size**, **Video Options**, **Marker Options**, and **Produce Video Options** dialog boxes work the same as in the **.wmv** and **.mov** production settings. Click **Finish** to start the rendering process and view production results.

NOTE ***The TechSmith Screen Capture Codec (TSC2)**, as the default Camtasia Studio video compressor for .avi file formats, might need to be changed depending on the video player.*

NOTE *The **.avi** format can be saved through the Camtasia Recorder.*

9.4e — M4V — iPod, iPhone, iTunes Compatible Video (.m4v)

The **.m4v** format is designed to be used by Apple products such as iPods, iPhones, and iTunes. The smaller video playback size for these devices highlights the SmartFocus and Zoom-n-Pan video animations. This format cannot support video features like hotspots and quizzes.

Advantages

- Synchronization with iPod and iPhone through iTunes
- Older iPods and iPhones can play the format

Disadvantages

- Smaller video dimensions
- Close to the popular .mp4 format without the advantages
- Will not support extra video options like quizzes and hotspots

Quick List: Custom .m4v Production

1. Open the **Production Wizard**
2. From the dropdown menu, select a **Custom production setting**, then click **Next**
3. Select **M4V-iPod, iPhone, iTunes compatible** output option, then click **Next**
4. From the **iPod Options** window, select video size
5. *Optional:* Click **Options** to enter video information
6. Click **Next**
7. In the **Produce Video**, select save file destination and name
8. Click **Finish** to render the video
9. Click **Finish** after verifying production results

There are fewer options for video features when using the **.m4v** format. To produce with the file format, navigate through the **Production Wizard** to the **iPod Options** window. Select a file size from the dropdown menu (See Figure 9.41).

Use the **Produce Video options** dialog box to enter file name, folder structure, and save location. Click **Finish** to start the rendering process and view production results.

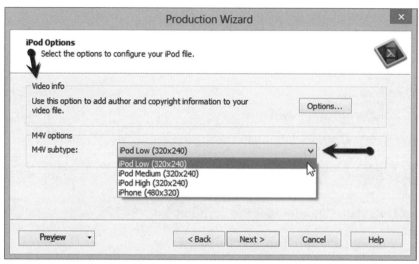

FIGURE 9.41 — iPod Options (video info, M4V subtype, and preview).

9.4f — MP3 — Audio Only (.mp3)

There are times where you might need to send or post only an audio track of your project. The **.mp3** file format is an audio only format and does not contain video.

Advantages

- Excellent audio quality
- Standard audio format

Disadvantages

- Audio only format

Quick List: Custom .mp3 Production

1. Open the **Production Wizard**

2. From the dropdown menu, select a **Custom production setting**, then click **Next**

3. Select **MP3-audio only** output option, then click **Next**

4. From the **MP3 Encoding Options** and select a bit rate from the dropdown, then click **Next**

5. *Optional:* From the **Options** button, enter video metadata

6. In the **Produce Video**, select save file destination and name

7. Click **Finish** to render the video

8. Click **Finish** after verifying production results

Navigate through the **Production Wizard** to the **MP3 Encoding Options** window. Select the bit rate from the dropdown menu (See Figure 9.42). Mono, Stereo, kHz, and Bits/sec selections are available in the list with the larger the number the larger the quality and file size.

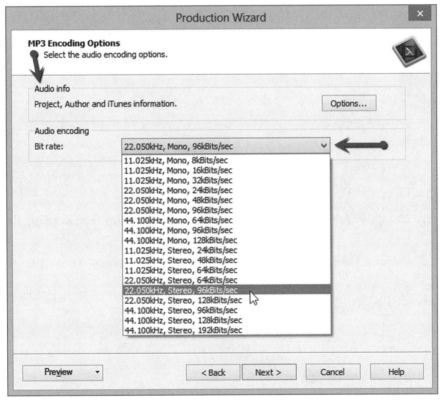

FIGURE 9.42 — MP3 Encoding Options (audio info, audio encoding, and preview).

In the **Produce Video options** dialog box, enter file name and save location. Select the folder structure. Click **Finish** to start the rendering process and view production results.

9.4g — GIF — Animation File (.gif)

The **.gif** format overall is a low quality video format. Its advantage is that the file sizes are very small and they can be embedded in Websites or e-mails where the sizes of the files are an issue.

Advantages

- File sizes are small

- Can be embed in e-mails or Websites

Disadvantages

- This file format does not include audio tracks

- Low overall quality

- Only 256 colors

- Supports only short videos

- Will not support extra video options like quizzes and hotspots

Quick List: Custom .gif Production

1. Open the **Production Wizard**

2. From the dropdown menu, select a **Custom production setting**, then click **Next**

3. Select **GIF-animation** output option, then click **Next**

4. From the **Animated GIF Encoding Options**, adjust settings, then click **Next**

5. Set the dimensions of the video in the **Video Size** dialog box, then click **Next**

6. Set the **Video Options** settings

7. *Optional:* Add meta data and a **Watermark**

8. *Optional:* Use the embed to HTML option for a marker based table of contents

9. *Optional:* Create multiple videos based on the markers in the **Markers Options**

10. Click **Next**

11. In the **Produce Video**, select save file destination and name

12. Click **Finish** to render the video

13. Click **Finish** after verifying production results

Even though the quality and video sizes are small, the **.gif** format production process acts similar to the **.wmv**, **.mov**, and **.avi** formats.

Select the **.gif** file format in the **Production Wizard**. A **warning** pop-up window will show alerting you if your video has features like quizzes, captions, hotspots, table of contents, or markers, will be tuned off or changed.

Navigate through the **Production Wizard** to the **Animated GIF Encoding Options** dialog (See Figure 9.43). Select from 4, 8, 16, 32, 64, 128, 256 colors, and video looping options.

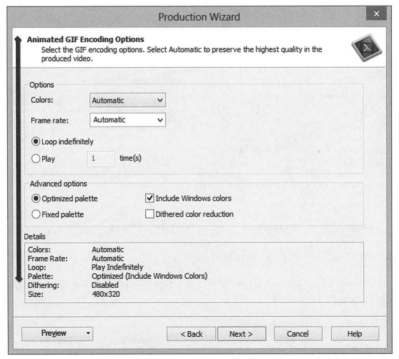

FIGURE 9.43 — Animated GIF Encoding Options (color, frame, loop, play, advanced options, details, and preview).

Next are the **Video Size**, **Video Options**, **Marker Options**, and **Produce Video Options**. Click **Finish** to start the rendering process and view production results.

9.5 — Add or Edit Presets

After using a custom setting to produce your video, you can save that setting and make it into a preset to use for other videos without having to redo all of the settings again. You can also share the new save preset with coworkers and friends (See Figure 9.44).

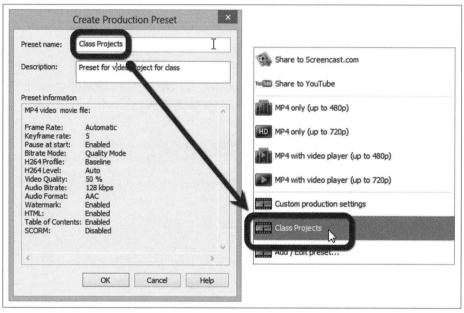

FIGURE 9.44 – Create Production Preset (preset name, description, and preset information).

Quick List: Save a Custom Production Setting as a Preset

1. Open the **Production Wizard**

2. From the dropdown menu, select a **Custom production setting**, then click **Next**

3. Adjust the settings through the wizard

4. Click **Finish** on the Produce Video screen to render the video

5. When the **Production Results** screen appears, click the **Create a Production Preset** button

6. The **Create Production Preset** dialog appears

7. Enter a name and description for the preset, then click **OK**, then click **Finish**

8. The new production preset is now in the **Production Wizard** dropdown list

Add or Edit a Production Preset

From the **Production Wizard** dropdown menu, select the **Add/Edit preset** selection to open the **Manage Preset** dialog box (See Figure 9.45).

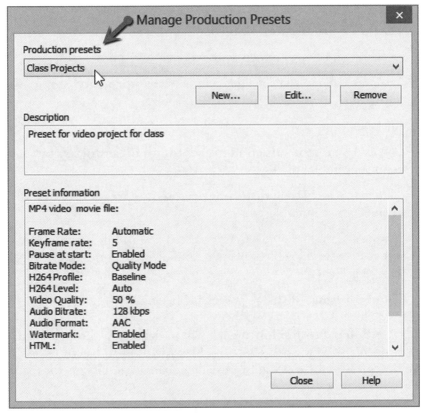

FIGURE 9.45 — Manage Production Presets (production presets, description, and present information).

Select the preset that you wish to edit or remove from the dropdown menu, then select the appropriate button. Click **New** as another way to add a preset.

9.6 — Batch and Advance Processing

If you have multiple video projects that are ready to be rendered, you can batch the production process to render the videos at the same time.

Quick List: Batch Produce Using Presets

1. Open the **Editor**

2. Select from the from the Menu Options, **Tools > Sharing > Batch Production**

3. The **Batch Production** wizard opens

4. Click the Add Files/Projects button then select the video files

5. Acceptable file formats include **.camrec**, **.camproj**, **.avi**, **.mpg**, **.wmv**, **.mov**, **.avi**

6. Click **Next**

7. Choose **Use one production preset for all files/projects** option to use one preset for all files

8. *Optional:* Select **Use a different production preset for each file/ project** to use multiple presets

9. *Optional:* If multiple presets are selected, the **Batch Production — select Preset** dialog box will open for individual preset to file selection, then click **Next**

10. Click **Finish** and the batch processing begins

The **Batch Production** wizard will navigate you through each step. After opening the wizard, select the files you want to batch render. Click **Next**, then select if you want to use one or multiple presets for the video files (See Figure 9.46).

If the using multiple presets option is selected, the **Batch Production — Select Preset** will have dropdown menus for each file (See Figure 9.47).

Once the presets are selected, click **Finish** to start the **Rendering Batch Production** (See Figure 9.48).

FIGURE 9.46 — Batch Production — Preset Options (preset or different production preset).

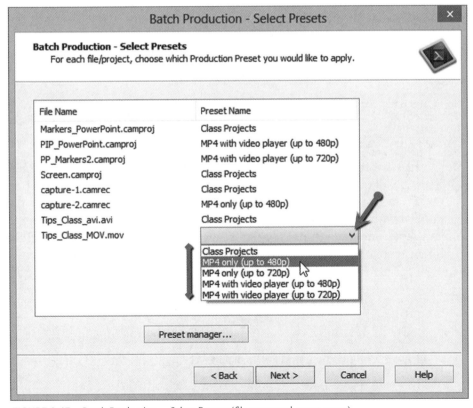

FIGURE 9.47 — Batch Production — Select Presets (file name and preset name).

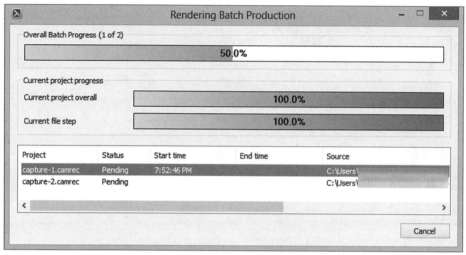

FIGURE 9.48 — Rendering Batch Production (Overall Batch Progress, current project progress, current project overall, current file step).

You can view the production results and files once the rendering is complete.

CHAPTER SUMMARY

In Chapter 9, we have learned a variety of ways of producing and sharing videos using the Production Wizard. There are many production presets available to use and it is suggested you use them until you become familiar with customizing your own settings. Each format has its advantages and disadvantages and you need to be careful which you choose. Snagit in the next chapter will expand your knowledge of screen captures.

CHAPTER PROJECTS

1. Review a short movie/presentation and find five ways to improve it.

2. How do you produce a MP4 flash/HTML5 with player and why?

3. How would you share and publish your video on YouTube, or Screencast.com?

4. Name four production formats. Why and when would you use them?

5. Explain how you would customize a video and audio recording setting.

6. List nine important ideas you learned from the first nine chapters (one from each chapter) of this book and why do you think they are important?

7. Plan a presentation using five things you have learned in this chapter.

8. Perform a search about video resolution and the differences between 480p and 720p and how they interact with the aspect ratio.

9. Perform a search on the Internet to see how and when SCORM can be used in your project. If it can't, why not?

10. Explain the six production preset options in detail and their advantages.

11. What is Screencast.com? Who developed it and how do you use it?

12. How are the .mp4 presets different and which would you use and when?

13. Describe a Moodle project and how you would use its features?

14. What do you need to know about the aspect ratio box and why is it important?

15. Make a chart showing the advantages and disadvantages of using .mp4, .wmv, .mov, .avi, .m4v, .mp3, and .gif.

3

SNAGIT AND JING

CHAPTER 10

SNAGIT

IN THIS CHAPTER

Over the next two chapters, you will learn to develop and produce high-quality screen captures using Snagit, the capture media application developed by TechSmith. In these chapters, we will cover the most current Snagit versions available, Snagit Version 11 for Windows OS and Snagit Version 2 for Mac OS X. Within the application, the main capturing and editing capabilities are divided into two separate interfaces. In this chapter, we will introduce you to the capability and design of Snagit and learn to operate the capture interface. You will learn how to use the capture interface to define a capture's region, method, and type. By the end of this chapter, you will be able to create still and moving images from the visual output of your computer.

Once you've completed this chapter, you will be able to:

- Introduce Snagit
- Learn to navigate the Snagit Capture Interface for Version 11 and Version 2
- Cover the different types and modes of screen capture in Snagit
- Isolate and select image and video capture regions
- Use the different capture tools to enhance and customize your captures

Files: All figures in this chapter are in color located in the chapter folder on the DVD.

10.1 — Introduction to Snagit

Businesses and individuals are often faced with the task of presenting an idea or concept that does not translate well into words. In some instances, visual communication can be more effective and efficient than a long written explanation or tutorial. Visuals can also be a great supplement for a presentation or report. Using Snagit, the capture media tool developed by TechSmith, you can create and produce images for visual communication using the visual output from your computer. This software can be used as a standalone application or in conjunction with other software applications such as MS Office, Adobe Photoshop, and Camtasia Studio. The necessary system requirements to run Snagit on a Windows OS and a Mac OS X are shown below in Figure 10.1.

Windows System Requirements
Microsoft Windows XP with (32-bit only), Vista, Windows 7, or Windows 8 (32-bit and 64-bit) installed and configured for Video
NET 4.0 or later required for Video
2.4 GHz single core processor (2.4 GHz dual core required for video)
1 GB of RAM (2 GB required for video)
125 MB of free hard disk space
Internet Explorer 8.0 or later
Mac OS X System Requirements
10.6.8 (Snow Leopard), 10.7 (Lion), 10.8 (Mountain Lion), or higher
Intel processor (dual core 2.0 GHz or faster)
2 GB of RAM or greater
64-bit only

FIGURE 10.1 — Snagit Version 11 for Windows and Version 2 for MAC system requirements.

Within Snagit, the bulk of capturing and editing functionalities are separated into two separate interfaces. The capture interface allows you to turn visual output such as a desktop, software application, or menu into a screen capture that can be edited in the editing interface.

Screen Capture — a still or moving snapshot of a computer's visual output. A screen capture is also known as a screen dump, screen grab, or screenshot.

From the **Snagit Editor**, you can manipulate the captured image with visual enhancements in order to tell a story, convey a message, or create a mood. With Snagit, step-by-step instructions are a thing of the past. You can now use images to convey your message or compile a set of images to create a storyboard. Your audience can follow along with you visually and you can illustrate your intended meaning with clarity increasing their chances of retention and understanding.

In this chapter, we will learn how to operate the capture interface and adjust capture settings according to the content of your visual output. The **Snagit Editor**, which houses the bulk of your editing tools and capture management functionalities, will be covered extensively in the following chapter.

10.2 — Capture Interface

Screen captures are a virtual photograph or recording of your computer's visual output. The capture interface functions as your virtual camera. You can use the capture interface as we have throughout this book to capture images of an application, tool, menu, or object. You can also create images from content on the Internet by snagging snap shots of your browser. No matter the visual content on your computer screen, it can be captured if you have the right settings selected in the capture interface.

By default, the capture interface opens whenever you run Snagit. This is where you will define your capture type, method, and region for your still and moving captures. While certain functionalities overlap, the interface will look completely different depending on which operating system you are using. In addition, Version 11 has additional tools and functionalities that you will not find in Version 2. Therefore, it is important that you acquaint yourself with the version of Snagit you will be working in.

10.2a — Snagit Version 11 Capture Interface

The capture interface for Version 11 that you see in Figure 10.2 is commonly referred to as **Snagit**.

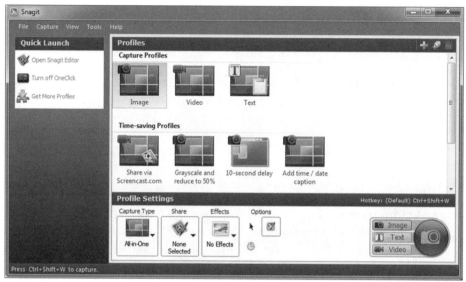

FIGURE 10.2 — Version 11 Snagit interface.

Across the top of the window is a traditional **menu bar**. A majority of the tools and capabilities found within the **Snagit** menus can be directly accessed from the interface. In addition to the menu bar, **Snagit** is divided into three separate sub-windows: the **Quick Launch** window, the **Profiles** window, and the **Profile Settings** window. The Quick Launch window allows for easy accessibility to additional functionalities in Snagit. From here you can access the Snagit Editor or download and install additional accessories from TechSmith to further customize Snagit. In this window, you can also access **OneClick** shown in Figure 10.3. This is an additional capture pop-out window designed so that it can be easily accessed from your desktop.

FIGURE 10.3 — Snagit OneClick.

You may not always know exactly when or what you will want to capture. Having the Snagit window open all the time would make it difficult to navigate your desktop and other windows. OneClick allows you to capture something at a moment's notice, but stays minimized along the edges of your desktop when not in use. To move OneClick to a different location on the edge of your desktop, click and drag the window. Whenever you need to create a screen capture, hover over OneClick to reveal the capture functionalities. Take a quick capture by pressing the red capture button. The two icons directly to the left of the **capture button** will allow you to change between video and camera mode. To take captures even faster, select from the predefined **profiles** by selecting the **arrow icon**.

Profiles are an easy and efficient way of storing information about commonly used captures and capture settings. A profile is made up of the capture **mode**, capture **type**, **sharing output**, and various **effects** for a commonly used screen capture.

Key Term

Profiles — allow you to store a number of settings and functionalities for commonly used screen captures. When selected, the profile will initiate a capture according to its preformatted properties.

This will be a little easier to understand once we have fully covered all of the components that make up a **Profile**, but think about the following example to illustrate a Profile's functionality: You are a local food critic and write a daily blog about the latest new eatery or tasty find. The blog always includes a variety of pictures from the different restaurants' Websites to keep your posts dynamic and visually appealing. It is important that all of the pictures are cohesive so they match the theme of the blog. Therefore, all of the images need to include a custom trim with a watermark of your logo. You can include all of these settings in your profile along with sending it directly to your blog at WordPress.com. With this newly configured profile, you can now easily create captures for your blog that are sent directly where you need them while still maintaining image and design continuity. The default Capture and Time-Saving Profiles can be found in the Profiles window on the Snagit interface. As you start to recognize and develop your individual capture needs, you will most likely want to begin customizing these default profiles and adding new ones to the list.

NOTE *Profiles are exclusive to Version 11 and are currently not available if you are running Version 2 of Snagit on your Mac OSX.*

The last sub-window of Snagit is the **Profile Settings** window. This is where you will create those new profiles we just discussed and edit any of the preexisting profiles. However, you can also make selections in this window for a single capture. If you are just beginning and don't have a lot of preformatted profiles to choose from, you can set up and start your capture from the Profile Settings window shown in Figure 10.4.

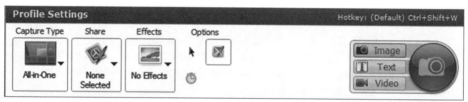

FIGURE 10.4 — Profile Settings window in Snagit.

The far left-hand icon, **Capture Type**, contains a dropdown list of capture types to help you select and define the area of the computer screen you are capturing. The next icon, **Share Output** offers different destinations to upload your capture to.

Share Output — a capture destination that has been configured with Snagit for quick and easy sharing. A number **Key Term** of outputs come preinstalled or you can download additional outputs from the TechSmith Website. You will learn more about outputs in Chapter 11.

If you choose the share output for your capture in Snagit, it will automatically be uploaded to the selected destination. If you want to edit your capture before sharing, select **None Selected**, shown in Figure 10.4. This will automatically open your capture in the Snagit Editor.

The **clock icon** in the **Options** panel of Figure 10.4 allows you to delay a screen capture or set up a specific date and time for Snagit to take a screen capture. Additionally, you can set up a timer that will take screen captures at scheduled time intervals. This could be especially useful if you need to monitor the activity on a personal or company machine. For example, if you are concerned about your child's Internet activity, you can set up the capture timer to take a screen capture every hour. Now you have a series of images that can give you an indication of the type of sites and content viewed on your home computer. The **arrow icon**, if selected, will include your cursor in your capture.

NOTE *You can also include your cursor in a screen capture by selecting Capture > Capture Type > Include Cursor. A check mark will appear next to the menu selection whenever activated.*

The last icon in the options panel is the **Snagit Editor Icon**. Selecting this icon will send your screen captures to the Snagit Editor before uploading them to your selected share output.

NOTE *The icons in the Options panel will have a square, grey border surrounding them whenever they are selected.*

The most important button of all in Snagit is the easiest to operate. The large red **capture button** in Figure 10.4 is used to initiate a capture whenever you are ready. The three icons to the left are used to select the **capture mode**, which we will cover later in the chapter. You can also use the **Hotkey** to initiate your screen capture, which is set to **Print Screen** by default.

Key Term **Hotkey** — the keyboard shortcut assigned to a command or tool in Snagit Version 11.

In most cases, you will want to hide Snagit while you are using capture to get a clear view of your screen capture and make it easier for your capture types to recognize any of the preselected regions. To do so, select **Tools > Program Preferences**. This will open the **Program Preferences dialog box**. From here select **Program Options** as illustrated in Figure 10.5.

From this tab, select **Hide Snagit before Capturing** if it is not already check marked. This will minimize Snagit as soon as you initiate your capture using the red capture button or one of the Snagit Profiles.

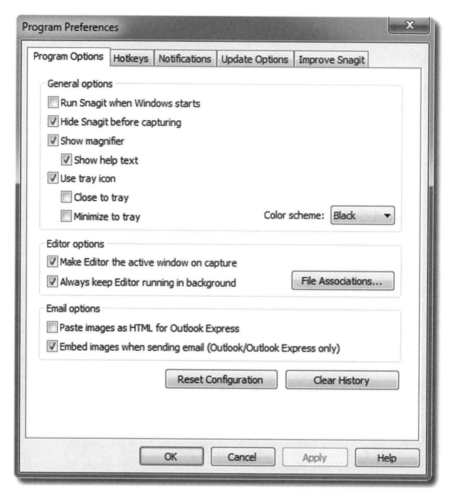

FIGURE 10.5 – Program Options tab in Program Preferences dialog box.

10.2b — Snagit Version 2 Capture Interface

The major capture tools and functionalities in Version 2 are condensed into a small pop-out interface referred to by Snagit users as the **Capture Window**. When the application is running but not in use, the window is minimized by default on the right side of your desktop. To maximize the window, hover over the minimized tab and it will expand out to the window shown in Figure 10.6. If you want to move the window from its default location, click and drag the window along the edges of your desktop.

FIGURE 10.6 — Version 2 capture window.

FIGURE 10.7 — Floating capture window.

You can permanently expand the capture window by dragging it away from the edge and dropping the window onto the desktop. This creates the **floating capture window** you see in Figure 10.7.

This floating capture window also contains options to **maximize**, **minimize**, or **exit** the capture window. If you exit out of the capture window, it can be reopened from the **Snagit menu icon** located on **desktop menu bar** shown in Figure 10.8.

FIGURE 10.8 — Snagit icon on the Mac menu bar.

You probably have noticed many of the icons in Figures 10.6 and 10.7. Let's explore the different functions these icons have to offer. The red circular button you see in Figure 10.9 is the **capture button** used to begin taking a screen capture.

FIGURE 10.9 – Capture button.

However, before you begin capturing, you have a few choices to make. First, you need to determine what mode you want to use to take your capture. Do you want to take a video or image capture? You can make this selection with the two **capture mode icons** to the immediate left of the capture icon in Figure 10.9. The **camera icon** will perform an **image capture** and the icon that displays a filmstrip will initiate a **video capture**. A blue color fill is used to indicate a selected icon. Additionally, the icon on the capture button will change to reflect your currently selected capture mode. So using Figure 10.9 as an example, the camera is highlighted blue and the camera image appears on the capture button so you are in image capture mode.

There are some other additional selections that you can make in the capture window. If you don't want the mouse cursor to appear in the capture, unselect the **arrow icon** as is done in Figure 10.9. When selected, the **clipboard icon** directly to the right of the cursor icon will automatically store your capture to the clipboard. This is useful if you wish to copy your capture directly into another application, such as Microsoft Word without first editing the image.

(Key Term)

Clipboard – a temporary storage area on your computer where data that is copied from one application, such as text or an image, is stored for use in another application.

Continuing to work our way down the capture window, we will find some important shortcut icons. These icons have been circled in Figure 10.10 for easy identification.

The first of these shortcuts is the **text field**, which displays the **capture**

FIGURE 10.10 – Shortcut icons in the capture window.

keyboard shortcut. Using the keys displayed in the text field allows you to quickly initiate your screen captures according to the selected capture mode.

*The default capture shortcuts for Version 2 are **Control + Shift + C** for image capture and **Control + Shift + V** for video capture. You can assign your own shortcuts by selecting **capture preferences** in the dropdown menu from the Snagit menu bar icon in Figure 10.8. This will open the keyboard dialog box in Figure 10.11.*

FIGURE 10.11 — Keyboard shortcut preferences dialog box.

Lastly, from left to right in Figure 10.10 are the Snagit Editor icon, Help icon, and the Setting Preferences icon. The **editor icon** allows you to quickly access the Snagit Editor for capture review and editing. **Help** provides you with helpful tips and explanations if you get lost or confused while taking a screen capture. Selecting the **Setting Preferences icon** will expand the capture window so you can select additional options for your captures. The expanded capture window is displayed in Figure 10.12.

FIGURE 10.12 — Expanded capture window.

From this view of the window, you can assign the Editor to run immediately after you get done taking your screen capture by checking the **Preview in Editor** box. You can also give yourself time to set up for your capture by selecting the **Delay Capture** box and choosing your desired time from the dropdown menu.

10.3 — Capture Modes

Capture Modes are very similar to the shooting modes of a camera. You may not be readily familiar with the term shooting modes, but you are likely to recognize them by their name or function. There are a number of different images that a photographer might take. He might take an action shot, a still shot, or a night shot, for instance. To capture any one of these he needs to adjust the shooting mode to correspond with the shot he wants to take. For an action shot, he would need the camera's shooting mode to be in Sports Mode; when taking pictures at night, he would need the camera to be in Night Mode. The different shooting modes adjust the settings needed for that particular kind of shot. The camera's shooting mode is equivalent to the **capture mode**. The different capture modes adjust the capture settings to capture and produce a particular kind of screen capture.

(Key Term) **Capture Mode** — a group of settings that define the method of screen capture.

The two most common capture modes in both versions of Snagit are **Image Capture Mode** and **Video Capture Mode**. The next few sections will break down when and how to use the different modes for each of the two versions.

NOTE *Remember that for both versions, the available capture mode icons are adjacent to the* **capture button** *in the capture interface and should be selected before you initiate your capture. However, Version 11 has one other additional capture mode,* **Printer Capture***, which will not be found with the other capture mode icons. This mode is used for turning the print materials from external applications into digital media. You can access this mode directly from the external application by selecting* **File > Print** *and selecting* **Snagit 11** *from the dropdown list of printers.*

10.3a — Image Capture Mode

Image capture mode is the default capture mode in both Snagit versions. This mode creates still images from any number of screen selections: your entire screen, a portion of your screen, an object, a window, or almost anything else that appears on the computer screen and a few selections that don't. This mode functions the same for both Versions 11 and 2 of Snagit. First, make sure to have open on your desktop the application, Website, or image you are trying to capture. Then once image mode is selected, use the capture button or the keyboard shortcuts if you prefer to begin capturing. You are now officially in capture mode! Now you will need to define your capture region using the orange lines or crosshairs.

Key Term

Screen Capture Region —the designated area for a screen capture. That is to say, everything you want to include in your capture is your capture region.

Snagit already has a number of region types built in to help you quickly identify regions. If you scroll your mouse across the screen, Snagit will highlight any of the recognized regions with an orange border. You can click anywhere inside the region to use the preselected region when it is highlighted or you can click and drag the crosshairs to define your own capture region.

NOTE

The image capture mode works closely with capture types to help you select and customize your capture region. We will learn how when we look at the different capture types and their functions.

10.3b — Video Capture Mode

The Video Capture mode is a new edition to Snagit. You can now capture video in Snagit to share with Camtasia or other third party applications as well as use it to isolate still frames from a continuous video capture for instruction manuals or presentations. Just like with image capture mode you can use video capture to take a recorded capture of a specific region, window, or the entire desktop. Additionally, you can record accompanying audio with an internal or external microphone.

It is important to note that while Snagit allows you the ability to capture and record videos from your screen, it does not have the capabilities in the Snagit Editor to manipulate and edit your recorded screen captures. You can only edit the individual frames as still images from your video recording. You can,

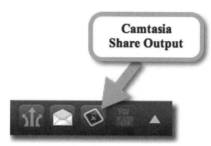

FIGURE 10.13 — Camtasia output in Version 2 Snagit Editor.

*however, export your video file into Camtasia, which as you already know, has a multitude of video editing tools and functions available for your use. Using the **Camtasia Output** in Snagit you can export a selected capture to the **Media Bin** and onto the timeline in a Camtasia project. In Version 11, you can locate the Camtasia output in the **Profile Settings window** of Snagit. In Version 2, however, you will have to visit the Snagit Editor to locate the Camtasia output button seen in Figure 10.13. We will discuss the Snagit Editor in depth in the following chapter.*

In Snagit, video captures are encoded using the **h.264 codec** and saved as **MPEG-4 files** (**.mp4** file extension). The MP4 format is great for sharing your videos because it is compatible with a number of modern video editors and Websites, such as YouTube, that host and play video.

Video Capture mode is brand new to the Mac version of Snagit. However, the previous Windows version of Snagit, Version 10, used AVI files for video capture. If you are upgrading to Version 11 from Version 10, you can still use any AVI files that were created with Version 10 with other video programs including Camtasia, but they cannot be played in the Version 11 Snagit Editor. Once you upgrade to Version 11, any unsaved AVI files remaining in your Library can be saved to a location of your choosing.

After initiating the Video Capture mode, you will need to select your capture region just as you would when capturing a still image. After you select your region, you will enter into capture mode. However, you can still readjust your region size when in capture mode by clicking and dragging the orange region border.

In video capture mode, you will notice a **control panel** appears at the bottom of the capture region. This panel, shown in Figure 10.14, is the same in both Snagit versions and allows you to control and adjust your capture recording.

FIGURE 10.14 — Video capture controls panel.

Begin your recording with the red **Record button**. While recording, this button will change to a **pause/play button** to start and stop your recording as needed. Also when recording, the faded **Stop icon** will become active. Press this button when you have finished recording and the capture will then automatically be exported to the designated output.

Snagit's video capture mode allows you to also record sound to accompany your capture. The **microphone icon** turns audio recording on or off, appearing green when on. The **Audio Meter Bar** is directly to the right of the microphone icon and measures the influx of sound detected by your audio recording device. The amount of sound detected is represented by the green bars you see in Figure 10.14. The adjacent **dropdown menu** allows you to select the device you want to use to record your audio. The last icons we have not yet covered allow you to restart or cancel your video capture. These icons are the **backward curved arrow** and the **circle 'X' icon**, respectively. In addition to the icons on the video controls panel in Figure 10.14, there are two important sets of numbers. The top number tells you the dimensions of your recording, while the bottom number keeps track of the duration of your capture.

10.3c — Text Capture Mode

This special capture mode, available only in Version 11, isolates text by removing any accompanying images or background graphics. This is great for capturing notes or important information from your screen without any supplemental materials. It is especially useful for capturing text when your **Copy and Paste** function is inoperable or incapable of transferring formatting between selected applications. The **text capture mode** will allow you to maintain the basic style and formatting of the text while giving you freedom to edit its appearance in the Snagit Editor from context-sensitive Edit ribbon shown in Figure 10.15.

FIGURE 10.15 – Text edit ribbon in Snagit Editor Version 11.

By default, your text captures will be saved as a **text file** (.rtf) in your **Snagit Images folder**. You can customize your file type and other text capture mode properties in Snagit by selecting **Capture > Share > Properties**. The dialog box in Figure 10.16 will appear where you will select the **Text File tab**.

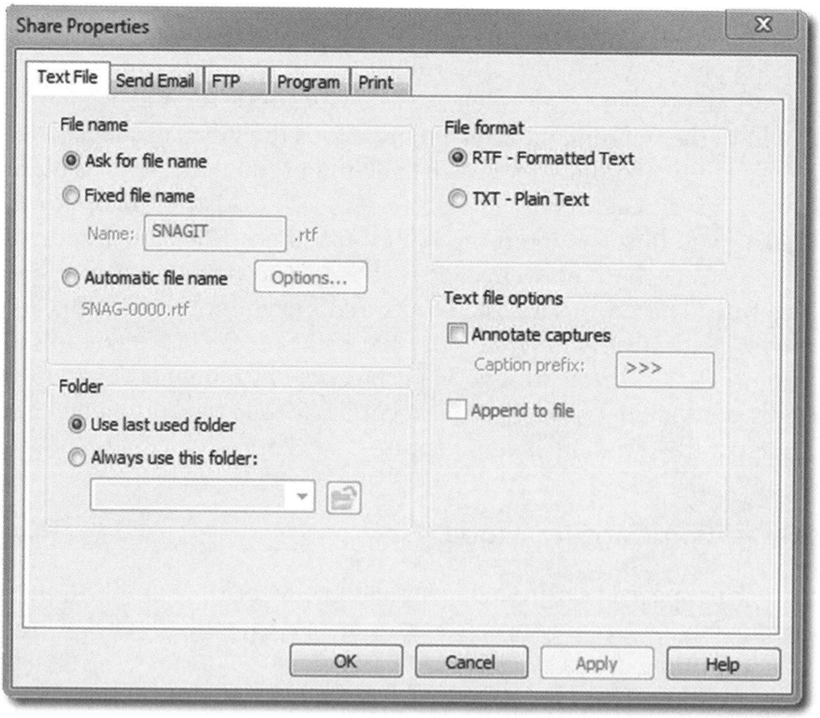

FIGURE 10.16 – Text capture mode properties in Share Properties dialog box.

10.4 — Capture Types

Capture types are designed to help you easily and efficiently select your screen capture regions. There are various different capture type, each specializing in a particular region boundary such as objects, free-hand, or windows. In addition there is the universal All-in-One capture type that identifies a number of different regions.

Key Term **Capture Type** — helps you to select and capture the image, video, or text according to its capture region.

Let's return to the camera analogy once again. On every modern camera you have a viewfinder. On most of the digital cameras today, the viewfinder is a digital screen where you seen an image of what your camera is going to capture. Everything within the borders of the viewfinder will appear in the picture you capture. In Snagit, you have to create your viewfinder using either a **capture type** or the **crosshairs tool**, which we will discuss later on in the section on **Capture Tools**. Capture types work within the individual capture modes to define the region for the type of image, video, or text you are selecting for screen capture.

10.4a — Locating Capture Types in Version 11

In Version 11, you can easily select and customize your capture types from the **Profile Settings window** in Figure 10.17.

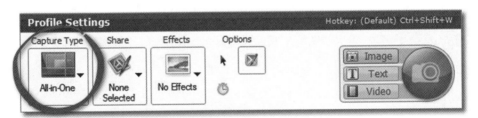

FIGURE 10.17 — Capture type icon in Version 11 profile settings window.

The **capture type** icon displays the currently selected capture type. To select a different capture type, you point and click on the capture type icon.

You can also select a capture type from the **Snagit menu bar** *by choosing* **Capture > Capture Type**. *A square yellow icon with a circle in the center appears next to the currently selected capture type.*

From here a pop-up menu will appear with all of the different capture type selections. Be sure not to forget that there are additional capture types located in the Advanced cascading menu.

Part of the advantage of individual capture types is the customization and specification tools. If you want to customize any of the different capture types select Properties in the pop-out menu. This will open the Capture Type Properties dialog box seen in Figure 10.18. You will need to use this dialog box in conjunction with many of the different capture types in order to customize them to your capturing needs.

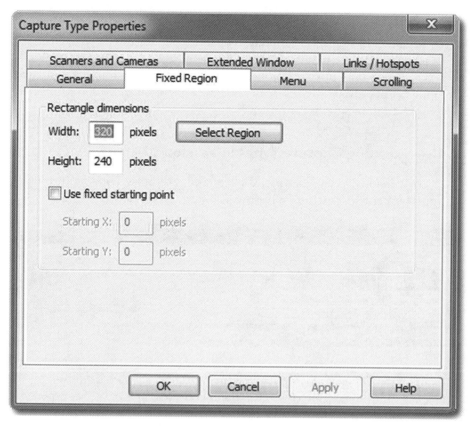

FIGURE 10.18 — Capture type properties dialog box.

After you learn about the individual capture types, you can explore their customization options in this dialog box to produce specified and customized capture types for various types of screen capture regions.

10.4b — Locating Capture Types in Version 2

Version 2, does not allow for any capture type selection from the capture window. To enter into a capture type other than the All-In-One Capture in Version 2 you must use the assigned keyboard shortcut. Due to the versatility of the All-in-One Capture type, the limited capture type selection in Version 2 poses no major disadvantages for successful screen capture. However, there are certain circumstances where it would be much more efficient to use more specific capture types in Version 2. Therefore, it is very much important for you to familiarize yourself with the shortcuts for the Version 2 capture types before learning their function or how to operate them. The capture type shortcuts along with a few video keyboard shortcuts are shown in Figure 10.19.

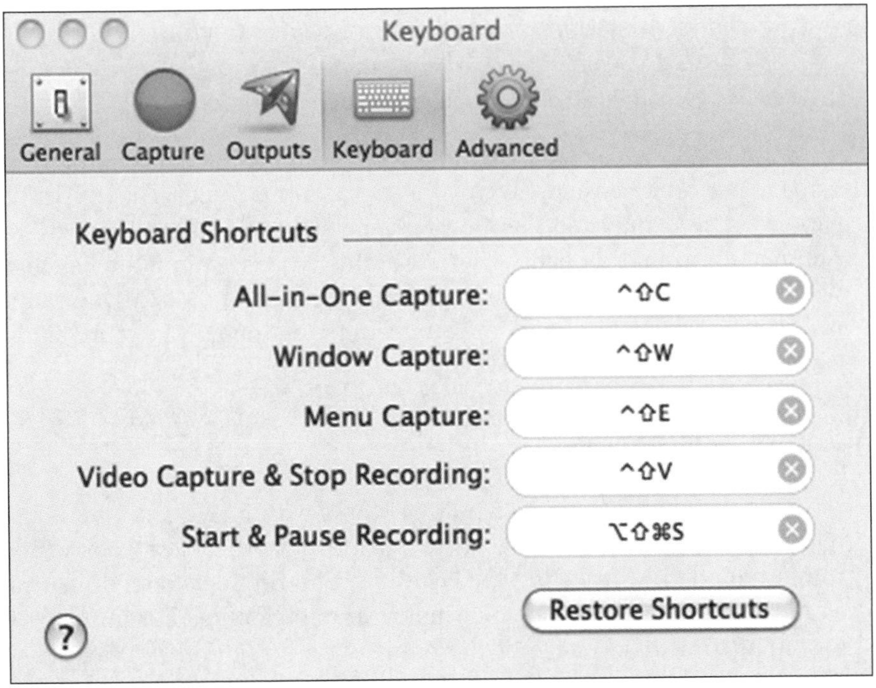

FIGURE 10.19 — Version 2 keyboard shortcuts in Capture Preferences Dialog box.

You can locate this window for reference anytime by going to the **Apply Menu bar** and clicking **Snagit Icon > Capture Preferences** and choosing the **Keyboard tab** in the **Capture Preferences Dialog box**. If you want to customize any of the shortcuts, click in the text field for the desired function and enter the new shortcut.

10.4c — All-In-One Capture

The All-In-One capture type is the default capture type for both versions of Snagit and is available for use with all capture modes because of its flexibility and efficiency in recognizing and highlighting predefined capture regions. This capture type uses your mouse to scan your screen searching for recognizable areas such as an open window or toolbar and highlights these areas as you hover over them with your cursor. You can simply click on the highlighted region to select it for screen capture.

NOTE

Is the All-in-One Capture not recognizing the region you want to select? That's an easy fix. Use the orange lines, known as crosshairs, to specify your own capture region. Click and drag the crosshairs to create a border around desired region. Once you release your mouse, Snagit will capture the selection.

It is important to note that many of the more specific capture types can be performed using the All-In-One Capture type. The All-In-One capture is like a one stop shop to snag images, video, and text quickly with minimal effort and thought. Therefore, this type is often interchangeable with some of the other more customizable types. If the All-In-One capture is not allowing you the freedom you need, try out one of the more tailored capture types discussed below.

10.4d — Scrolling Capture

This is a special capture type that works with image and text capture mode to snag screen captures that are outside the normal desktop or window frame boundaries. Selecting the Scrolling Capture lets you automatically capture an entire Web page or window in one capture. For instance, say you want to take an image of the entire Home Page of the Website you are currently browsing and not just the portions currently viewable in your browser. For this type of capture, you will need to utilize the Scrolling Capture type.

In addition to being a stand-alone capture type in Version 11, the scrolling capture type is embedded in the All-in-One Capture type for both Snagit Versions. Whenever you hover over a region that has a recognizable scrolling region while using All-in-One capture the corresponding icons in Figure 10.20 will appear. These icons will appear in the corners or on the sides of the scrolling region.

FIGURE 10.20 — Scrolling capture icons.

The **up and down arrow** and the **side-to-side horizontal arrow** icon suggest **vertical** and **horizontal scrolling regions**, respectively. Select the **diagonal arrow icon** if you want to capture the entire scrolling region. Clicking on the desired scrolling icon will automatically scroll through the entire selected content to create one cohesive capture. This will be extremely helpful when working with large capture regions, which would have to be broken up into multiple, separate screen captures if you were using the screen capture functionality built into your machine.

NOTE

If you cannot remember what scrolling region each of the arrow icons indicates, simply hover over the icon with your mouse and a description of that icon will appear as shown in the example in Figure 10.21.

FIGURE 10.21 — Icon functionality tooltip for scrolling capture icon.

This is true of most icons and tools available in Snagit. If you need Snagit to remind you of an icon's function hover over it with your mouse and wait for the tooltip to appear.

Version 11 Scrolling Capture Types

Version 11 boasts a few different capture types specific to scrolling images and text. However, due to the advanced functionality and nature of this capture type, sometimes the simplest method is to stick with the All-in-One capture. This will recognize the available regions for scrolling captures and will highlight them the available scrolling icons. We recommend the more novice users of Snagit stick with this capture type until you become more familiar and comfortable with the different scrolling capture types and how they can be customized in Version 11.

For those of you with a little more experience or who feel comfortable testing out some of the other capture types, you can start by changing your capture type selection in the **profile settings window** to **Scrolling Window**. This capture type functions just as the All-in-One capture type but specifies that your region will be a window.

NOTE

A number of different regions can be defined as a window as it is the standard user interface for most applications. For example, the Internet browser appears in a window; the traditional Microsoft Office applications operate using a window; a dialog box opened from a menu is a window. You can quickly start to see how a number of different regions could be considered as a window when your desired capture region includes the complete user interface.

If you are using the Scrolling Window capture type and the graphical interface of the window you select does not extend beyond what is currently displayed, Snagit will capture the defined region as a normal still capture. Otherwise, the scrolling icons corresponding to the available scrolling directions will appear.

Window scrolls are not the only scrolling option available in Version 11. You may have noticed **Advanced** in the **capture type drop-down menu**, which opens the cascading menu in Figure 10.22. Here you can find even more content specific types. Among these types are two additional scroll types: **Scrolling Active Window** and **Custom Scroll**.

Use **Scroll Active Window** as opposed to Scrolling Window when you have multiple different windows open so you can be sure to capture the desired window. For this type, the window you desire to capture should be the last window you click on, the **active window**, before opening or clicking

Capture Type

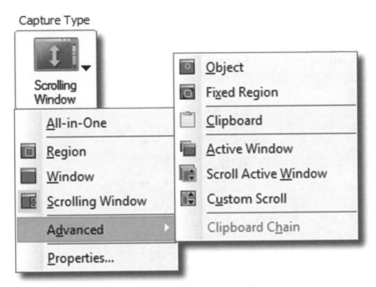

FIGURE 10.22 — Capture type cascading menu for Advanced capture type options.

on Snagit. **Custom Scroll** is necessary when you do not want Snagit to auto scroll your screen capture. Instead, with this type, you use the **vertical** or **horizontal scrollbars** of the window or application to define the scrolling boundaries yourself.

Optimizing Scrolling Captures in Version 2

In Version 2 of Snagit, there is not a designated Scrolling Capture type available. Therefore, you must rely on the All-In-One capture type as we discussed above in the **Scrolling Capture** section, to recognize the possible scrolling regions for your capture. Because you can only rely on the one capture type to identify scrolling regions for you, you will want to optimize the scrolling recognition performance of your All-in-One capture type. For optimum Scrolling capture performance on a Mac, select the **Apple icon** on the **Apple menu**

FIGURE 10.23 — Apple icon dropdown menu.

bar at the top of your desktop interface as shown in Figure 10.23. You will then want to click on **System Preferences** in the dropdown menu.

This will open the **System Preferences dialog box**. Select the **General icon** circled in red in Figure 10.24.

FIGURE 10.24 – System preferences dialog box.

In the **General dialog box** that opens, select **Always** for **Show Scroll Bars** as demonstrated in Figure 10.25.

If you followed along with the text to activate the Scroll Bars on your Mac OS X, you have now optimized Scrolling Captures in Version 2.

NOTE

While Version 2 does not offer a specific Capture Type for Scrolling Captures, it does offer a unique capture method specifically for Web pages. If you wish to capture a Web page that extends beyond the frame of your browser, you can click the URL icon, located directly to the left of the URL, and drag it to one of two places: the Snagit Editor or the Snagit Dock Icon. This will automatically initiate a scrolling capture on the entire Web page.

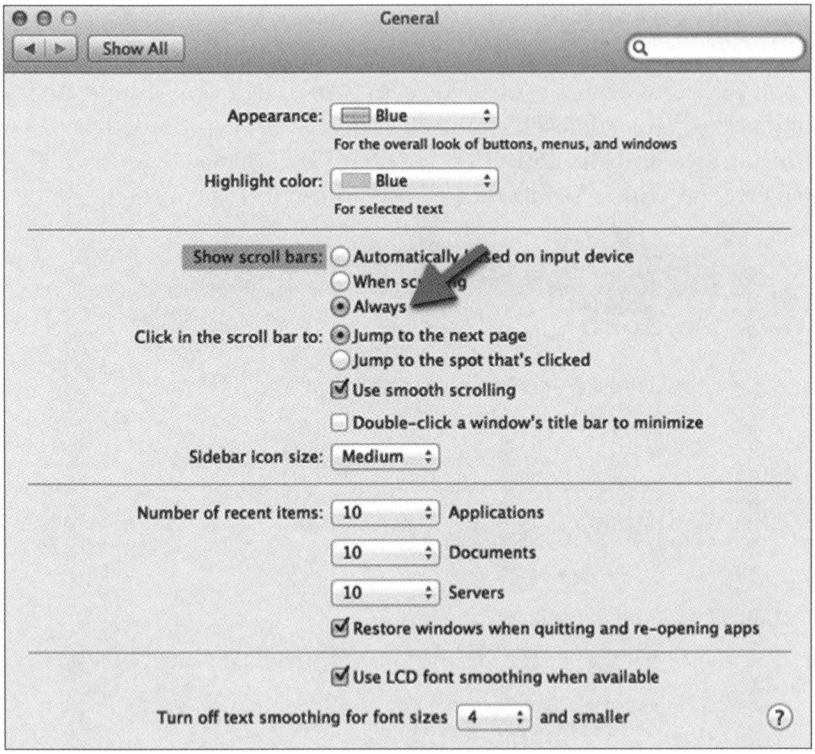

FIGURE 10.25 — Scroll bars activated in General Preferences dialog box.

10.4e — Menu Capture

Sometimes you will want to be able to capture a dropdown or cascading menu as we have done throughout this chapter to help illustrate instructions. Or, you may need to capture a menu to explain a process or location. Whatever your reason for wanting to capture the menu, in **image capture mode**, you can use Snagit to focus specifically on the menu itself without superfluous distractions in your capture and using minimal editing efforts.

NOTE

You will learn the tools necessary in Chapter 11 to edit your capture so that it will only include a menu or certain menu portion. However, using the capture type will allow you to minimize your efforts and help you to produce your captures quickly while also avoiding human error when editing.

Version 11 Menu Capture

Version 11 has a specific Menu Capture type available in image capture mode. For this capture type to work effectively, it must be used in conjunction with a delayed capture. To delay your capture, select the **clock icon** on the **Options Panel** of the **Profile Settings window**. This will bring up the **Timer Setup dialog box** shown in Figure 10.26.

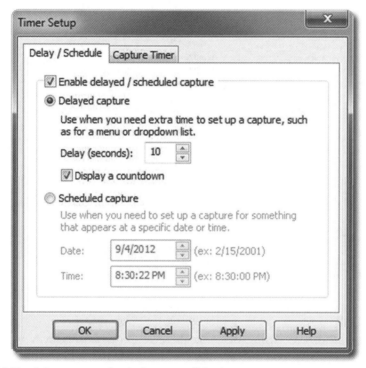

FIGURE 10.26 — Delay capture settings in timer setup dialog box.

By default the **Delay/Schedule tab** is selected. To setup of the capture delay, check **Enable delayed/scheduled capture > Delayed Capture** and select how many seconds, up to sixty, you want to delay Snagit entering into capture mode. Then select **Menu** from the **Capture Type pop-out menu**. You may also want to include the menu bar with your Menu capture. In this case, you will need to open the **Capture Properties Dialog box** that we discussed in the earlier section, Locating Capture Types in Version 11, and shown in Figure 10.18. From this dialog box, select **Menu > Include Menu Bar**. Additionally, select **Capture Cascade Menus** to include any cascading menus as a part of your Menu screen capture.

NOTE   *The All-In-One capture will not capture an entire cascading menu in Version 11 of Snagit. It will only highlight individual windows of the menu for capture.*

Version 2 Menu Capture

For Version 2, the simplest method of menu capture is the capture keyboard shortcut, **Shift + Control + E.** Before initiating your capture, select the dropdown menu along with any cascading menus you wish to capture. Once the menu is displayed properly, use the keyboard shortcut and Snagit will automatically capture the menu using a transparent background. Your capture will appear in the Snagit Editor and, without any editing, will look similar to the capture in Figure 10.27.

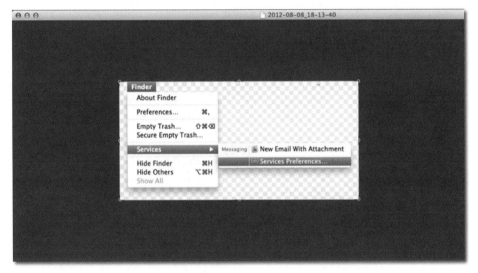

FIGURE 10.27 — Unedited menu capture in the Snagit Editor.

NOTE   *The Menu Capture will highlight your menu selections just as they are highlighted on your interface and include the menu name from the menu bar it was selected.*

You can also use a **delayed capture** with **All-in-One Capture** to capture a menu in Version 2. Set your capture delay to give you enough time to open the desired menu before the capture initiates. Then select the desired menu being sure to expand any cascading menus that you want to include.

NOTE *Refer to back to the earlier section, Snagit Version 2 Capture Interface, for an explanation of setting up delayed screen captures.*

It can often be difficult for the All-in-One capture to recognize the entire menu as a capture region. Therefore, since you can use the menu keyboard shortcut to easily capture an entire menu, we recommend using All-In-One capture if you want to isolate and select only a particular submenu from a cascading menu region. This can be helpful if it is not necessary to guide your audience along through the menu selection process. To select a portion of the menu, hover your mouse over the desired submenu region so that it is highlighted and click your mouse when you are ready to capture.

10.4f — Version 11 Advanced Capture Types

As you are beginning to see, Version 11 has an extensive list of capture types. Combining these with the different customizations, capture modes, and profiles makes it virtually impossible to exhaust all of the possible types of screen captures you can create in Snagit. However, we will briefly discuss the functionality of some of the more popular and useful advanced capture types in Version 11.

The **Full Screen** capture type captures the entire desktop as an image in any of the available capture modes. The entire desktop can easily be recognized using **All-In-One Capture**. Therefore, we suggest using this capture type specifically for users with two monitors. This will take a capture of both screens as one image. If you have two screens and only wish to capture one, use **All-In-One Capture** or **Region Capture**.

Earlier when we discussed the All-In-One Capture type, we explained how to use **crosshairs** to select a specified region for capture that was not to be recognized by Snagit as one of the preselected regions. However, Version 11 has an additional **Region** capture type available. We recommend using this type when you want to include multiple regions on your screen of varying type and size in one screen capture. To do so, you will need to also select **Multiple Area** from the **Capture Type pop-out menu**. Then, while in capture mode, click and drag the crosshairs over each of the areas you want to include in your capture. The colors of the selected area will invert to indicate they have been selected. When you have selected all of the regions you want to include, **right-click** and select **Finish**.

If you already know the dimensions of your screen capture region, you can use the **Fixed Region** capture type in place of **Region** or **All-In-One** to accurately define the size of your capture region. To designate the dimensions in pixels of a region or designate the starting point of a region, select the **Fixed Region tab** in the **Capture Type Properties dialog box** in Figure 10.18.

The **Free Hand** capture type is used for capturing regions that you do not wish to define with using a rectangular perimeter. This type is designed with the idea of manually cutting out your selection from the background. Think of using scissors to cut around object. If you initiate a capture using this type, a pair of scissors will appear on the screen. Use your mouse to draw around the object to "cut" it out of the screen. You can cut a conventional square, follow along the boundaries of an object or use the scissors to "cut out" any number of other regions. Figure 10.28 illustrates using the mouse to "cut" around an object. Everything highlighted will be included in the screen capture.

FIGURE 10.28 — Free hand capture type used to define screen capture region.

The last capture type we will cover is Clipboard. The Clipboard capture is available for you to easily capture the contents on your system's clipboard. This can be both graphics as well as text. Simply select the Clipboard capture type and then select if you would like the capture mode to take an image capture or text capture of the contents.

NOTE

If you are capturing text from your clipboard, but want to create an image capture of the text as opposed to a text capture, simply use the image capture mode with the Clipboard capture type. You might want to do this if you wish to share text to a destination that only accepts images, such as Screencast.com. Otherwise, you can use the text capture mode to create an ASCII text file.

10.4g — Version 2 Advanced Capture Types

As we have already mentioned, all capture types in Version 2 other than All-in-One require the use of keyboard shortcuts. If you have multiple windows running and need to quickly capture the one at the bottom of the pile, you can use the Windows keyboard shortcut, **Shift + Control + W**, to capture a buried or hidden window. Simply press the keyboard shortcut and then point and click on a viewable portion of the window. It's as simple as that.

NOTE *Be advised, the Windows capture shortcut will not include the cursor in your screen capture.*

You can use the Command key in conjunction with the All-In-One capture type to select multiple regions on your screen and combine them into one screen capture. When in capture mode, hold down **Command** while dragging your cursor over the desired windows or objects. These will appear in your editor on the same canvas but as separate vector objects.

NOTE *Canvas? Vector objects? Feel a little bit lost? No need to worry. These and many other editing terms will be covered in the following chapter.*

 ## 10.5 Capture Tools

Capture tools are what allow you to take and customize your screen captures. If you have been following along, you have already encountered a number of these tools. For instance, the red capture button is the tool that allows you to initiate a screen capture. There are a number of other tools, however, that operate beyond the point-and-click functionality. We will look at a few of these tools, some of which you may have already started using, and discuss their function and how they operate in both versions of Snagit.

10.5a — Crosshairs and Magnifier

The Crosshairs and Magnifier tools look and function similarly in both Snagit versions. Once you have initiated your capture, Snagit will enter into capture mode. In this mode, the Crosshairs and Magnifier tools

FIGURE 10.29 — Crosshairs and Magnifier tools.

shown in Figure 10.29 appear. These are important selection tools that help you identify and define your screen capture region.

Crosshairs are the orange perpendicular lines that appear on the screen in capture mode. The lines extend the width and length of the screen. The crosshairs act as a cursor that moves with the movement of your mouse. As you hover the crosshairs over objects or windows on the screen, they will highlight any predefined regions they recognize with an orange border. Figure 10.30 shows an example of the crosshairs identifying a predefined capture region with an orange border. Everything that is faded is outside of the capture region.

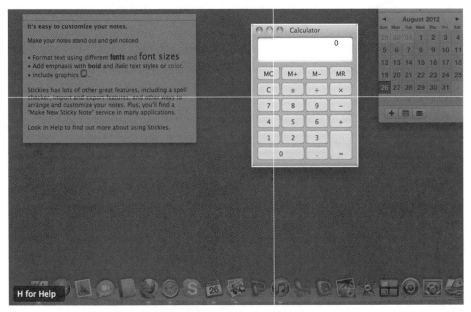

FIGURE 10.30 — Example of a highlighted capture region in Version 2.

If the crosshairs identify your desired capture region, then point and click to take the capture. If they do not recognize the region you want to capture, you can use the crosshairs to click and drag your own border. The **magnifier** will display the dimensions of the region in pixels. You can show/ hide the magnifier by pressing **M**.

NOTE

You may notice in Figure 10.29 the Help keyboard shortcut displayed in the lower left-hand corner. This is a tooltip available only in Version 2. Pressing the keyboard shortcut H, designated in the tooltip, brings up the Help window in Figure 10.31.

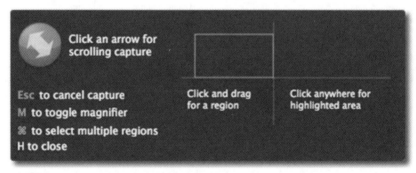

FIGURE 10.31 — Version 2 capture mode Help window.

This window provides helpful reminders for you while in capture mode. When in video capture mode, a similar help menu is available with reminders and tips for video screen captures.

10.5b — Tools for Video Capture Mode

Once you have entered into video capture mode, you will need to select your recording region. For this, decide which video-hosting platform you will be using to share your video. In other words, where will your video be viewed? You can use common video outputs such as Screencast.com or YouTube or it may be meant for display on a device like an iPod. Most of these options will have fixed aspect ratios that should be used when creating your video to avoid any distortion.

(Key Term)

Aspect Ratio —the longer dimension divided by the shorter dimension. The two standard aspect ratios for video are 4:3 (for every 4 pixels of width there are 3 pixels of height) and 16:9.

Resolution	Dimensions	Aspect Ratio	Display	Usage
	320 x 240	4:3	Standard	Classic IPods
480p	640 x 480	4:3	Standard	Web Videos
720p	1280 x 720	16:9	Widescreen	HD Web Videos
1080p	1920 x 1080	16:9	Widescreen	1080p HD Video

FIGURE 10.32 — Standard dimension guide for video capture.

The standard aspect ratios and their corresponding dimensions and usages can be seen in the table shown in Figure 10.32.

Aspect Ratio Selection Guides

To help you create your video according to the common aspect ratios we discussed in the previous section, Version 11 features a tool called **Aspect Ratio Selection Guides**.

NOTE *Version 2 has a comparable tool called Video Guides, or Guides for short.*

These guides help you recognize and select the common dimensions and aspect ratios as they appear on your screen.

(Key Term) **Video Guides** —a video capture tool that uses the Magnifier and Crosshairs in video capture mode to highlight the standard video dimensions for common video outputs.

The keyboard shortcut G turns the guides on or off. Once you have turned on the guides, you can click and drag the crosshairs over your desired region. As you drag the crosshairs, standard dimensions will appear dimly when your selection region is within close range. The dimmer orange lines represent the boundaries of the standard dimension region. The guides you see in Figure 10.33 are for a 4:3 aspect ratio.

Drag your crosshairs over the guides. Whenever you are directly over the guides, the crosshairs, standard dimension size, and aspect ratio will highlight in bright orange as seen in Figure 10.34.

If you are happy with the suggested region, point and click to being recording. In Version 11, the guide tool also gives you the ability to specifically define if you desire a 4:3 or 16:9 aspect ratio by holding down the **Control key** to lock the guides on a 4:3 aspect ratio or the **Shift key** for a 16:9 ratio.

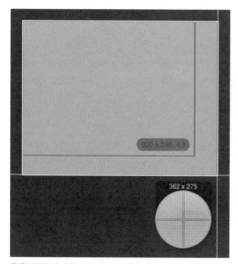

FIGURE 10.33 — Aspect ratio selection guides activated in video capture mode

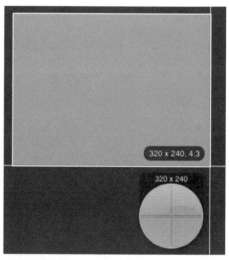

FIGURE 10.34 — Standard dimension capture selected with video guides.

10.5c — Capture Effects

In Version 11, you can get a head start on editing before you ever even begin capturing. The Effects icon in the Snagit Profile Settings window allows you to apply various image effects while still in capture mode. From the dropdown window, you can control and alter the overall color scheme of an image with color modes substitution and correction. With Image Scaling, you can scale images up or down with preset or custom settings. Borders or Edge Effects can outline or frame any image capture to give it that little something extra. Or, you can trip down your capture borders with the Trim effect. You can also add objects to your capture. These objects include watermarks, timestamps, or captions to identify and narrate your captures. You should note that of all these effects, only the caption effect with the timestamp option if available for text capture mode. Additionally, the no editing rule for video captures applies to capture effects as well.

10.5d — Profiles

Now that you are familiar with capture modes, types, and effects and have read a little about share outputs, we can return back to Profiles, which we introduced briefly earlier in the chapter.

NOTE *Profiles, like Capture Effects, are exclusive to Version 11.*

Individually selecting each of the different options every time you want to take a capture can be cumbersome and slow down your productivity. **Profiles** give you the ability to preconfigure your settings for common captures to speed up capture productivity and efficiency. Snagit comes with a few profiles already built in for you, which are organized into two separate categories, **Capture Profiles and Time-Saving Profiles**. They have also created a **My Profiles** category for you to store any profiles that you may want to configure yourself.

You can reorganize your profiles and profile categories individually or collectively by **right clicking** on any one of the desired profiles. This opens the **context sensitive profile menu options**. From this menu, you can select **Organize Profiles**, which will open the **Capture Profiles dialog box** shown in Figure 10.35 that allows you to move profiles from one category to another, create new categories, or delete old ones.

Using one of the preexisting profiles or an earlier profile you created, you can make changes, updates, or adjustment to create a new custom profile. Simply select the profile you wish to modify and begin making any additions or changes you want to implement. For example, if you want to change the preinstalled Screencast.com time-saving profile to work for image mode as opposed to the already selected video mode, you will first need to select the preexisting **Time-Saving Profile** by pointing and clicking the **Share via Screencast.com** icon. The profile will highlight with a yellow box whenever selected. Then change the mode from the **Capture menu** or by selecting the **image capture mode icon** in the **Profile settings window**. The profile will automatically apply the changes. If you only want to use the change once, you can simply initiate your capture. If you want to apply

FIGURE 10.35 — Organize profiles dialog box.

this to the selected profile from now on, select the **Save Profile's Current Settings** icon located in the far right-hand corner of the Profiles window, shown in Figure 10.36. Also in this figure, you will see two other icons in the upper right-hand corner. The green plus sign will save the profile with your updates and changes as a new profile. The other remaining icon, a green plus sign with pages, is the **Add New Profile Wizard icon**, which allows you to create a new profile using the **Profile Wizard**.

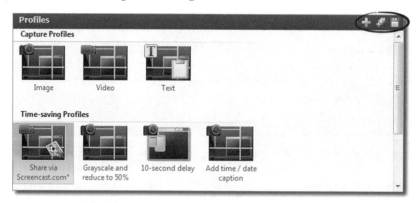

FIGURE 10.36 — Profile option icons to add, create, or save profiles and their settings

NOTE

Speed up the capture process even more by assigning a hotkey to your most commonly used profiles so you can take your capture with the click of a button. Right-click on any one of the profiles to assign your desired hotkey.

CHAPTER SUMMARY

This chapter provided you with an in-depth look into Snagit capture tools, types, and practices. We have covered how to optimize the capture interface for quick and easy screen capture. It will most likely take you some time to fully tailor Snagit for your own screen capture purposes and needs. As you are learning your capture habits, strategies, skills, and handicaps, you can use the preinstalled options, settings, and profiles we have covered in this chapter to get you started. Over time, you can begin to slowly edit and customize the default options to meet all of your screen capture demands. Next, we will explore the second half of Snagit, the Editor. We will spend time learning to transform our captures into visual statements using editing tools and styles. We will also expand on our discussion of share outputs and touch on where and how to store and manage our captures.

CHAPTER PROJECTS

1. In this project, you will plan out your own screen capture scenario. Think of a way you can utilize Snagit in a professional or academic setting. Create a one page paper that identifies what you would want to capture and how you will capture your selection. This includes the mode, type, and region of your capture. Discuss whether this would be a sporadic or consistent capture need. How could you configure Snagit to quickly access the settings required for your capture? Include captures of the tools you will be using in your document.

2. **Video Capture Project:** Use video capture mode to create a tutorial of Snagit. Select your destination that you will later upload your capture to. Research what aspect ratio they require for video uploads. Use the video/aspect ratio selection guides to format your capture according to your selected output's specifications. In the recording, setup audio to discuss the different features and ways to customize the interface during your illustration. Send your finished capture to the Editor for preview. Be sure to save your video so you can use it again in Chapter 11.

3. **Version 2 Project:** Complete this project if you are running Snagit on a Mac. If not, skip to Project #4. For this project, you apply what you learned about Version 2 Menu captures. Open any desired application. Using your chosen application take a menu capture of a cascading window. Your capture needs to include the original menu tab and a minimum of one cascading window. Save your capture to your clipboard. Then paste the capture into a word processing document. Include a paragraph that explains in detail how you captured your menu selection. Also, be sure to list what application you were using for the viewer's reference.

4. **Version 11 Project:** Those using Snagit on a Windows OS will need to create their own custom profile. You can choose to either update a preexisting profile or use the wizard to start from scratch. If you are using a preexisting profile, you will need no less that four additions and/or modifications in the newly generated profile. You will then need to create a logical category for your new profile and assign a hotkey that you will easily remember. The profile also needs to be applicable to your capture needs. In a one-page paper, describe the profile you created. Explain how it addresses your own screen capture needs and what method you used to create your new profile. Include a screen capture of your new profile icon in your write-up.

CHAPTER 11

SNAGIT EDITOR

IN THIS CHAPTER

In this chapter, we will cover the second Snagit interface, the Snagit Editor. We will explore how to navigate the Snagit Editor and use the available editing tools to develop and produce images for visual communication. We will cover how to apply annotations, callouts, and effects to an image, which can help you to alleviate unnecessary verbiage and jargon from many of your different personal and professional projects. In addition, you will learn how to share and manage individual captures and projects from the Editor. By the end of the chapter, you will have the tools necessary to add information to your captures; guide the flow and audience of a capture; and develop a cohesive collection of images.

Once you've completed this chapter, you will be able to:

- The Snagit Editor interface for Versions 11 and 2 of Snagit
- Drawing, annotation, and callout tools
- Capture organization and management
- Available file formats and share outputs

 Files: All figures in this chapter are in color located in the chapter folder on the DVD.

11.1 — Introduction to Snagit Editor

The Snagit Editor is where your captures begin to develop meaning and purpose. This is where the bulk of your capture editing, design, and management will take place. In the Editor, you will work with selection, drawing, annotation, and callout tools as well as capture effects and vector-based objects. You can also use the Editor to open, preview, and edit image files saved on your system that were created from other capture devices. The capabilities and layout of the Editor will vary with each of the different Snagit versions and are designed with their required operating system and user in mind. We will start by examining the interface for both versions and then discuss what you can do in each of the different Editors.

11.1a — Snagit Editor Interface for Version 11

By default, the Snagit Editor is set to open immediately after capturing an image. If a share output is not designated in the capture interface, this default setting cannot be changed. However, if you have chosen an output in the **Profile Settings window**, you can unselect the **Editor** icon from the **Options panel** to send the capture directly to the share destination without previewing in the Editor.

The Snagit Editor for Windows utilizes a mixed style interface where the tools and functionality are housed in the **Ribbon interface** portion of the Editor and Panes help manage and organize your capture. The Snagit Editor shown in Figure 11.1 may seem very complex with numerous sections and tools. However, we will break down the ribbons and panes in order for you to efficiently utilize the Editor.

Across the top of the window is the **Quick Access Toolbar**. The Quick Access Toolbar is a customizable toolbar with preformatted default icons that allow you to open, save, or print a capture and undo and redo an action. From the dropdown arrow on the toolbar, you can add or delete icons for your editing convenience. To the right of the Quick Access Toolbar is the interface name, **Snagit Editor**, followed by the capture **filename**, which is by default the timestamp. Moving across the top to the far right-hand side, you have icons to **minimize**, **maximize**, and **exit** the Snagit Editor window.

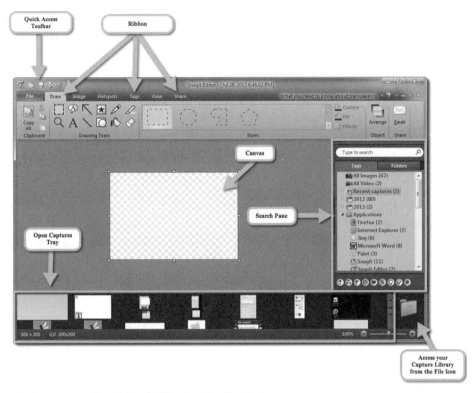

FIGURE 11.1 — Version 11 Snagit Editor interface for Windows.

*You can also **maximize**, **minimize**, and **close** out of individual captures using the corresponding icons located directly beneath **Minimize**, **Maximize**, and **Exit** icons for the Snagit Editor window. Located to the left of the Capture Minimize, Maximize, and Exit icons are helpful dropdown menus for tutorials and tricks for Snagit and the Snagit Editor.*

Directly below the Quick Access Toolbar are the ribbon tabs. The first tab, the File tab, gives you access the backstage view shown in Figure 11.2 where you can change your settings and import and export your captures.

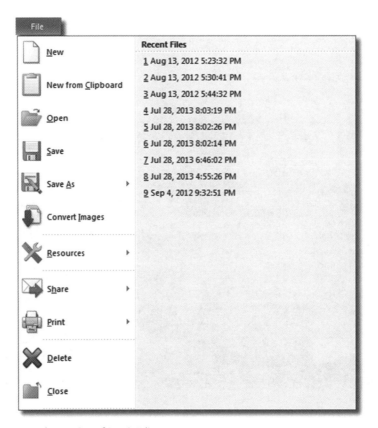

FIGURE 11.2 – Backstage view of Snagit Editor.

You can also access your most recent captures in the backstage view.

The **Canvas**, indicated in Figure 11.1, is where you preview and edit your captures. By default, the Canvas background is **transparent**, which is to say that the Canvas is invisible in any destination outside of the Editor. This means that the capture's background is see through or will not appear when it is shared to another location.

Key Term

Transparent — the condition of being completely see through or invisible. For example, glass would be transparent because you can see from one side through to the other. Therefore, the Transparent Canvas is one that cannot be seen as part of the finished screen capture.

For editing purposes, the transparent background is represented by a grey and white checkerboard. This allows you to see the dimensions of your editing region and the transparent areas of your capture but will not appear in your final capture. This is great if you are inserting a capture into an output that is already equipped with a background image or color fill, and you do not want your capture to conflict with the sharing destination or if you simply want all of the focus to be on the content of your capture. However, if you want to include a background color or image you can change the default canvas from the **Image tab**. Locate **Canvas Color** on the **Canvas panel** shown in Figure 11.3 and select your desired color from the dropdown menu.

FIGURE 11.3 — Canvas color on canvas panel.

NOTE

Any objects or visual enhancements in the grey area around the Canvas will only appear in the Snagit Editor. If you save your file and paste your capture into a word processing document, for example, anything outside of the canvas will not be included. You can think of the grey area as storage for annotations or callouts that you may want to place on your capture at another point.

At the bottom of the Snagit Editor interface you have important information and viewing settings. On the left-hand side there are some different sets of numbers similar to the ones shown in Figure 11.4.

FIGURE 11.4 — Capture sizing and location information in the Snagit Editor.

The numbers to the left of the dividing bar are the dimensions of the Canvas in pixels. The numbers to the right of the dividing bar are the X, Y coordinates of your cursor location.

NOTE
The cursor coordinates are in relation to the (0,0) starting coordinate, which is registered at the upper-left-hand corner of the Canvas.

The dimensions to the far right are of the currently selected region. You can select a region of your capture by using the **Selection tool**. A dotted line border will appear outlining the region. This will allow you to cut out and manipulate different regions of your capture.

On the bottom far right-hand side of the interface is the **Zoom Slider** shown in Figure 11.5.

FIGURE 11.5 — Zoom slider in the Snagit Editor.

You can slide the indicator left or right to minimize or maximize the Canvas, respectively. The zoom percentage will appear to the left of the slider with 100% being the actual size of the Canvas. The dotted triangle in the lower-right-hand corner of the Zoom Slider allows you to use your mouse to adjust the size of the Snagit Editor window. Simply place your mouse over the dotted triangle and click and drag to your desired size.

11.1b — Snagit Editor Interface for Version 2

After taking a screen capture, Snagit opens the image or video in the **Snagit Editor** by default. This allows you to immediately edit your capture and prepare it for sharing. However, if you are working on a project that requires you to take a large number of captures, it might be easier to edit all of the captures at once. In this case, you will want to adjust the default settings so that you must manually open the Editor to preview your captures. To change the default settings, unselect **Preview in Editor** from **Settings** in the **capture window** shown in Figure 11.6.

FIGURE 11.6 — Snagit Editor preview preferences in capture window.

You can also use the capture window to manually open the Editor at any point by clicking the **Snagit Editor icon** located in the bottom-right-hand corner of the window, shown in Figure 11.7.

If you are accustomed to working with a traditional ribbon interface layout, the Version 2 Editor may look a little unfamiliar. If you look at Figure 11.8, you will notice there are only two tabs setup up using **panes** instead of the panels you may be accustomed to working with in a ribbon. These two tabs are the **Tools** and **Effects** tabs where you will find the bulk of the editing capabilities for Version 2.

FIGURE 11.7 — Snagit Editor icon in Version 2 Snagit capture window.

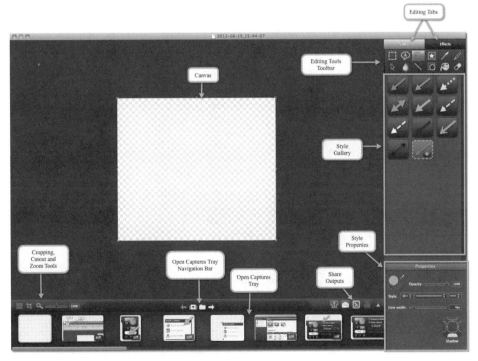

FIGURE 11.8 — Version 2 Snagit Editor for Macs.

The **Canvas** functions the same in both versions as your capture preview and editing surface, and just as in Version 11 the default Canvas type for Version 2 is **transparent**. The Red, Yellow, and Green icons at the top of the interface in the far left-hand corner are for **closing**, **minimizing**, and **maximizing** your window, respectively. Located on the same bar, at the top-center of the Snagit Editor is the **capture filename**, which is the capture **timestamp** by default.

Not all of the Editor's functionality is housed within the Editor interface. You will find important dropdown menus located outside of the Snagit Editor in the **Apple Menu Bar**, shown in Figure 11.9.

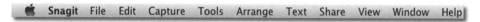

FIGURE 11.9 – Snagit Editor menu bar on a Mac.

A number of the functionalities found within the menus are duplicated within the Editor, but they are especially helpful in customizing your preferences. Additionally, you can create a new file, open existing files, or save capture files using the File menu.

NOTE *The Apple Menu Bar only displays the menus for the active application. Therefore, if the Snagit Editor is running but is not the application currently selected, the Snagit menu options will not display in the Menu bar.*

At the bottom of Snagit Editor, just above the Open Captures Tray, are a few important icons that you can see in Figure 11.10.

FIGURE 11.10 – Capture and Zoom icons in Snagit Editor.

The left two icons are important cropping tools we will get to shortly. The other two tools are the **Zoom Slider** and the **Magnifier**. The magnifying icon does not work how you would typically imagine if you are use to using the more traditional zoom magnifier. When you click on the magnifier icon in the Editor, the Zoom Slider will disappear and the dimensions and cursor coordinates will appear in its place. Figure 11.11 shows an example of how this transformation looks in the Editor.

FIGURE 11.11 — Canvas dimensions and cursor coordinates displayed by clicking the magnifier icon.

The top numbers are the dimensions of your canvas and the two numbers on the bottom are the X and Y coordinates of your cursor, labeled accordingly with (0,0) defined as the top-left-hand corner of the Canvas.

<hr>

NOTE

Version 2 displays the coordinates for the location of your cursor anywhere inside the editing window. This includes the Canvas along with the grey space surrounding the Canvas. In Version 11, coordinates are only displayed when the cursor is within the canvas region.

11.2 — Capture Editing

To start off, it is a good idea to have a working knowledge of what tools are available in the Editor and how to use them.

<hr>

NOTE

*To help you identify these tools, Version 11 uses tooltips that remind you of a tools name and functionality. A **tooltip** is a small window that appears when you hover over an area or icon. The window displays information about the usage and functionality of the said area or tool. These tooltips are available for a number of other icons and functionalities as well. Always try hovering over an icon with your mouse if you have forgotten or are unsure of the functionality of one of the tools.*

Both versions feature a number of identical editing tools that will become your go-to design tools in the Snagit Editor. These common tools are shown in the table in Figure 11.12 along with a picture of their corresponding icons and a short functionality description.

You will find all of these tools in the **Draw tab** of the Ribbon interface in Version 11 and the **Tools tab** of Version 2. We will talk more about customizing and using these tools in Sections 11.2a and 11.2b, but for now, take a look over the Figure 11.12 table to familiarize yourself with the icons.

Icon	Name	Description
	Selection	Click and drag on the canvas to select an area that you want to move, copy or cut.
	Callout	A callout combines shape and text to visually add a message or instruction to your capture
	Arrow	Add arrows to point out something in your capture
	Stamp	Stamps are Snagit graphics that can be added to your capture for visual enhancement and instruction.
	Pen	Used to draw free hand lines on your capture
	Highlight Area	Used to highlight a specific, rectangular, region on a capture
	Zoom	Magnifies an area of the of the canvas
	Text	Add comments or information to your capture with unadorned text
	Line	Add a line on your capture. Great for underlining!
	Shape	Insert one of the many different Snagit shapes into your capture. Good for drawing a frame around a portion or all of your capture.
	Fill	Fill an enclosed area with color or make it transparent using the Fill icon.
	Erase	Erase unwanted objects or image from your capture exposing the Canvas underneath.

FIGURE 11.12 – Common editing tools in Versions 11 and 2 of the Snagit Editor.

Project: Use project files and use each editing tool to practice adjusting the effects.

11.2a — Editing Captures in Version 11

When you are editing your captures, you will find helpful tools in the **Draw**, **Image**, **Hotspots**, and **View** tabs of the ribbon interface. We already got a look at a number of different icons located on the Draw tab in Figure 11.12. Those icons can all be found on the **Drawing Tools panel**. This panel works in conjunction with the **Styles panel** shown in Figure 11.13.

FIGURE 11.13 — Styles panel in the Snagit Editor's drawing tab.

This panel houses what is known in Snagit as the Quick Styles Gallery, because it is where you can quickly select from a number of different tools that have been predesigned with a variety of different styles and/or effects.

The **Quick Styles Gallery** contains the preformatted objects for each individual Drawing Tool. In this window, you can select one of the already designed Shapes, Stamps, or other visual enhancements and quickly add it to your capture.

The gallery options change based on the tool you have selected in the Drawing Tools panel. In Figure 11.13, the **Stamp** tool is selected. Figure 11.14 shows the Style Gallery options with the Shapes tool selected.

FIGURE 11.14 — Styles panel with shapes tool selected in drawing tools panel.

Notice how changing the icon selection changes the style options that are available from Stamp designs to Shape designs.

NOTE

When an icon is selected, it will appear with a yellow box surrounding it as the Shapes icon does in Figure 11.14.

Use the arrows to the right of the Quick Styles Gallery to scroll through additional style options. The bottom downward facing arrow with an additional line above it is the **More button**. If you click on this button, it will open a dropdown window with all of the available style options. An example of this window using the Shapes icon is shown in Figure 11.15.

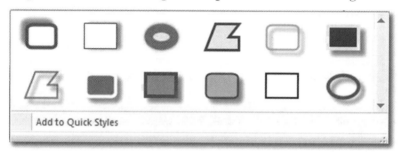

FIGURE 11.15 – Quick Styles Gallery pop-out window.

However, you may not like the predesigned options that Snagit has to offer. If not, you can customize the different tools and tailor the effects and styles to your personal editing needs by using the **Outline**, **Fill**, and **Effects** options at the far right of the Styles panel, shown in Figure 11.16.

FIGURE 11.16 – Customizing options for drawing tools in the styles panel.

If a customization option is not available for the currently selected draw tool, it will appear faded. Click the downward arrow for the available options to view the different options available for each type of customization. Once you have customized a tool exactly the way you want it, you can select the **Quick Styles Gallery pop-out window**, shown in Figure 11.15, and click **Add to Quick Styles** to save that specific customization for later use.

The last panel on the Draw tab we want to look at in regards to editing is the **Object panel** shown in Figure 11.17.

FIGURE 11.17 – Object panel on the Draw tab.

Some of the drawing tools create what are known as **Vector-Based Objects**. These are objects that can be manipulated in Snagit using the customization options. For the layering of objects, do note that objects are layered in the order that they are added. This means that the last object added will be on the top layer; that is to say, the one in full view not covered by any other objects.

Vector-Based Object — a tool in Snagit that has properties that allow it to be resized and manipulated by other editing tools and effects in Snagit. These include Callouts, Arrows, Stamps, Freehand Pen, Highlight, Line, and Shapes.

Key Term

Vector-Based Objects can be repositioned or layered within the Canvas by selecting the desired object with your mouse and visiting the object panel. From here, you can move objects behind another object, group them together as one object, reorder, flip, or flatten them as needed.

Flattening — to make a vector object a part of the background. The object becomes a part of the image and can no longer be edited apart from the image as a whole. This is necessary to use with certain functions or tools in Snagit such as a flood fill or erasing. If you save a capture file with any format other than a .SNAG file, the vector objects are flattened and will no longer be separate editable objects.

Key Term

Other captures can become a Vector-Based Object by copy and pasting it into another capture. The pasted capture then functions as a vector object to which you can apply applicable editing tools and effects.

Now we will look at the Image Ribbon shown in Figure 11.18. This ribbon is broken up into three panels: the Canvas Panel, Image Style Panel, and Modify Panel.

FIGURE 11.18 — Image ribbon in Snagit Editor.

The Canvas Panel name is a little deceiving because this panel also allows you to perform many of its functions directly onto your capture. For example, you cannot only resize your Canvas but your image as well. You can also **Crop** and **Rotate** the image from the Canvas Panel. A notable tool on the Canvas Panel is the **Cut Out Tool**. This tool allows you to select a section of your image to cut out using various cutting styles. Say, for example, we wanted to illustrate the top and bottom of the Snagit Editor Interface, but wanted to leave out the editing window in the middle. We could click the **Cut Out drop-down arrow** to choose from the different styles in Figure 11.19.

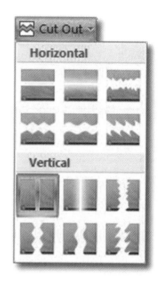

FIGURE 11.19 — Cut out options in the Cut out dropdown window.

The horizontal zigzag option would be a good choice to clearly indicate to the viewer that a portion of the interface has been removed. Once selected, click and drag to indicate the selection you wish to remove. Snagit will apply the changes and produce a capture image similar to what you see in Figure 11.20.

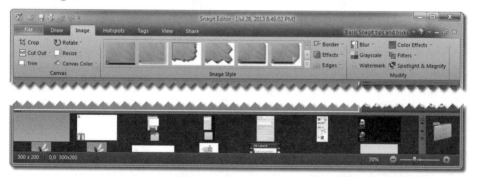

FIGURE 11.20 — Capture with cut out tool applied to remove the middle section of the image.

The Quick Styles Gallery in the Image Styles panel functions like the Quick Styles Gallery we looked at on the Draw tab. However, in Image ribbon, you can apply edge effect to your capture. The **Modify panel** also allows you to alter your capture with more advanced effects. You can apply a grayscale, blur the image, or add your own watermark from this panel.

Remember those tooltips we mentioned earlier? Did you ever wonder how they got those on the interface? Well, in Snagit, you can add your own tooltips or link your capture to other information using the **Hotspots tab**. From here, you can click and drag to select a desired object on your capture or a certain area and use tools to create links or tips that your viewer can read when they hover over the indicated area with their mouse.

The last ribbon we will mention to help you edit your captures is the **View ribbon**, shown in Figure 11.21. This ribbon does not specifically apply visual enhancements to your captures but allows you to manage the capture windows to make the process easier.

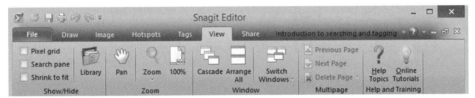

FIGURE 11.21 — View ribbon in the Snagit Editor.

With this ribbon, you can manage multiple capture windows at one time making it easy to switch back and forth between captures and apply similar effects across a selection of multiple captures. You can also use the Pan tool to click and drag a capture that is larger than the editing window so you can pan different areas of the capture.

11.2b — Editing Captures in Version 2

The Mac version of the Snagit Editor combines various panes and the Snagit Menu bar to help you achieve all of your editing needs. The major editing functionalities in the Snagit Editor are housed in the Editing Pane shown in Figure 11.22.

This pane features two tabs, Tools and Effects, along with the Properties Pane. The Tools tab is where you will find all of the editing tools we discussed in the table shown in Figure 11.14.

FIGURE 11.22 — Editing pane in Version 2 of the Snagit Editor.

NOTE

*You may have noticed an unfamiliar icon in Figure 11.22 that does not appear in the table in Figure 11.12. That would be the **cursor** icon. This tool is exclusive to Version 2 of Snagit and is used for removing those bothersome cursors from your captures. If you forgot to unselect the cursor during capture mode or just decided that it is no longer necessary, simply select the tool. Snagit will then recognize the cursor as an editable object, which you can move or delete from your capture.*

The pane directly beneath the tool icons houses your **Quick Styles Gallery**. Here you see the tool types that have been preformatted using the Properties Pane. If you do not see what you are looking for, you can use the Properties Pane to apply the available additional effects, designs, and/or modifications to own any of the tools. Using Figure 11.22 as an example, the **Eraser** tool is selected for use.

NOTE

A selected tool is indicated in Version 2 by a blue box surrounding the icon.

There are a number of different erasing widths preformatted for using in the Quick Styles Gallery. If you want your Eraser tool to cover more or less area than any of the preformatted styles seem to offer, you can use the available **slider** in the Properties Pane, moving it left or right to widen or minimize the erasing field. When you make customizations in the Properties Pane, a faded style with a dotted border and plus sign, like the example in Figure 11.23, will appear. You can click on the plus sign to add your newly created style to the Quick Styles Gallery for later use.

The second tab is the Effects tab shown in Figure 11.24.

FIGURE 11.23 — Add a style to the Quick Styles Gallery icon.

FIGURE 11.24 — Effects tab in the Snagit Editor editing pane.

In this tab are effects that you can apply to your whole capture such as adding a shadow or border around your image. If you hover over any one of the effects with your mouse, a **gears** icon will appear like on the Border Effect shown in Figure 11.25.

FIGURE 11.25 — Settings icon on the Border Effect option in the Effects tab.

This is your **settings** icon, which you can click to customize that effect.

NOTE

The Border effect icon in Figure 11.25 appears green to indicate that it has been currently selected for use in the capture. If an effect is unselected, it will be grey in color.

Figure 11.26 shows the Border effects customization window. You can use the sliders to determine how transparent and thick your border is and determine its color using the color wheels below.

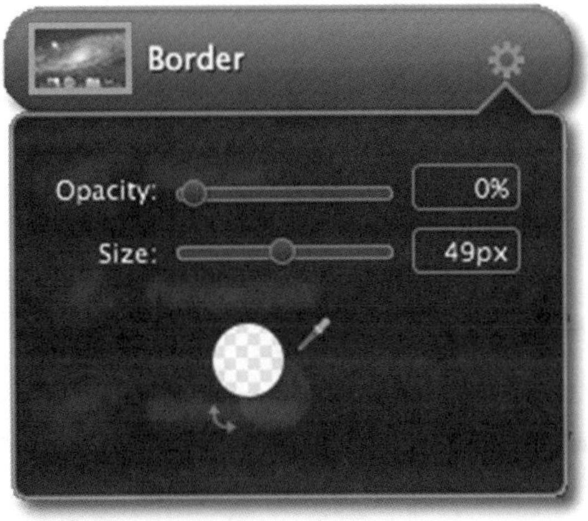

NOTE

By clicking on the transparent circle you see in Figure 11.26, a dropdown list of colors appears for you to choose from. This allows you to select the color of your border. If you want to match the color to one of the colors in your capture, click on the eyedropper icon next to the circle. Then a magnifier will appear as your cursor. Hover and click over the desired color. It will then be used as your background color. This function can be performed anytime you see the eyedropper icon.

FIGURE 11.26 — Customization window dropdown window from the Border effect's Settings icon.

The **Style Pane** on the **Effects tab** acts as your **Quick Styles Gallery** for **Effects tab**. The preformatted styles contain combinations of different customized effects. For instance, if you are creating a photo album where all of the images will have a sepia tone with brown border, you can create an **Effects Style** that is preformatted with these specific **Border** and **Color Filter** settings. The style can then quickly be added to all of your photo album captures.

To crop your captures in Version 2, you can use the Cut Out and Crop tools, as shown in Figure 11.27, located in the bottom-left-hand corner of the Editor, just above the Open Captures Tray.

FIGURE 11.27 – Crop tools in Snagit Editor.

The far left icon is the **Cut Out tool**, which allows you to remove a portion of your capture. If you point and click on the icon, a pop-out window will appear with the different edge effects to apply to the remaining sections of your capture. Select your desired effect and then a blue line will appear when you hover your mouse over your capture. Click and drag the blue line to highlight the section of your capture you wish to remove. Snagit will automatically remove the section from your capture and apply the edge effects you previously selected. The **Crop tool** directly to the right of the **Cut Out tool** will allow you to cut off the outer portions on your capture. Click and drag the Canvas edges so they include only the portions of your capture you wish to keep. Everything that will be cropped out of your capture will appear grey and the region that will remain will be highlighted. Figure 11.28 shows an example of a capture that has been highlighted for cropping.

Everything outside of the highlighted borders Canvas border will be removed from the capture. Once you have defined the Canvas region, click the **Crop icon**. Once the capture in Figure 11.28 has been cropped, it will appear in the editor as shown in Figure 11.29.

Vector objects can be arranged and layered in Version 2 from the **Arrange menu** located on the Snagit menu bar. From the **Tools menu** on the **Snagit menu bar**, you can also locate all of the tools and their keyboard shortcuts. The **View menu** allows you to adjust your zoom settings and move back and forth between the Tools and Effects tab.

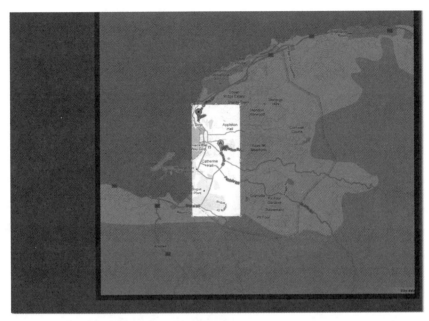

FIGURE 11.28 — Capture with cropping region defined.

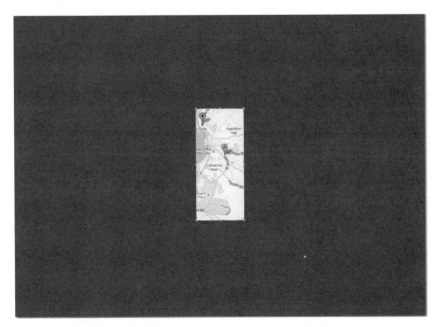

FIGURE 11.29 — Cropped capture.

11.2c — Previewing Video Captures

Although Snagit has video recording capabilities, the main focus of the application is to produce high-quality still images and does not allow for the editing of video captures. To edit your video recording, you can export your video captures into Camtasia Studio. However, you can still preview your captures in the **Editor**. When you open a video capture in the **Editor** the **Recorder Controls toolbar** will appear in both Versions 11 and 2. Figure 11.30 shows these toolbars for both versions.

FIGURE 11.30 — Recorder controls toolbar in Versions 11 and 2 of Snagit Editor.

Most of the recording tools perform your typical video recording functionality and toolbars are set up with similar layouts. The center arrow icon is your **Play button** to playback your recording. The icons directly to the left and right of the Play button are respectively for **rewinding** and **fast-forwarding** the recording. The **double arrow icon on the left** will navigate you back to the very beginning of your video recording and the **double arrow icon on the right** will navigate you to the very end of the recording. However, you are more than likely unfamiliar with the filmstrip and the arrow icon located to the right of the video playback controls. This is the **Capture Frame tool**, which allows you to capture a frame from your video recording as an image capture. Select a spot during the video capture recording and click the Capture Frame icon. Snagit will add the individual frame as an image capture into the **Open Captures Tray** for you to then edit and share as you desire.

11.3 — Capture Organization and Management

Over time, you will develop a large number of captures for a variety of different projects. Learning to organize and sort through your captures in the Editor will make it easier for you to manage your different projects and quickly edit and share your captures. While capture management is far more sophisticated in Version 11, both versions have an **Open Captures Tray** that displays thumbnails of recently taken captures and accessed media files. Whenever you capture an image using the capture interface, it will automatically appear in your Capture Tray. From here you can manage and edit your most recent capture files. You can drag captures from the tray onto the canvas for editing. You can also drag multiple images from the tray onto one canvas to combine them into one capture.

The thumbnails in the tray also have important information or icons associated with them. Figure 11.31 shows the **Delete** and **Unsaved Changes** thumbnail icons.

FIGURE 11.31 — Capture icons in the Snagit Editor capture tray.

The **'X' icon** appears when you hover over one of the captures in the tray. This allows you to delete the thumbnail from the tray, but does not permanently delete the capture. An **orange starburst icon** on a thumbnail indicates that there are unsaved changes made to one of your captures that must be saved before closing the **Editor**. This can help avoid losing any of your capture updates. The thumbnails in Figure 11.31 also have "tiff" in the lower-right-hand corner. Saved files will indicate their **file format type**, such as tiff, while in the capture tray. You can also view the file format and capture dimensions by hovering over the desired thumbnail with your mouse.

11.3a — Open Captures Tray and Editor Library in Version 11

The Open Captures Tray for the Version 11 Snagit Editor is shown in Figure 11.32.

FIGURE 11.32 — Open capture tray in Snagit Version 11

The **navigation arrows** are located to the far right of the capture tray. They allow you to scroll up and down through the thumbnails in the tray. Above the navigation arrows is the **Quick View Button**. Clicking this icon will open all of the thumbnails in an easy to navigate window directly above the Capture Tray.

In addition to the Open Captures Tray, Version 11 also allows you to manage your captures from the **Snagit Editor Library**. While the tray is useful for working with recent captures, the Editor Library is the main hub of capture organization in Version 11. By clicking the **Library icon**, the large file folder icon in the bottom-right-hand corner of the Snagit Editor Interface, you can open the Editor Library shown in Figure 11.33.

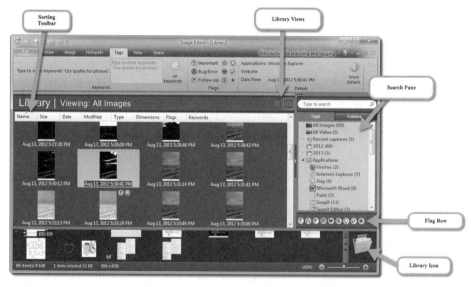

FIGURE 11.33 — Snagit Editor Library.

The Library has two views. You can display captures as they are in Figure 11.33 using **Thumbnail View** or use **List View** to display captures by their details and properties. You can also sort captures with the **Sorting toolbar**. Click on the different options to list your captures chronologically or alphabetically by name, size, or date, for example. This allows you to easily view, sort, and access your captures through a number of different avenues. You can also **tag** your captures by using the **Flag panel** in the **Tags ribbon** or using the **Flag Row** at the bottom of the **Library Search Pane**.

Key Term

Flags or tags — markers that allow you to assign your capture to one or more different categories that can later be searched and sorted in the Search Pane.

Click on the thumbnail in your library of the capture you want to tag. Then click a flag, such as **Important**, that you want to apply to your capture. The flags will appear in the upper-right-hand corner of the capture thumbnail. You can then later use the **Search Pane** to sort through the Library by flag categories. You can also search thumbnails by keywords, capture type, and a number of other properties. For optimum organization, the Library should be used in conjunction with the Search Pane and Tags ribbon.

To assign a **keyword** to captures, click on the desired thumbnail in the Library. In the **Keywords panel** on the **Tags ribbon** you will see a **text field**. This text field will allow you to type the keyword you wish to assign to the selected thumbnail.

Key Term

Keyword — descriptive text that is applied to a capture in the Editor. Once applied, the text can be entered into the search bar on the Search Pane to identify and group images and videos by common properties.

If you have previously used a keyword for a different capture, it can be located in the **dropdown menu** of the **All Keywords** icon on the **Keywords panel**.

NOTE

If you wish to apply a key phrase to your captures, place quotes around your text in the Keyword text window.

11.3b — Open Captures Tray in Version 2

Capture organization and management is fairly limited in Version 2 of Snagit, especially when in comparison with Version 11. In Version 2, all of your capture organization and management is confined to the Open Captures Tray, shown in Figure 11.34.

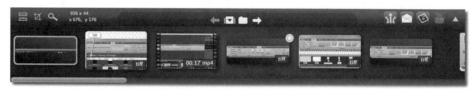

FIGURE 11.34 — Open capture tray in Snagit Version 2.

The far left thumbnail is your most recent capture. You can use the grey scroll bar at the very bottom of the tray to quickly scroll through all of the capture thumbnails. If you want to scroll through each of the thumbnails individually and display them in the editing window, use the left and right **arrow icons** at the top-center of the tray. Additionally, you can select an individual capture by using your mouse to point and click on the desired thumbnail. To hide the capture tray, click the folder icon with a downward arrow. When the tray is hidden, the arrow will turn upwards. Click the icon again to maximize the tray.

All of the screen captures you create using the Version 2 capture interface are automatically saved for you as **Snagit Project File (.snagproj)** and uploaded to your Captures Tray. However, the tray will only hold up to twenty-five thumbnails at a time. The older captures are stored in the **Autosaved Captures folder**. To view this folder, select the plain folder icon to the right of the **Hide/Unhide Capture Tray icon**.

> NOTE
>
> *Snagit will automatically store any captures that you do not specifically save yourself as a **Snagit Project File (.snagproj)**. These project files are located in **Documents > Snagit > Autosaved Captures folder**. Once you save a capture with a different file format, it will automatically be deleted from the Autosaved file.*

11.4 — Saving and Sharing Captures

After you finish designing your captures and you know how to easily access them, you will most likely want to save and share them with your friends, coworkers, and relatives. The Editor is equipped with a number of commonly used outputs to easily upload your captures to your favorite destination.

NOTE *If it is your first time using an output, you will be prompted to provide your respective account information and verify access.*

However, you will first want to make sure you have saved your capture with the appropriate file format for your selected sharing destination. By default, all of your captures are saved using the **Snagit Project File Format**.

NOTE *SNAG (.snag) is the Snagit file format on a Windows OS.*
SNAGPROJ (.snagproj) is the Snagit file format on a Mac OS X.

As a rule, you should save all of your captures with this format in addition to any other file formats. If you save a capture file with any format other than a Snagit Project file, the vector objects become a permanent part of the capture and will no longer be separate editable objects. Although the Snagit Project file format is only compatible with Snagit, it will allow you to edit captures and vector objects at a later time, if needed. When you are ready to share your capture, however, you will need to save it with a file format that can be opened by applications outside of Snagit. The file formats supported by Snagit are JPEG (Joint Photographic Experts Group) File Interchange Format, Tag Image File Format (TIFF), Portable Network Graphic (PNG), Bitmap, Graphic Interchange Format (GIF), Portable Document Format (PDF), and Small Web Format (SWF). When a specific file format is not required, it is best to save captures using the PNG format. This format saves your captures in a reasonable file size and maintains the original image quality allowing you to easily share your captures in other documents, presentations, and online.

11.4a — Locating Share Outputs in Version 11

As mentioned in Chapter 10, you may use the capture interface to select the output for your screen capture. However, the Editor also allows you to share your captures using the Share ribbon shown in Figure 11.35.

FIGURE 11.35 — Share ribbon in Version 11 of the Snagit Editor.

Here outputs are divided into two panels with an additional panel, the **Downloads panel**, for accessing additional outputs available on TechSmith's Website. The **Outputs panel** contains generalized sharing destinations such as **Program**, which allows you to upload a capture to an external program or software application. The **Output Accessories panel** contains application-specific outputs such as **Camtasia**, which are designed to share your compatible captures directly to the specified application. You can customize these output types by clicking the small **dropdown menu** in the lower-right-hand corner of the two panels.

NOTE

Although Versions 11 and 2 have different output icons, they perform the same functions in both versions. A list of these functions can be seen in Figure 11.36 in the following section, Locating Version 2 Share Outputs.

11.4b — Locating Share Outputs in Version 2

Version 2 comes with a number of preinstalled outputs located on the lower-right-hand side of the **Editor**, just above the Open Captures Tray. In Figure 11.36, you can see a list of these preinstalled outputs along with their respective icons and sharing functionality.

To share your capture to one of the preinstalled outputs, open the desired capture in the editing window and then click the desired output icon from the **Output Panel** shown in Figure 11.37.

Icon	Output Destination	Function
	Camtasia	Imports a capture into the Media Bin and timeline in a Camtasia project for additional editing
	Screencast.com	Uploads capture to your Screencast account
	E-mail	Embeds image captures into a new e-mail message in either Mail, Microsoft Entourage or Outlook
	YouTube	Uploads video captures to YouTube
	Twitter	Allows you to tweet a link to your capture
	Facebook	Uploads captures to your Facebook wall
	Evernote	Uploads captures to the Evernote application or directly to a Evernote
	FTP	Uploads to a FTP server for Website publishing
	Copy All	This copies the entire capture with edits to your clipboard to be pasted into another compatible application

FIGURE 11.36 — Available Snagit outputs.

FIGURE 11.37 — Share outputs.

You can access additional preinstalled and downloaded outputs by clicking the **up arrow icon** in Figure 11.37. If an output does not support the capture type of the selected screen capture, it will appear faded like the **YouTube output** in Figure 11.37. You can customize your outputs as well as download additional outputs from the TechSmith Website by clicking the **up arrow** and selecting the **gears icon** shown in the **additional output options**.

CHAPTER SUMMARY

In this chapter, we covered the basics of using the Snagit Editor. We learned how navigate the interface and maximize our sharing and managing capabilities within the application. There are numerous specifications and customizations that can be made with each tool and function. The key is to master all of the basic commands and then explore the effect that each adjustment makes. With time and practice, you will be developing advanced high-quality captures that can be introduced to your friends on your favorite social media site or easily transitioned into the work environment. Combining Snagit with the more advanced Camtasia Studio will allow you to integrate your screen captures into a lecture or presentation for any setting.

CHAPTER PROJECTS

1. You will use the video capture you created in Chapter 10 for this project. You will need to create an instruction manual using frames from your video capture. You will need no less than five frames that are edited using callouts, arrows, and other necessary editing tools to instruct your viewer. Your manual should use minimal text explanation, focusing on using images to explain and illustrate your chosen topic.

2. Explore the different capture effects available in either Version 2 or Version 11 of the Editor. Use no less than three effects to create a preformatted style to add to your Quick Styles Gallery. Create a set-up of images that explain why you chose your effects and the process of adding a style to the gallery. Your set of instructions should include a minimum of four captures (feel free to create a video capture at least 2 minutes in length) and utilize your newly created style.

3. Use Snagit to capture an image of the Editor. Then edit your image capture using the available tools to point out different features. Use callouts to help name and/or define key elements. The idea is to create an image that works as a Guide for your Editor. You may choose to focus on a specific area such as a ribbon or pane. Then use one of the Snagit Outputs to share your image with a friend, coworker, or instructor. Visit TechSmith's Website using the Editor

CHAPTER 12

JING

IN THIS CHAPTER

This chapter will cover what makes Jing the perfect screen capture application for informal online communication, or **chatting**. By looking at the different capturing, editing, and sharing capabilities of Jing, we will learn to capture and share images and video recordings at high-speed intervals. We also explore the limited editing tools to help provide additional meaning, information, or instruction in your image captures.

Once you've completed this chapter, you will be able to:

- How to operate Jing's interface, the Sun Launcher
- The available capture methods and file formats used in Jing
- Ways to annotate your image captures with visual enhancements in the Jing Editor
- How to utilize share outputs in Jing

Files: All figures in this chapter are in color located in the chapter folder on the DVD.

12.1 — Introduction to Jing

Many of the most popular social media sites now incorporate image sharing into their platform. Some of the more notable sites include Facebook, Twitter, and Pinterest, the popular online pinboard application. Jing is an on the fly screen capture application offered by TechSmith that is made to keep up with this fast-paced speed. This application is perfect for quickly capturing clips from your favorite Website and sharing it to a variety of different viral communication platforms. With many of business and personal conversations going viral, Jing provides the ability to include images instantaneously to the ongoing dialogue. Designed to move with the speed of online conversation, Jing is used to capture images and video that can be quickly inserted into an instant message to provide visual instruction or clarification. Therefore, it is primarily intended for taking quick-and-easy screen captures that need minimal editing or enhancements. You can think of Jing as your grab it and go capture application. It also offers a free alternative to Snagit or can work with its more advanced sibling to enhance its quick snapshots.

12.1a — Jing Interface

The Jing interface is known as the Sun Launcher due to its resemblance of the sun. The Launcher appears as a minimized window on your desktop, visible as a quarter or half sun. The whole sun appears when you are working within certain Jing menus. By default, the interface appears as a half sun in the top center of the desktop as shown in Figure 12.1.

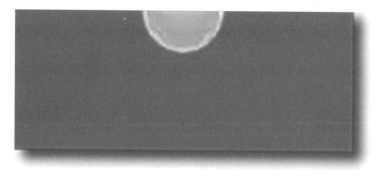

FIGURE 12.1 — Default Jing Interface appearance.

NOTE *MAC: While there are separate downloads of Jing for Windows OS and Mac OS X, there are only slight variations. These notes will be used while introducing Jing to highlight any important differences in functionality or layout when running Jing on a Mac OS X. By default, the Launcher appears as a quarter sun in the top-right-hand corner of a Mac desktop as shown in Figure 12.2.*

FIGURE 12.2 — Default Jing Interface appearance on a Mac OS X.

You can choose to move the location of your launcher by clicking and dragging on the sun, but the Sun Launcher does not have the capability to appear as a free-floating window. It must remain anchored to the edges of your desktop. Additionally, there are a few places the Launcher cannot be placed. The Sun will not anchor on the desktop edge near the **Start Menu**.

NOTE *MAC: Unlike other applications, Jing does not have the capability to placed on the **Dock** on a Mac desktop.*

To maximize the Launcher, hover over the sun with your mouse. Three separate rays will appear: the Capture, History, and More rays. Their order will vary depending on the location of the Launcher along the desktop. However, they can easily be identified by their respective crosshair, polaroid, and gear icons shown from left to right in Figure 12.3.

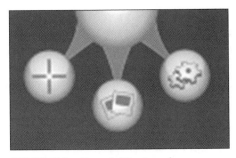

FIGURE 12.3 — Expanded Sun Launcher.

FIGURE 12.4 — Expanded Ray Selection.

To select a ray of the Jing interface, hover over the desired selection with your mouse. The ray will expand along with a tooltip with the name of the ray like the example in Figure 12.4. Click on the expanded ray to activate its functionality.

12.1b — Customizing the Sun Launcher

The **More** and **History** rays access their own separate interfaces with which you will interact. **More**, shown in Figure 12.4, accesses the **Jing Options icons**, shown in Figure 12.5. The primary functionality of these icons is to set up your Jing preferences and options.

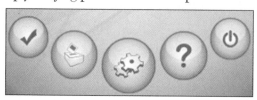

FIGURE 12.5 — Jing Options icons.

You will quickly notice that these icons are not in the standard rectangular window interface that you are most likely accustomed to seeing. However, it functions in much the same manner. The window has a set of five icons at the bottom of the interface used to close the window, access Option menus, and close the application. These icons function similarly to **tabs** and remain at the bottom of the interface regardless if you are in the main menu or are viewing a submenu of the Options window. From left to right these icons are **Finish**, **Send Feedback**, **Preferences**, **Help**, and **Exit Jing**.

NOTE

*MAC: Figure 12.6 shows the layout of the **Jing Options icons** on a Mac. Excluding the icon to quit the application, the Options window on a Mac has the same layout and function as on the Windows version. However, the Mac version has slightly different names for some of the icon functionalities. From left to right the icons are labeled **Done**, **Send Feedback**, **Preferences**, **Help**, and **Exit**.*

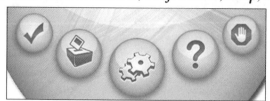

FIGURE 12.6 — Jing Options icons for Mac OS X.

The two icons on either end have an exit or close function. You close the Options window by using the icon at the far left of the selection. The icon on the opposite far right end is used to close the entire application. If you exit out of Jing or do not have it set up to run automatically when you start the computer, you will open it from **Start > Programs > TechSmith > Jing**.

NOTE   *MAC: If you need to access Jing from the Mac OS X, go to* *Finder > Applications > Jing.*

The **Send Feedback** and **Help** icons are Jing support functions. They both require an active Internet connection. **Send Feedback** takes you to TechSmith's community-powered support forum where users post tips, problems, and reviews of Jing and other TechSmith products. The Help Icon looks like a question mark and accesses the **Help Menu**. From this menu, you can find additional application support by visiting the **Jing Help Center** or selecting one of the commonly asked questions to watch different tutorials provided by TechSmith. You can also check on any available application updates and help improve performance.

The last icon located directly in the center of the icons is the **Settings** icon, which opens the **Preferences menu**, shown in Figure 12.7. This menu is broken up into eight subsections.

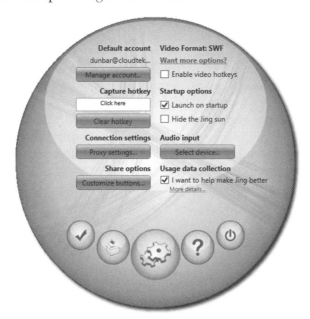

FIGURE 12.7 — Preferences window in Mac OS X version.

A number of these sections will be addressed later in the chapter. For now, we will look at the Jing **Startup Options**.

MAC: The Preferences window on the Mac version of Jing, shown in Figure 12.8, has only six subsections and slightly different labeling.

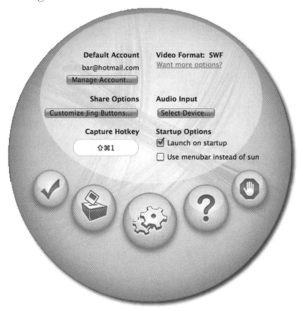

FIGURE 12.8 — Preferences menu on Mac OS X version.

From this section, you can customize how you view Jing. To run the application as soon as you boot up your computer, check the **Launch on Startup box**. You can also remove Jing from your desktop while still running the application by checking **Hide the Jing Sun**. When selected, the Jing icon will appear on the **Windows taskbar** as shown in Figure 12.9.

FIGURE 12.9 — Running Jing from the Windows taskbar.

If you do not immediately see the Jing icon, select the up arrow to the left of the Jing icon in Figure 12.9 to customize your taskbar icons. Be sure to select show icon under the Jing taskbar settings if you want it to remain visible on the taskbar.

NOTE

MAC: To remove Jing from your Mac desktop and place it in the ***Apple menu bar****, check* ***Use Menubar Instead of Sun*** *in the* ***Preferences Menu > Startup Options****. This will place the Jing icon indicated in Figure 12.10 in your* ***Apple menu bar****.*

FIGURE 12.10 — Running Jing from the Apple menu bar.

██ 12.2 — Capturing

If you read through the Snagit chapters, you are used to selecting the capture mode and other additional options before initiating your screen capture. In Jing, that order is reversed. To begin capturing, select **Capture** from the Sun Launcher interface. This will put you directly into capture mode where you will select your capture region. Jing is populated with a number of regions and dimensions to help you make your selection. As you scroll over the screen, Jing will highlight identifiable capture regions with a border and grey out anything outside of the capture field. However, if Jing fails to identify the menu, toolbar, icon, window, or other object you wish to capture, you can click and drag the crosshairs to create a frame around your desired region.

NOTE

If you hold down the ***Control key*** *or* ***Shift key*** *as you click and drag over your desired capture region, you can adjust the capture size to standard dimensions. Holding down the* ***Control key*** *locks your capture to a 4:3 aspect ratio and* ***Shift*** *locks to a 16:9 ratio. As we explained with Snagit, this is helpful when working with other video editors or creating images that will adhere to a particular Website standards.*

Once you let go of your mouse or click on a preselected region, the Capture Toolbar in Figure 12.11 will appear.

FIGURE 12.11 — Capture tools toolbar.

The **polaroid icon** and **filmstrip icon** allow you to select your **capture mode**. In Jing, you can perform an **image capture**, which creates a still image of your screen capture, by selecting the **polaroid icon** on the far left. Or, you can create a short **video capture** by selecting the **filmstrip icon**. If you do not like the frame for your capture, you can redefine your capture region by selecting the **back arrow icon**. This will take you back to capture mode. If you want to cancel your capture and exit out of capture mode, select the **(X) icon**. The last item on the toolbar is your **capture dimensions**, or capture size, located on the far right-hand side.

12.2a — Video Capture

For an image capture, you simply select the **polaroid icon** from the **Capture Tools toolbar** and Jing will automatically open your capture in a **preview window** where you can make additional edits or enhancements. Video capture, however, has a few more steps that we will need to look at. Immediately after you select the **filmstrip icon**, Jing will enter into **video capture mode**. While in video capture mode, filmstrips will appear on the right and left of the capture region as shown in Figure 12.12. You will have a three second countdown before the recording begins. A countdown of three seconds along with the audio settings will appear on the screen, as shown in Figure 12.12, immediately after you enter video capture mode.

"Mic On" indicates that the audio recording device is on and ready to record sound along with the visual recording. If the microphone is turned off "Mic Off" will appear on the screen during countdown.

FIGURE 12.12 — Video capture mode countdown.

NOTE

*When you use video capture for the first time in Jing, it will give you an opportunity to select your Audio Input device. However, if you missed that opportunity or if your input device has changed, you can visit the **Preferences window** in Figure 12.7 to make your selection. Just click **Select Device** under **Audio Input** and Jing will allow you to select from the devices currently recognized on your machine.*

Additionally in Figure 12.12, there is a capture toolbar to control your video recording. This **video capture toolbar** has been maximized in Figure 12.13 so we can take a closer look at the different tools and options available.

FIGURE 12.11 — Capture tools toolbar.

The first two icons are your traditional stop, ■, and pause, ‖, icons. If you select the pause icon to timeout your recording, the icon will switch to the **resume icon**, ●. Select this icon to start your recording back after it has been paused. The **microphone icon** is used to mute and unmute audio recording. If there is a 'X' through the microphone, the video capture is not recording sound. If you messed up the start of your video capture or just want to start over, select the **back arrow icon**. This will exit you out of video capture mode back into capture region and mode selection. Just as with the capture tools toolbar in Figure 12.11, the **(X) icon** will exit you completely out of capture mode. You may have noticed the bar above the icons. This bar along with the numbers to the far right-hand side of the toolbar, mark your current recording time out of a five-minute maximum.

NOTE *Jing focuses on quick captures that can be shared instantly with others. Therefore, your video captures are limited to five minutes and cannot be edited.*

Once you are finished recording, select the **stop icon**. Your video capture will open in a **Preview Window**, as demonstrated in Figure 12.14

FIGURE 12.14 — Video capture preview window.

By pressing the **play button** in the middle of the window, you can playback your capture for review. If you are not satisfied with your capture, you can press the **cancel icon**, (**X**), in the **Jing Buttons toolbar**, shown in Figure 12.12. As you can see in Figure 12.15, this toolbar is located at the bottom of the **Preview Window interface**.

FIGURE 12.15 — Default Jing buttons toolbar in video capture preview window.

NOTE *The **Jing Buttons** toolbar shown in Figure 12.15 is the default toolbar. Shortly, we will learn how you can customize this toolbar with additional share outputs.*

By default, your capture name is the **timestamp stamp** of your capture. You can select a customized name for your video capture by clicking in the **Name text field**. If you want to edit your capture and have Camtasia downloaded to your computer, click the **Edit in Camtasia Studio icon** to upload your capture into the application. If you do not have Camtasia or do not need to edit your capture, you can use the far left icon to share your video to **Screencast.com** or you can save the capture to your computer using the **save icon** to the right of the Screencast icon. This will open the dialog box shown in Figure 12.16 where you can select the name and location for you video capture.

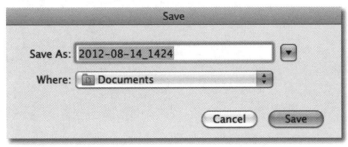

FIGURE 12.16 — Save as dialog box.

You can add additional sharing outputs by clicking the **wrench icon**. This will open the dialog box you see in Figure 12.17.

FIGURE 12.17 – Customize Jing buttons dialog box.

To add additional outputs select "**New.**" This will open yet another dialog box, shown in Figure 12.18.

FIGURE 12.18 – Button settings dialog box.

From this dialog box, you are able to add additional output options to your toolbar for quick and easy sharing. We will learn how to add and customize these additional outputs shortly.

12.2b — File Formats

Jing uses the **Portable Network Graphics (.png)** file format to save all of your image captures. A PNG format is a common choice for sharing images on the Web and specializes in storing visuals and text at a small file size. This format helps the application maintain its fast paced tempo by allowing you to quickly upload your captures to various Web platforms. The **Macromedia Flash file** or the **SWF file format** is used to save Jing video captures. By default, this format type requires the viewer to open the video file in a Web browser or Flash player. If you want to save a capture using a format other than SWF or PNG, you will have to upgrade to the more advanced image capture application, Snagit.

12.3 — Editing

As we have already mentioned, video captures cannot be edited in Jing. Therefore, as we mentioned, video captures are opened directly into the Preview window. Image captures, however, open in the **Jing Editor window** as seen in Figure 12.19.

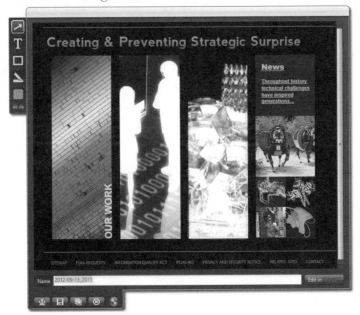

FIGURE 12.19 – Jing Editor window.

You should already be familiar with a number of the tools in the **Editor**. The toolbar located along the bottom of the **Editor** is very similar to the toolbar from the video capture preview window in Figure 12.14. In this toolbar, you can share your image to Screencast.com, save it to your computer and cancel your capture using all of the same icons. There is one new icon we should mention and that is the **copy icon** highlighted in Figure 12.20.

FIGURE 12.20 – Default Jing buttons toolbar in Jing editor.

Selecting this icon will copy your image to the Clipboard so you can paste it into a supported location such as a Microsoft Word document.

(Key Term) Remember back in Chapter 10 we defined the **clipboard** as a temporary storage area on your computer where data, such as text or an image, that is copied from one application is stored for use in another application.

The other toolbar you will notice in the Jing Editor is the very important Editing toolbar shown in Figure 12.21.

The top **Arrow tool** is used to add arrows to your capture. This can be helpful in drawing your audience's attention to something in your capture. You can also frame an object or your capture using the **square icon**. The icon with a "T" is your **Text tool**. This icon adds a text box to your capture where you can add descriptive text. Click and drag the text box to your desired size. When you release the text box, the **formatting toolbar** in Figure 12.22 appears.

You can use this toolbar to select the font, size, and color of your text. Click the dropdown arrow to see the different **font types** available and drag the ball to the right or left to increase or decrease the font size. The two color boxes you see to the far right-hand side of the toolbar are your **border and background Color tools**. They allow

FIGURE 12.21 – Editing toolbar.

FIGURE 12.22 — Text formatting toolbar.

you to select the font color, border color, and background color for a text box. Click on the top color box and a dropdown menu will appear. This color selection will be for both the **border** of your text box as well as your font color. The color box directly beneath it selects your **background color**.

Because the border color also determines the font color, you cannot have the same border and background color. Otherwise, your font will blend into your background and not be legible. However, selecting the same background and border color is a good way to cover up any sensitive material in your capture. Simply select the same color for both the background and border and place your textbox over any material you wish to conceal. See the example in Figure 12.23.

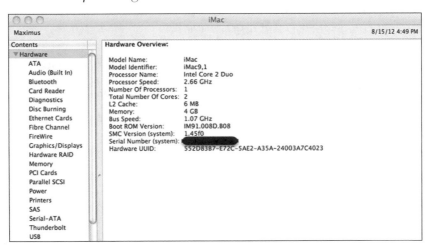

FIGURE 12.23 — Jing textbox used to conceal sensitive data in a screen capture.

Do note that you will need to enter text or hit the spacebar in order for the textbox to remain visible. Otherwise, it will disappear once you click outside the text area.

You can also change the colors of your arrows and frames using the Color tool located in the **Editing toolbar**. Select the editing tool you want to apply to your capture. Then, click on the color icon to bring up a list of color options in a dropdown menu. The last visual enhancement tool available in Jing is the **Highlighter tool**. This allows you to highlight different words or objects in your text by clicking and dragging over your desired selection or text while in highlight mode. The traditional highlight color is yellow but Jing allows you to choose from other available colors using the **Color tool** as well.

The last two tools you will want to learn in the Editing toolbar are **Undo** and **Redo**. These icons are located at the bottom of the toolbar. The arrow icon on the left is to undo your previous action and the arrow icon to the right reverts the previous undo action. These are important editing tools because you cannot right-click or use keyboard shortcuts to remove one of the visual enhancements after it has been placed on your capture. This means you will have to pay careful attention when you are editing. If you get everything placed exactly where you like it and create multiple different arrows and frames, you will have to undo each action just to delete something you inserted in the very beginning.

NOTE

*There are multiple reasons for paying close attention to your visual enhancement order in the Jing Editor. There is first the issue of removing a shape or text box that was inserted before one or multiple other objects. There is also an issue of **layering**. Layers are added in the order that an object is added. Therefore, whatever you wish to be in the foreground should be added last. As an example, say you want to add a text box with some important information. You also want to add an arrow that will connect your text box to something in your capture. If you add the text box first, your image will look similar to the capture in Figure 12.24.*

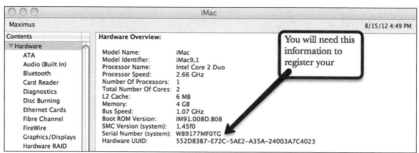

FIGURE 12.24 — Layering objects in the Jing editor.

This arrow makes your capture look unprofessional and covers up important information. If you had added the arrow first and then created your text box, your image would look like the capture in Figure 12.25.

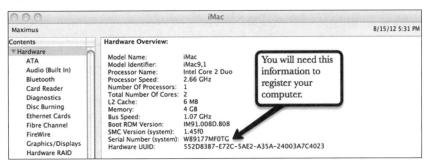

FIGURE 12.25 — Layering objects in the Jing editor.

Note how the arrow is now behind the text box. This is because the arrow object was added before the text box and, therefore, on the bottom layer. This gives the capture a more polished, professional design.

12.4 — Customizing Jing Buttons

If you have been following along, you should already know that additional share outputs can be added to your **Jing Buttons toolbar**. We learned how to customize these outputs from the toolbar itself by selecting the wrench icon. Now we will learn how to add additional buttons to the toolbar using the **Sun Launcher** and talk about the different share output options available.

The **Preferences window** allows you to customize your toolbar by clicking **Customize Buttons** in the **Share Options** section. This will open the **Customize Jing Buttons dialog box**, shown in Figure 12.17. Use the **trashcan icon** to delete any buttons off the toolbar that you do not want or need.

NOTE *You can have a maximum of eight output buttons on your Jing Buttons toolbar at any one time. So, plan to include your most frequently used sharing options.*

You can edit any of the buttons already on the toolbar by clicking on the desired share output icon. Now, we will look at how to configure the different share outputs to our specific capture needs.

12.4a — Screencast.com Output

TechSmith designed Jing to not simply be compatible with their media hosting solution, Screencast.com. They integrated Screencast.com into the functionality of the application. This hosting platform provides users a place to securely store and host their captures. Whenever you download Jing, you automatically have access to a free Screencast.com account. The first time you run the application, it will prompt you to choose an existing account or sign up for your free account.

NOTE *Your free account allows you 2 GB of storage and 2 GB of bandwidth per month. You can get additional storage and bandwidth by purchasing a Screencast.com Pro account.*

Whichever account you chose will be automatically linked with the application and become your default Screencast.com account for Jing. If you have multiple Screencast.com accounts and want to switch the default account after setup, you can click **Manage Account** in the Preferences Window shown in Figure 12.26.

FIGURE 12.26 — Default account options in Preferences Window.

After you have chosen an account, you are ready to start sharing your captures to Screencast.com. The Screencast.com output comes preinstalled on your Jing Buttons toolbar and can be recognized by the icon in Figure 12.27.

FIGURE 12.27 — Screencast.com Output icon.

You can use this default button and your video or image capture will automatically be uploaded to your account. Once the capture has successfully uploaded, the dialog box in Figure 12.28 will appear. From here, you can access Screencast.com by clicking on the link.

FIGURE 12.28 — Screencast.com capture upload confirmation dialog box.

You might have also have noticed from the dialog box that Screencast. com creates a URL for you to paste into another platform. Jing simultaneously copies this distinct URL created for your capture by Screencast.com onto your **clipboard** so you can quickly paste it into an online chat or into an e-mail.

To create a new Screencast.com output or edit the existing default output, open the **Button Settings dialog box**. The default view of the dialog box allows you to edit your Screencast.com output. In Figure 12.29, you will see the **Screencast.com Button Settings dialog menu**.

FIGURE 12.29 — Screencast.com button settings dialog menu.

You can change the default name of your button in the **Button Description field**. The name you choose will appear as a **Tool Tip** whenever you hover your mouse over the button icon in the **Jing Buttons toolbar**. The **E-mail Address field** allows you to select any of your Screencast.com accounts.

NOTE
Say you have a separate Screencast.com account for work and for personal use. You may choose to create two different Screencast.com share output buttons for each account. This will make it easy for you to upload your captures for the office and ones at home separately and quickly.

There are two options in the **Clipboard Contents field: URL and HTML Embed Code**. We already mentioned how you would want the URL copied to your clipboard in order to paste it directly into your platform of choice. The **Embed Code** is necessary if you want to include your capture into a Web page or other similar HTML authoring tool. This option will copy the HTML Embed Code for your capture directly to your clipboard in place of the URL. You can then paste the code, into your blog post for instance, to share your capture with others.

NOTE
This works for image and video captures alike, provided that the service provider of your chosen HTML authoring tool allows for video embed code.

Next you can select the **Screencast.com folder** you want your captures to upload to. If you have not created any of your own Screencast.com folders yet, click **Edit Folders** shown in the dropdown menu in Figure 12.29. Here you can create a specific folder and an output button configured for this Screencast.com folder location.

NOTE
*By default, all of your captures shared to Screencast.com are uploaded into your **Jing folder**. This folder is automatically created the first time you upload a capture to Screencast.com and is hidden from the public. This means no one will be able to access or view any content in the Jing folder. In order to share a capture in a hidden folder, you must manually provide the URL address to your desired audience.*

Selecting the **Allow Comments box** will enable viewers to comment on your captures. This option provides a good way to get feedback from your audience either on the content of a capture or the capture itself. Once you have made this last configuration, you can look back over the dialog box. If you are happy with the settings you selected, click **Save** to create your new Screencast.com Output button.

12.4b — Social Media Outputs

You can customize output buttons in Jing to quickly upload your captures to your favorite social media site. To use the **Twitter output**, you will need to authorize Jing to use your Twitter account by providing an assigned pin number. To get your pin, click **Get Twitter Pin** in the Twitter dialog menu shown in Figure 12.30.

FIGURE 12.30 — Twitter button settings dialog menu.

This will take you to the **authorization page**. Here you will enter your **Twitter username** and **password**. If you do not already have a Twitter account, you can sign up for one on the authorization page as well.

Once you authorize the account, you will automatically be provided with a pin, which you should copy and paste into the Twitter dialog menu. Click **Authorize** and your **Twitter account username** will appear in the dialog menu. You are now ready to **Save** and create your Twitter output button.

Similarly, you will need to authorize Jing to use your Facebook account if you want to create an output button for this social media Website. Click the **Start Authorization** button seen in Figure 12.31.

FIGURE 12.31 — Facebook button settings dialog menu.

You will then be prompted to login to Facebook and allow Jing access to your account. Follow the listed steps and your account will appear in the dialog menu. Click **Save** and your button will be added to the Jing Buttons toolbar.

12.4c — Additional Media Hosting Outputs

Screencast.com is highly recommended as your choice output for hosting your captures because of its close integration with Jing and easy visual sharing abilities. However, Jing also provides you with alternative hosting output options. You can choose to host your captures on your own FTP server by setting up the FTP output in the Button Settings dialog box. You can also host your image captures on the popular image-hosting site, Flickr. To configure this button on your Jing Buttons Toolbar, you will need to authorize your Flickr account in a similar process as your Facebook or Twitter account authorizations.

The YouTube output option is only available when running Jing Pro, Jing's predecessor, which is no longer available for purchase. If you want to share your video captures with this video hosting output, you will want to get Snagit from TechSmith.

12.5 — Jing History

The last ray we have left to cover in the Jing Sun Launcher is **Jing Capture History** shown in Figure 12.32.

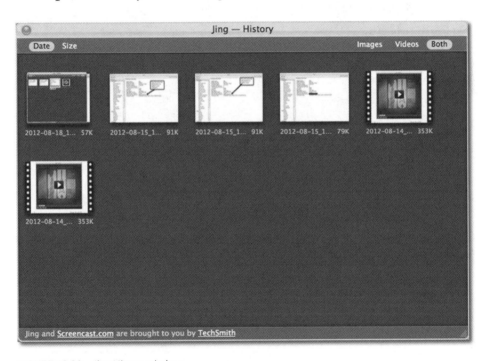

FIGURE 12.32 — Jing History window.

This is where Jing stores all of your image and video captures as thumbnails for your preview. The **menu bar** at the top of the History window allows you to sort your images either by **Date** or Size and lets you view your captures by capture type: **Image**, **Video**, or **Both**.

If you hover over any one of the thumbnails, a window will appear that will enlarge the capture and provides the capture specifications including dimensions and date of capture. Figure 12.33 shows an example of this Capture Details Window.

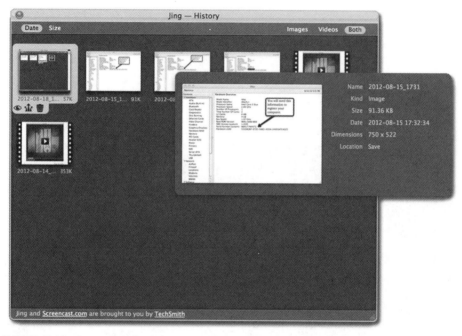

FIGURE 12.33 —Capture Details window in Jing History window.

Clicking once on a thumbnail will allow access to the **thumbnail toolbar**, shown in Figure 12.34. From this toolbar, you can **View**, **Share**, or **Delete** the highlighted thumbnail.

The first icon on the far left-hand side of the toolbar will open your capture either in the **Jing Editor** if it is an image capture or in the **Preview window** for a video capture.

FIGURE 12.34 —Thumbnail toolbar in Jing History window.

NOTE *You can also view your captures in the Jing Editor or Preview window by double-clicking on the thumbnail.*

When you open an image capture from your History in the Jing editor, you can add additional visual enhancements and share it to another output of your choice. However, you cannot delete any of the visual enhancements that were previously saved to your capture. Additionally, when you save the new additions, this will create an entirely new capture. This allows you to use both the original and edited captures as needed.

To the right of the **View icon** is the **Share icon**. This allows you to re-copy your capture back onto your **Clipboard** to easily share it with a friend or coworker. The **Share tool** provides you the capability to take multiple captures and then copy them all back to back into your online conversation. Therefore, you can take all of your captures at once and then later paste them together into an e-mail or chat. Lastly, the **Trashcan icon** allows you to delete any unwanted captures from your History.

NOTE

*Captures are not just deleted from your History. When you select the **Delete tool**, this will remove the actual content from its share output as well. This means if you have your image saved on your machine, deleting it from your History will also delete it off your computer.*

CHAPTER SUMMARY

With the knowledge from this chapter and the two previous chapters, you now know when and how to utilize each screen capture application to fully meet your capturing needs. We have discussed the Jing functionalities and tools accessible in both the Windows and Mac versions of the application and took a close look at when and where to use them. Jing's sharing versatility makes it your user-friendly visual content solution for the modern computer user. You don't have to be "computer savvy" to keep up with the flow of conversation any longer. Capturing and sharing your view is one quick click away.

CHAPTER PROJECTS

1. Use the following link to download Jing from TechSmith's Website: http://www.techsmith.com/download/jing/default.asp. Follow the download instructions. Choose an e-mail account, password, and username to sign up for your free Screencast account. During your download, you will be prompted to sign up. Once you have everything set up, you will need to create a new folder for your Screencast account. Now, use what you have learned in this chapter about Jing Buttons to create your new Screencast folder and title it "Personal". Once you are done, create a new button in Jing for uploading captures to this folder. Upload one capture and one video to this new folder.

2. This project is designed to test your understanding of layering in the Jing Editor. You will need to capture an image of your favorite Website. Open your capture in the Editor and create a tutorial of this Website using the available tools. You need to indicate specific tools, instruments, pictures, and/or icons in the capture and provide explanatory text. Your capture should be professionally formatted with properly overlapping objects. If you do not already have one, create a Facebook account and upload your finished image to your wall.

3. Move your Sun Launcher to either your Menu bar or your taskbar, depending on the operating system you are using to run Jing. Now, set Jing to open automatically when you turn on your computer. You will also need to reset your capture hotkey combining Shift and X. Once you have completed these setting modifications, take a series of captures that record all of your changes. Use the Editor to point out any new modifications. Feel free to add an explanatory text. Now share your captures to your preferred destination.

PROJECTS AND REFERENCE LISTS

▪ A.1 — DVD information

The DVD included in this book contains a number of additional files and features. Project tutorials, scripts, videos, images, captions, audio files, blank storyboard frames, and exercises are included for further practice. Although the project files are split into chapters, you can use any of the files for any of the projects in the book.

Some of these features include:

- **Mini tutorial videos** — showing the actions talked about in the book

- **All images in color** — to see more detail color coding used by the programs

- **Project files** — create your own projects using supplied sample files

- **Sample projects** — completed project created by the programs

A.2 — Quick Clips

Chapter 02

- messy verses a clean recording background

Chapter 04

- recording a screen capture
- recording a custom selection
- recording with audio
- recording with a camera
- drawing on the screen
- adding markers to the recording
- adding cursor effects
- adding automatic keystroke callouts

Chapter 05

- PowerPoint recording
- PowerPoint notes and captions
- PowerPoint markers and table of contents

Chapter 06

- importing and adding media from the clip bin to the timeline
- previewing and using the library media
- adding clips to the library media

Chapter 07

- grouping clips and arranging the layer order

- resizing, rotating, and move media
- add and lock tracks
- making a selection with the playhead
- cutting, splitting, and trimming clips
- changing the speed and duration of a clip
- adding markers to the timeline

Chapter 08

- using the Callout tab
- using the Zoom-N-Pan tab
- using the Audio tab
- removing background noise
- using the Transition tab
- using the Cursor Effects tab
- using the Visual Properties tab
- using the Voice Narration tab
- using the Record Camera tab
- using the Captions tab
- using the Quizzes tab

Chapter 09

- producing a video
- custom .mp4 production

A.3 — Chapter Projects

Chapter 01

- **Files:** All figures in this chapter are in color located in the chapter folder on the DVD

- **Project:** Watch the sample projects representing a few different types of projects created using Camtasia Studio
  - *Torchwork* — a sample of a story or blog report
  - **Presentation Tips video** — sample of a work or school teaching tool
  - **Presentation Tips presentation** — a sample of a PowerPoint presentation recording
  - **InDesign tutorial** — a sample of a screen capture tutorial
  - *Overtime* — a sample of an animated storyboard
  - *Cat's Inner Thoughts* — a sample of a home movie

Chapter 02

- **Files:** All figures in this chapter are in color located in the chapter folder on the DVD

- **Project:** Fill blank script and storyboard frames

Chapter 03

- **Files:** All figures in this chapter are in color located in the chapter folder on the DVD

Chapter 04

- **Files:** All figures in this chapter are in color located in the chapter folder on the DVD

- **Project:** Open a photo in the project folder to draw and highlight areas using ScreenDraw

Chapter 05

- **Files:** All figures in this chapter are in color located in the chapter folder on the DVD

- **Project:** Add text to notes field and add slide titles in a PowerPoint presentation to create captions and markers when the recording is opened in the Editor

- **Project:** Use the files in the project folder to assemble a PowerPoint presentation and record it

Chapter 06

- **Files:** All figures in this chapter are in color located in the chapter folder on the DVD

- **Project:** Import the selection of files in the project folder to the Clip Bin

- **Project:** Open project file and add clips to the Library

- **Project:** Import .libzip file in the project folder into the Library

Chapter 07

- **Files:** All figures in this chapter are in color located in the chapter folder on the DVD

- **Project:** Use the media in the project folder to resize, rotate, and movie media on the canvas

- **Project:** Use the media in the project folder to align and crop media

- **Project:** Use the practice files to cut, split, trim, and change the duration of the clips

Chapter 08

- **Files:** All figures in this chapter are in color located in the chapter folder on the DVD

- **Project:** Use the illustrations in the project folder and add zooms and pans to create a moving storyboard

- **Project:** Use the media in the project folder and use the Visual Properties tab to adjust the clip settings

- **Project:** Add Cat Thoughts captions to add captions and arrange clips to create a video project

Chapter 09

- **Files:** All figures in this chapter are in color located in the chapter folder on the DVD

- **Files:** All production presets and custom formats are rendered using the same video project as reference examples located in chapter folder on the DVD

- **Project:** Use project files and create a video project and Screencast.com account, then use the Production Wizard Screencast.com preset to uploaded the practice file

Chapter 10

- **Files:** All figures in this chapter are in color located in the chapter folder on the DVD

- **Project:** Knowledge Check questions

Chapter 11

- **Files:** All figures in this chapter are in color located in the chapter folder on the DVD

- **Project:** Use project files and use each editing tool to practice adjusting the effects

- **Project:** Knowledge Check questions

Chapter 12

- **Files:** All figures in this chapter are in color located in the chapter folder on the DVD

- **Project:** Knowledge Check questions

A.4 — Practice Script and Storyboards

Use the blank script storyboards to practice writing an outline, script, or drawing a storyboard. (See Figure A.1)

Outline or Script

Blank storyboard frames for practice

Blank storyboard frames for practice

FIGURE A.1 — Blank script storyboard.

Use the storyboard to practice writing an outline or script, describing the action in the storyboard. (See Figure A.2)

FIGURE A.2 — Blank script or outline with illustrations.

A.5 — Hotkey Commands (Camtasia Studio)

Hotkeys are keyboard shortcuts that use keystrokes for activate menu or task actions.

Recorder Hotkeys (default, customizable)

Hide Tray Icon	None Assigned
Marker	CTRL + M
Record/Pause	F9
ScreenDraw	CTRL + SHIFT + D
Select Region	None Assigned
Stop	F10

ScreenDraw Hotkeys (not customizable)

Enable/Disable ScreenDraw	CTRL + SHIFT + D
Exit ScreenDraw	ESC
Redo	CTRL + Y
Tool Width	1 - 8
Undo	CTRL + Z

Shape

Arrow	A
Ellipse	E
Frame	F
Highlight	H
Line	L
Pen	P

Color

Black	K
Blue	B

Cyan	C
Green	G
Magenta	M
Red	R
White	W
Yellow	Y

PowerPoint Add-in Hotkeys (default, customizable)

Record/Pause	CTRL + SHIFT + F9
Stop	CTRL + SHIFT + F10

Editor: Canvas Hotkeys

ALT Key	toggles the crop function
CTRL Key + Mouse Scroll Wheel	scale a zoom animation for the selected media
CTRL Key	while resizing media, overrides maintaining the aspect ratio
Keyboard Arrow Keys	moves selected media in the direction of the arrows
Mouse Scroll Wheel	increase or decrease the magnification view
Shift Key	holding down the shift key will resize media from the middle point, while when in pan mode it moves the canvas view

Editor: Timeline Navigation Hotkeys (not customizable)

Beginning of the timeline	CTRL + SHIFT + Home
End of the timeline	CTRL + SHIFT + End
Jump to beginning of timeline	CTRL + Home
Jump to end of timeline	CTRL + End

Make a selection step-by-step	CTRL + SHIFT + Right Arrow or CTRL + SHIFT + Left Arrow
Next clip	CTRL + ALT + Right Arrow
Next marker	CTRL +]
Play/Pause	Spacebar
Previous clip	CTRL + ALT + Left Arrow
Previous marker	CTRL + [
Select between markers	CTRL + SHIFT [or CTRL + SHIFT]
Select next clip	CTRL + SHIFT + ALT + Right Arrow
Select previous clip	CTRL + SHIFT + ALT + Left Arrow
Step backward	CTRL + Left Arrow - Hold the keys down to rewind
Step forward	CTRL + Right Arrow - Hold the keys down to fast forward
Stop	CTRL + ALT + Space
Zoom in	CTRL + Plus or CTRL + Mouse scroll wheel up
Zoom out	CTRL + Minus or CTRL + Mouse scroll wheel down
Zoom to fit	CTRL + F9 or CTRL + SHIFT + Mouse scroll wheel down
Zoom to maximum	CTRL + F11 or CTRL + SHIFT + Mouse scroll wheel up
CTRL + F10	Zoom to Selection
Move the playhead	Double-click

Generic Windows Hotkeys

These hotkeys work in most operating systems

Copy	CTRL + C
Cut	CTRL + X
Exit menu, or close dialog box	Escape
New	CTRL + N
Open	CTRL + O
Paste	CTRL + V
Print	CTRL + P
Save	CTRL + S
Select all	CTRL + A
Undo	CTRL + Z

A.6 — Audio Meter Ranges

Range of the Audio	State or Problem	Action
None	no range is showing	Check source: connected and activated, unmuted, the correct source selected
Low Green	high point only hits a low green	Drag the volume slider to the right
Green to Yellow	high point does not pass middle	Drag the volume slider to the right
Yellow	high point just past middle	No change needed
Yellow to Orange	clipping might occur	Drag the volume slider to the left
Orange to Red	clipping occurs	Drag the volume slider to the left

FIGURE A.3 — Audio Meter Ranges

A.7 — Production Formats

MP4 — Flash/HTML5 Player (.mp4)

Advantages

- Comparatively small file size
- Excellent overall quality
- Plays on browsers, smartphones, and tablets

Disadvantages

- Not supported by all browsers or devices if the Flash player is not installed

WMV — Windows Media Video (.wmv)

Advantages

- Excellent quality
- Smaller file size

Disadvantages

- Limited mobile device support
- Not all players will be able to play this format, not native to Mac
- Will not support extra video options like quizzes and hotspots

MOV — QuickTime Movie (.mov)

Advantages

- Native video format for Macs
- Plays in iTunes, QuickTime or other 3rd party players on Windows

Disadvantages

- Limited mobile device support
- Not all video players will be able to play this format
- Not native to Windows
- Will not support extra video options like quizzes and hotspots

AVI — Audio Video Interleave Video File (.avi)

Advantages

- Standard video format
- Excellent overall quality
- Good to use with additional video editors
- Neutral format that is not bound to Mac or Windows programs

Disadvantages

- Not recommended as a sharable format because it uses specific audio and video codecs that will be required if played on another machine
- Will not support extra video options like quizzes and hotspots

M4V — iPod, iPhone, iTunes Compatible Video (.m4v)

Advantages

- Synchronization with iPod and iPhone through iTunes
- Older iPods and iPhones can play the format

Disadvantages

- Smaller video dimensions
- Close to the popular .mp4 format without the advantages
- Will not support extra video options like quizzes and hotspots

MP3 — Audio Only (.mp3)

Advantages

- Excellent audio quality
- Standard audio format

Disadvantages

- Audio only format

GIF — Animation File (.gif)

Advantages

- File sizes are small
- They can be embed in e-mails or Websites

Disadvantages

- This file format does not include audio tracks
- Low overall quality
- Only 256 colors
- Supports only short videos
- Will not support extra video options like quizzes and hotspots

A.8 — Types of Importable Media

Camtasia Recording file

- **.camrec** — Camtasia Recording File

Image files

- **.bmp** — Bitmap image file
- **.gif** — Graphics Interchange Format
- **.jpg/.jpeg** — Joint Photographic Experts Group
- **.png** — Portable Network Graphics

Audio files

- **.wav** — Waveform Audio File Format
- **.mp3** — MPEG 1 or MPEG 2 audio layer 3
- **.wma** — Windows Media Audio

Video files

- **.avi** — Audio Video Interleave
- **.mp4** — Motion Picture Expert Group 4
- **.mpg/.mpeg** — Motion Picture Expert Group 1
- **.wmv** — Window Media Video
- **.mov** — Quick Time Movie
- **.swf** — Adobe Flash

A.9 — Common Aspect Ratios

- **Standard** — 4:3 with resolutions — 640x480, 800x600, 1024x768

  Traditional television and computer monitor standard

- **Widescreen** — 16:9 with resolutions — 854x480, 1280x720, 1366x768, 1600x900

  Video widescreen standard, used in high-definition television

Resolution	Dimensions	Aspect Ratio	Display	Usage
	320 x 240	4:3	Standard	Classic IPods
480p	640 x 480	4:3	Standard	Web Videos
720p	1280 x 720	16:9	Widescreen	HD Web Videos
1080p	1920 x 1080	16:9	Widescreen	1080p HD Video

FIGURE A.4 — Standard dimension guide for video capture.

A.10 — Credits

All screen shorts and screen recordings were taken using the program Camtasia Studio and Snagit and on the Windows operating system.

Torchwork Video

Cara Torta

Jonathan Torta

Stephanie Torta

Presentation Tips Video

Allison DiRienzo

Antonio Lopez

Stephanie Torta

Presentation Tips Presentation

Allison DiRienzo

Antonio Lopez

Stephanie Torta

***Overtime* Animatic**

Vladimir Minuty

Stephanie Torta

Ramona Taj *(voice)*

Leighsa Burgin *(voice)*

Fiore Leo *(voice)*

Alisha Finneran *(voice)*

InDesign Tutorial

Stephanie Torta

***Cat's Inner Thoughts* Project**

Diana Torta

Jonathan Torta

Stephanie Torta

Video Talent

Allison DiRienzo

Antonio Lopez

Cara Torta

Photographs

Jonathan Torta

Diana Torta

Stephanie Torta

Illustrations

Vladimir Minuty

Scripts

Cat's Inner Thoughts

Diana Torta

Presentation Notes

Diana Torta

Cameras

Canon 7D

GoPro

Canon Power Shot SD1100 IS

Logitech Webcam C210

Microphones

LogitechG35 Headset

Olympus VN-6200PC Digital recorder

A.11 — References

www.techsmith.com

www.lynda.com

Daniel Park. *Camtasia Studio 6*. Wordware Publishing Inc. 2009.

Stephanie Torta, Vladimir Minuty. *Storyboarding: Turning Script to Motion*. Mecury Learning and Information. 2011.

Stephanie Torta. *Graphic Design: Adobe InDesign CS4*. Jones and Bartlett Publishers, Inc. 2009.

GLOSSARY

Many of the words in this list have multiple meanings or uses. This glossary lists their definitions as they apply to recording and editing with Camtasia Studio, Snagit, or Jing.

.avi — (Audio Video Interleave video file) — video file format that can be used with multiple playback programs and is not bound to the Editor

.bmp — Bitmap — raster graphic file format to save image files

.camproj — Camtasia Studio Project file format extension

.camrec — (Camtasia Recording File) — default recording file format used by the Recorder, it can only be used by the Editor, but saves a wide range of data that is collected during the recording

.flv — Flash Video — container file format using Adobe Flash Player for delivery

.gif — (Graphics Interchange Format) — graphic Images on the Web that may be in the cross-platform file format

.jpg — (Joint Photographic Experts Group) — compressed image file, picture quality bitmapped images in a file format

.libzip — zipped Camtasia Studio library file

.m4v — MPEG-4 Video file from iTunes — iPod, iPhone, iTune compatible video

.mov — Quick Time Movie

.mp3 — MPEG 1 or MPEG 2 audio layer 3, a codec CD worth sound files

.mp4 — Motion Picture Expert Group 4

.mpeg — Motion Picture Expert Group 1, a codec especially intended for video compression

.mpeg 4 — Motion Picture Expert Group 4

.mpg — Motion Picture Expert Group 1

.pdf — (Portable Document File) — on a multi-platform by Adobe Systems

.png — (Portable Network Graphic) — compressed bitmapped raster graphic file format

.snag — the Snagit file format on a Windows OS

.snagpro — Snagit file format on Mac OS X

.swf — Small Web Format

.tiff — Tag Image File Format

.wav — audio file by Microsoft, and the native digital audio file format for Windows

.wma — (Windows Media Audio) — audio sound compression developed by Microsoft

.wmv — (Window Media Video) — video compression format supported by Windows Media Player along with other types of players

.zip — compressed file, multiple files can be compressed together inside a single .zip file and stored as one file until extraction

1.33:1 — an aspect ratio; includes television and computer screens; also called 4:3 or Academy Standard

1.78:1 — an aspect ratio; high definition; the video widescreen standard used in high-definition television; also called 16:9

A

ADA — Americans with Disabilities (federal anti-discrimination act to make sure qualified people with disabilities have the same opportunities people have without disabilities)

ADDED SCENES — shots or script changes that are added after preproduction

ADD-IN — an enhancement to a base program

ADJUSTMENT HANDLES — little black outlined squares that can be clicked on with the mouse and dragged to adjust the recording are selection box to the desired dimension on both the sides and corners of the selection area box

ALIGNMENT — the position of lines and objects, and text relative to the margins including left, right, justified, and centered

ALT KEY — alternate key (key giving alternate meanings to other keys)

ANGLE SHOT/ANGLE — the directional relation between the camera and the object at which it is pointed

ANIMATED GIF — a simple animation using .gif images while repeating them in order

ANIMATIC — combined images of a storyboard or still photographs edited in a sequence and synchronized with a soundtrack

ANIMATION — the techniques used to simulate motion through creating frames individually and then editing them as one sequence

ANIMATION INDICATOR — an icon of a blue arrow that indicates an animation applied to the clip

ANNOTATION TAB — settings for system stamps and captions including the options to adjust the background, positions, font, color, effects, and style of the stamps and captions

APPLICATION — See program

ASPECT RATIO —longer dimension is divided by the shorter dimension. The two standard aspect ratios for video are 4:3 (for every 4 pixels of width there are 3 pixels of height) and 16:9

AUDIO CLIPPING —distortion that happens when the audio wave overloads the audio output clipping part of the sound

AUDIO IMPUT METER — shows the audio level for the recording

AUTOMATIC GAIN — adaptive system inside your audio recording device that reduces the volume if the sound is strong and raises it when it is weak

B

BACKDROP — the background of an event; setting that is created to represent an environment

BLOCK/BLOCKING — to plan or rehearse in order to work out the movement of the camera and placement of the cast and crew for a shot or scene

BLOG — a Website that represents information, views, or ideas from the creator to the general public

BLUESCREEN — actors and objects are placed in front of a large blue (or green) background to later be superimposed onto another image

BLUR CALLOUT — maintains privacy by hiding parts of the video of sensitive or confidential information from viewers

BOLD — characters formatted in boldface

BROWSER — a Web server's program allowing you to get their files

BUDGET — total amount of money allocated for a specific purpose during a specified period of time

C

CALLOUT — graphics on the top of a video to show an important process or object

CAMERA ANGLE — the point of view from which the camera photographs a subject or scene

CAMERA MOVEMENT — a change in subject view, frame, or perspective of a shot, made by the movement of the camera

CAMTASIA STUDIO — an innovative multimedia recording and editing program

CANVAS — an area in the preview window where you can rotate, arrange, resize, and order the content

CAPTION — text that overlays over a video project

CAPTURE — selections controlling the recording aspects of the program. These include starting and stopping the recording along with area selection and what input devices will be used

CAPTURE MODE — settings that define the method of screen capture

CAPTURE TYPE — helps you to select and capture the image, video, or text according to its capture region based on predefined sets of properties

CD — (Compact Disk) — media that stores from 650 to 700 megabytes of information

CHECKBOX —the option button when you click the box, you can enable or disable the item

CHROMA KEY COMPOSITING — an editing technique for combining two images or frames, making one color of one image or frame transparent to reveal the other image or frame behind it

CINEMATOGRAPHY — the artistic creation of moving images using light and cameras

CLIP ART — images (cartoons, pictures, or drawings) that are already made and can be bought

CLIP BIN — file that holds video, image, and audio clips imported into the project you are working on

CLIPBOARD — temporary storage area on your computer where data that is copied and stored for use in another application

CLIPPING — distorted sound that happens when the sound goes beyond the range that it can be recorded

CLIPS — the media pulled or imported from the Recorder, clip bin, and library

CLOSE CAPTIONS — captions that can be turned on and off and hidden

CMS — Course Management System

CODEC — (coder/decoder) — a program that enables digital data or streaming media to be compressed and decompressed

COMMERCIAL BOARDS — normally color on large sheets of paper and very detailed; at times, designed by advertising agencies for their clients

COMPUTER WINDOW — shows were all the drives are on the computer such as the hard drives, CPU, and flash drive

COMPUTER-GENERATED IMAGERY — (CGI) — art created with the use of a computer; can be static or dynamic

CONCEPT BOARDS — very detailed illustrations focusing on the location, set, background scenery, or a dramatic event

CONTEXT MENUS —menus that change to match the tool, location, or task you are working with

CONTINUITY — the seamless physical detail from one shot to another within a scene

COPY and PASTE — allows the copying to another place of a file, folder, text, or picture

CORNERS — these corners indicate the edge of the recording area and will change color and blink once the recording has started

COVERAGE — shooting a scene from many different angles in order to properly tells the story

CPU — (Central Processing Unit) — chip or circuit which controls how the computer operations

CREDIT — the recognition or approval for an act, ability, or quality

CUR — cursor abbreviation

CURSOR — shows where the user can type text

CURSOR EFFECT — data can be collected, stored, and then can be used to enhance video

CUT — in editing, to make an abrupt change of image or sound, or changing from one shot to another, and removes a section of track on a timeline

CUTAWAY — a shot of part of a scene, filmed from a different angle and/or focal length from the master shot, of action not covered in the master shot

D

DATA — information that can be grouped and arranged in many ways

DEFAULT — value that is preset when user does not set values

DIALOG BOX — an interface window that opens for user interaction, perform commands, or apply settings

DIGITAL CAMERA — digital photographs are encoded and stored on a camera

DISSOLVE — a transition between scenes; one scene fades away and the other fades in simultaneously

DOWNLOADING — copying files (network or Internet)

DRAG and DROP — moving objects from one position to another while clicking on an object and holding the mouse button down then releasing

DROP-DOWN — an arrow on the far right side in a dialog box that opens a menu

DROPDOWN MENU — a button when clicked opens a list of options that are selectable

DVD — (Digital Versatile Disc) — media made with four layers that can store up to 4.7 gigabytes per layer

E

EASE-IN/EASE-OUT — in animation, it is the continuing increase or decrease of motion to replicate the effect of gravity or other things

EDIT — the act of deleting, arranging, and placing together shots and sounds in order to construct a flowing sequence

EDITORIAL BOARDS — storyboards that tell a story and are sometimes taken from scripts

EFFECTS — visual enhancements that can be included into the screencast during the recording. These include captions, system stamps, and system sounds, sometimes abbreviated as "fx"

EMBED — to insert an object into another place or program

EMBED SIZE — frame size in the HTML page where the video is displayed

EXTRACTING — the process of pulling files or folders out of a compressed folder

F

FADE — the gradual diminution or increase in the brightness or visibility of an image in cinema or television

FADE IN — to appear or be heard gradually

FADE OUT — to disappear gradually

FILE — container for data and programs, a collection of data stored in one unit, under a single name

FILE COMPRESSION — compression shrinks the size of files and folders without affecting their content

FILE EXTENSION — one or more letters following the filename separated by a period, the extension may designate the program that created the file

FILE FORMAT — encoded information storage in a computer file, and vary depending on how they were encoded

FILE PATH — the route to a specific folder on a computer or server

FLAGS — markers that allow you to assign your capture to one or more different categories that can later be searched and sorted in the Search Pane, also known as Tags

FLASH DRIVE — a small, lightweight, removable, and rewritable data storage device that uses flash memory, also known as a USB drive

FLATTENING — a vector object means to make it part of the background, the object becomes a part of the image and can no longer be edited apart from the image as a whole

FOLDER — files are stored on your flash drive, hard disk, or other media

FONT — characters of text in a certain style and size

FORMAT — the specific type of media used to capture an image; also, the type of equipment used to photograph and project and screen the media

FORMATTING — setting up your file with margin settings, fonts, font size, spacing, and more

FRAME — the viewing area as seen by the camera lens

FREEZE FRAME — a still, motionless scene or image in the course of a shot made by running a series of identical frames or by stopping at one desired frame

FTP — (File Transfer Protocol) — protocol for exchanging files with another computer

G

GPU — (Graphic Processing Unit) — single chip processor

GREEN SCREEN — often used in Chroma key compositing because green is the least amount of color in skin; also, see BLUE SCREEN

H

HAND-HELD — a shooting technique; the camera is held in the operator's hands

HARD DRIVE — storage hardware in a computer for data

HELP MENU — additional recourses, documents, and help selections

HIGH DEFINITION — (HD) — video having higher resolution than standard definition (SD) and digitally broadcast using video compression

HOTKEY — keyboard key stroke shortcut assigned to a command, tool, or menu actions

HOTSPOT — added interactivity and links to a section of a clip, site, or document

HTML — (Hypertext Markup Language) — used to create WWW with hyperlinks and markup for texting

HYPERLINK — a hotspot that is linked to a new document or Website address, a connection between two data items in the same document or in an external file

I

ICO FILES — image file format that are icon images with multiple sizes and color depths

ICON — a graphic symbol that represents a location, object, or program on the hard drive or application

ICON BUTTON — an image graphic that also acts as a function button

INSERT — a shot of action already covered in the master shot but from a different angle or focal length

INTERNET — sharing data on a network

INTERNET EXPLORER — Microsoft's Web browser

ITALICS — the font is formatted into italics

J

JING — a TechSmith product primarily intended for taking quick and easy screen captures that need minimal editing or enhancements and used for informal online communication (Facebook, Twitter)

JUMP CUT — a edit that removes the middle section of a continuous shot and joins together the beginning and end of the shot; any moving objects in the shot will appear to jump to a new position

K

KEY FRAME — a drawing that defines the starting and ending points of any smooth transition

KEYBOARD SHORTCUT — keys on the keyboard which help you enter commands

KEYSTROKE CALLOUT — displays keyboard activity on the screen

KEYWORD — descriptive text that can be entered into the search bar on the Search Pane to identify and group images and video by common properties

L

LAYERS — when used in graphics, it is different parts of a picture on planes. The layers can be stacked, combined, locked together, or flattened

LAYOUT — an area to arrange objects, images, text, audio, and video on slides or the canvas

LETTERBOX — the practice of transferring film shot in a widescreen aspect ratio to standard-width video formats while preserving the film's original aspect ratio

LIBRARY — holds clips (timeline sequences, audio, image, and video) you can use in projects

LINK — it is the connection (word, image, or phrase) between the source and destination to another Web page

LMS — (Learning Management System) — software or Web-based technology used to plan, implement, and assess a certain learning processes

LOCATION SOUND — any sound recorded at the shoot

LOCK — closes the track or area down and will not be able to be changed or edited

LOCK ASPECT RATIO OPTION — makes sure correct aspect ratio is held if more resizing is needed

LOCK TO APPLICATIONS — lets you automatically size recording area to the size of the application you selected in Windows

LOOP INDEFINITELY — video playing continuously

M

MAC OS — Apple Macintosh's operating system

MACINTOSH — Apple computer

MARGINS — on a page, it is the blank space on the edges

MARKERS — creating recording notes, setting points to split long videos into multiple videos and making navigation points within the timeline and production

MATCH CUT/MATCH DISSOLVE — a cut from one scene to a completely different scene with the objects in the two scenes occupying the same place in the frame

MATTE SHOT — a small portion of the shot is a live action shot, the rest is masked to show a different background or foreground image

MAXIMIZE BUTTON — expands the window to the entire screen in Windows

MEDIA ASSETS — items in the library

MENU BAR — list of commands (Menu Options) on a bar at the top of the program

MENU OPTIONS BAR — a bar commonly located on the top of the interface that has selectable dropdown options and generally controlling the overall program

METADATA — information regarding the contents in files

MICROSOFT POWERPOINT — Microsoft Office's slide and multimedia presentation program that combines text, charts, animations, video, and photos into slide shows

MINIMIZE BUTTON — makes the window to a small button on the taskbar which glows when the mouse hovers over it in the Windows programs

MODEM — connects to the Internet and other networks

MONITOR — screen that shows what you enter and the response of the computer

MONTAGE — short shots edited into a sequence to condense narrative; often used to suggest the passage of time

MOODLE — (Modular Object-Oriented Dynamic Learning Environment) — an open source course management system used by educational institutions to create online courses

MOTION CAPTURE — the process of capturing movement and translating the information into a digital form or model

MOUSE — input device which lets you point and click at items on the screen

MOVING COMPASS — an icon that when clicked allows you to fully move and reposition the selection area while keeping the dimensions

MULTIMEDIA — using a digital piece of equipment, you can build, incorporate, and deliver many combinations of text, animation, graphics, sound, or video

MUSIC PLAYER — a small machine or program that lets you listen and play audio files and songs

N

NATURAL SOUND OR WILD SOUND — sound recorded in the environment of the recording area that might not be picked up in the initial recording or additional sound for enhancement

O

OBJECT — any shape, box, text, image, or something that you can manipulate using the program's commands. It can also be a certain area in an image

OPACITY — tells how opaque an object or layer is

OPEN CAPTIONS — can be set and cannot be turned off

OS — (Operating System) — the essential software on a computer

P

PAN — Panorama — to move a camera to follow an object or create a panoramic effect; in the preview, window will move the focus center of your video to the area you highlighted

PATH — the list of folders or menus that points to a location

PC — abbreviation for personal computer

PICTURE-IN-PICTURE — (PIP) — Camtasia Recorder and PowerPoint Add-in include a picture-in-picture feature where you can show PowerPoint or desktop screen actions with a video of yourself or lecturer speaking from a different place

PIP — see picture-in-picture

PIXEL — digital picture elements, represented by small dots that connect to create images

PIXILATE CALLOUT — maintains privacy by hiding parts of the video of sensitive or confidential information from viewers

PLAYHEAD — a slider that can select a frame and move throughout the duration of the timeline that is linked to the preview area

POINT — a unit of measurement

POSTPRODUCTION — the general term for all stages of production occurring after the actual shooting or recording ending with the completed work

POWERPOINT — Microsoft Office's presentation program

PRE-PRODUCTION — the process of preparing all the elements involved in a project before actual shooting

PRESENTATION — a speech, lecture, or slideshow

PREVIEW WINDOW — whole area showing canvas, playback controls, viewing options, and editing dimensions within Camtasia Editor, will show for preview the selected area of the timeline where the playhead is positioned

PRODUCTION BOARDS — sometimes taken from scripts to tell a story, they reflect the director's or developing team's ideas on the story and camera shots

PROFILES — allows you to store a number of settings and functionalities for commonly used screen captures. When selected, the profile will initiate a capture according to its preformatted properties

PROGRAM — computer software designed to perform tasks, see also application

PROGRAM WINDOW — a program is running in a window

PROPERTIES — attributes connected with drives, files, folders, and other items

Q

QUICK STYLES GALLERY — contains the preformatted objects for each individual Drawing Tool. In this window, you can select one of the already designed Shapes, Stamps, or other visual enhancements and quickly add it to your capture

QUICKTIME — developed by Apple Computer using .mov extension for energetic data (sound, animation, and video) using a cross-platform file format

R

RATERIZE — when displaying on a printed page or screen, this is the process of changing text or images into pixels or bitmap

RECORDING AREA SELECTION BOX — a dotted green box that outlines enclosing the area of the screen to be recorded

RENDER — video rendering is the process the computer takes to generate images

RIGHT CLICK MENU — a menu that will open when the right mouse button is clicked

ROTATING — object is moved around a precise axis

S

SANS SERIF — font that doesn't have decorative lines on letters

SCALE — a proportion used in determining the dimensional relationship of a representation to that which it represents

SCENE — the presentation in which the setting is fixed and the time is continuous

SCORM — (Sharable Content Object Reference Model) — standards for Web-based e-learning and shows how to transfer to zip files

SCREEN CAPTURE — a still or moving snapshot of a computer's visual output. A screen capture is also known as a screen dump, screen grab, or screen shot

SCREEN CAPTURE REGION — designated area for a screen capture and everything you want to include in your capture region

SCREEN DRAW — drawing on the screen while you are recording

SCREENPLAY — a script for a movie, including descriptions of scenes and some camera directions

SCREENSHOT — a image capture of a window, application, or desktop

SCRIPT — a written text of a film, play, presentation, television, and speech

SCRIPT BREAKDOWN — lists of the basics elements of the project, including special items, equipment, and effects that are necessary for the script

SCROLL BAR — you can move up, down, or left and right to see the information if the file is too large to see all at one time. You can use the bar to look at parts of the file not on the screen

SCRUBBER — shows progress of playback on timeline

SCV TEXT FILE FORMAT — ScanVec OAS mate file

SEARCH ENGINE — Internet program to find information on the Internet

SECTION 508 — an amendment to the Rehabilitation Act of 1973 where people with disabilities have access to technology

SELECTION AREA — full-screen, preset, and custom recording dimensions linked to the recording area selection box

SELECTION HANDLES — lets you resize an image by using the circle and square symbols that are on your border of your image

SERIF — font with decorative lines finishing letters

SHARE OUTPUT — a capture destination that has been configured with Snagit for quick and easy sharing, a number of outputs come preinstalled or you can download additional outputs from the TechSmith Website

SHOOTING SCRIPT — a version of a screenplay used during the production, using scene numbers, and following a well-defined set of procedures specifying how script revisions should be implemented and circulated

SHORTCUT — quick access to the original folder, program, or file using a link or pointer

SHOT LIST — a document listing all intended shots in a film

SHOTGUN MICROPHONE — a very narrow recording area that captures sound in an outward cone in front of the device

SINGLE — a shot with the frame encompassing a view of one person or subject

SKETCH MOTION CALLOUTS — shows animation on the screen over a time period that can change in color, fade length, and draw time

SLIDE — basic "page" including text, pictures, graphs, clip art, charts, and/or video in PowerPoint

SLUG LINE/SLUG — the text before each scene in a script that details the time and location of the action

SMART FOCUS — a feature that automatically zooms and pans

SMART PHONE — cell phone that can go on the Internet, access e-mail, store contact information, has personal assistant abilities, and has advanced features and capabilities

SNAGIT — screen capturing and image editing program, the capture media application developed by TechSmith

SNAP GUIDES — yellow guidelines that pull or snap clips to markers, media, or other clips

SNAPPING GUIDELINE — allows media be exactly aligned

SOCIAL MEDIA — people on the Internet can use it for social interaction and applications such as forums, message boards, wikis, podcasts, blogs, Google, Facebook, and YouTube

SPECIAL EFFECTS — see effects

SPLIT TOOL — divides one chip into two chips

SPOTLIGHT CALLOUT — adds a selected light and dims the rest of the screen

SRT — (Source-route transparent) — IBM's bridging of source-route bridging (SRB) and transparent bridging in token ring networks

STANDARD — 4:3 with resolutions — 640x480, 800x600, 1024x768, traditional television and computer monitor standard

STATISTICS TOOLBAR — gives information on recording performance such as duration of recording, frames, and frame rate

STICHING — combining clips after being cut or selected so animations can flow from one to another

STOCK FOOTAGE — a film or video footage that is not custom shot for use in a specific film or television program

STORYBOARD — a series of drawings, illustrations, or photographs that convey a story or series of events and sometimes includes dialogue

STYLE — a well-defined text characteristic that is easily recognized such as bold, underline, and italic

SUBFOLDER — a folder inside a folder

SYSTEM STAMP — puts in recording information (elapsed time into recording plus time and date)

T

TASK DEPENDED MENUS —menu or options only active during certain actions

TASK TABS — tabs that hold media and tools to create and perform selected features such as adding transitions, callouts, zooming, and panning

TASKBAR — a bar (usually at the bottom of the desktop) that contains tabs and icons that can be used to change from one task to another and open programs

TECHSMITH — a software company that publishes leading screen recording programs such as Camtasia Studio, Snagit, and Jing

TEXT BOX — a box where text can be typed into

THEME — shows a constant feel and look (colors, fonts, and more) to the presentation or the whole document

THUMBNAILS — images represented by small images

TILT/TILTING — a cinematographic technique in which the camera rotates up or down

TIME CODE — shows hours, minutes, seconds when each frame is recorded, also works as a frame's address and to synced video and sound

TIMELINE — area to assemble and show all of the frames, tracks, and features of your project including videos, images, audio, special effects, and other features

TIMELINE TOOLBAR — basic editing tools — zooming, cutting and splitting, copying and pasting, zooming in and out

TIMELINE TRACKS — shows the sequence of all clips and the effects in a video

TITLE BAR — shows the file or program being used and is at the top most area of the screen

TITLE CLIP — a clip or animation of a project with a title or other related information

TOC — table of contents

TOGGLE KEY — turned on and off each time you use them

TOOLBAR — it is the set of tools together on a menu bar

TOOLS — launches additional programs included within Camtasia Studio as well as opens the Tools Options and Recording toolbar dialog boxes

TOOLTIP — small window that appears when you hover over an area or icon, the window displays information about the usage and functionality of the said area or tool

TOUCH SCREEN — a digital display that can detect and track the location of a touch on the screen

TRACKS — shows both the vertical and horizontal in sequence on the timeline including videos, images, audio, and special effects

TRANSITION INDICATOR — an icon in-between or at the end of a clip to indicate a transition

TRANSITIONS — moving effects between clips and slides

TRANSPARENT — the condition of being completely see-through or invisible

TRIM — hiding part of a clip on the timeline

TSC2 — (TechSmith Screen Capture Codec) — rugged adaptable handheld data collector

TUDI — TechSmith User Design Initiative

TYPEFACE — styles and sizes of every letter including serif, sans serif, script, and all cases

U

UNDERLINE — a line is put under a character

URL — (Uniform Resource Locator) — global address of resources and documents of WWW

USB — (Universal Serial Bus) — computer port that connects secondary devices to the computer system

V

VECTOR-BASED OBJECT — a tool in Snagit that has properties that allow it to be resized and manipulated by other editing tools and effects in Snagit. These include Callouts, Arrows, Stamps, Freehand Pen, Highlight, Line, and Shapes

VIDEO FRAME RATE – lists the video frames per second with the more frames equaling higher quality and file size

VIDEO GUIDES — a video capture tool that uses the Magnifier and Crosshairs in video capture mode to highlight the standard video dimensions for common video outputs

VISUAL EFFECTS — audio or visual effects that alter reality and are edited postproduction after the live action shoot

VLE — (Virtual Learning Environment) — virtual classroom letting teachers and students to communicate online (class information, learning materials, and assignments)

VOICE OVER — (VO) — narration heard over a scene; also, narration heard at a higher level than a source of music or background sound

W

WATERMARK — pattern of bits that are embedded in a file but are not noticeable

WAVEFORM — pattern of sound waves

WEB CAMERA — camera that can be used to take pictures or video ideal for use on the Web and live streaming

WEBSITE NAVIGATION BOARDS — drawings or thumbnails that create connections and map out the navigation of a Website

WIDESCREEN — 16:9 with resolutions — 854x480, 1280x720, 1366x768, 1600x900, video widescreen standard, used in high-definition television

WI-FI — a wireless local networking protocol

WILD TRACK — sound recorded without images

WINDOW — an area holding a program, dialog box, or user interface and can pop up and overlay over each other

WINDOWS — Microsoft's operating system

WIPE — a gradual spatial transition from one image to another; one image is replaced by another with a distinct edge that forms a shape

WIZARD — a dialog box that will walk the user through a set series of steps

WORLD WIDE WEB — (WWW) — a group of hyperlinked Web pages accessed on the Internet

Z

ZOOM — gradual change in the focal length of the lens with a camera; or will magnify in and out parts of the area of your screen

ZOOM-N-PAN — gradual change in the focal area will magnify or move the view area

INDEX